The American Law Institute

MODEL PENAL CODE

Changes and Editorial Corrections in May 4, 1962
Proposed Official Draft

July 30, 1962

The Executive Office
THE AMERICAN LAW INSTITUTE
4025 Chestnut Street
Philadelphia, Pa. 19104

MODEL PENAL CODE

Changes and Editorial Corrections in May 4, 1962 Proposed Official Draft

The following changes and corrections in the Proposed Official Draft of the Model Penal Code reflect decisions taken by the Institute at the May meeting 1962 and editorial corrections authorized under the Institute's resolution of May 24, 1962, approving the Code. The Reporters are still engaged in preparing the Text and Comments for final publication. Some additional corrections of a minor character may therefore be anticipated.

Section 2.03(1). The comment is to make clear why the Reporter considers the formulation sufficient to include concurrent sufficient causes, and what language should be added if it is desired to deal with this problem explicitly.

Section 2.11(2)(b). The language is to be revised to extend to any concerted activity of a kind not forbidden by law.

Section 5.06. Insert "of" after "is" in Subsection (2)(c). Substitute "is" for "shall be" in the phrase "it shall be presumed".

Section 5.07. Change "bodily harm" to "bodily injury" in line 8.

Section 210.6. Put brackets at beginning and end of the section to signify the fact that the Institute has taken no position on the abolition or retention of capital punishment.

Section 210.6(2). The second sentence of the second paragraph is revised to read: "Any such evidence, not legally privileged, which the court deems to have probative force, may be received, regardless of its admissibility under the exclusionary rules of evidence, provided that the defendant's counsel is accorded a fair opportunity to rebut such evidence."

The same change is made in the equivalent sentence of the alternative formulation of Subsection (2).

Section 211.1. Change "bodily harm" to "bodily injury" in Subsection (1)(c). The words "entered into by mutual consent" are to be reconsidered to be certain that they do not negative consent as a total defense under some circumstances. Cf. notation for Section 2.11(2)(b), above. Correct spelling of "deadly" in Subsection (2)(b).

Section 213.0. Definitions of "sexual intercourse" and "deviate sexual intercourse" are to be transposed here from Sections 213.1(1) and 213.2(1).

Section 213.1. Substitute "mistakenly" for "falsely" in Subsection (2)(c).

Section 213.4. The first two lines are revised to read as follows: "A person who has sexual contact with another not his spouse, or causes such other to have sexual contact with him, is guilty," etc.

The last paragraph of the section is revised to read: "Sexual contact is any touching of the sexual or other intimate parts of the person for the purpose of arousing or gratifying sexual desire."

Section 213.6. Insert "by a preponderance of the evidence" after "to prove" in last sentence of Subsection (1). Correct numbering of last three subsections to 3, 4 and 5, respectively.

Section 220.2. Conform definition of "occupied structure" in Subsection (4) to definition given in Section 221.0.

Section 223.1. Change first sentence by inserting period after "offense" at end of line two of Subsection (1); balance of sentence is deleted. The sense of the deleted material is to be incorporated in comment. Insert after "automobile" in line three of Subsection (2) "airplane, motorcycle, motor boat" so that the language parallels Section 223.9.

Section 223.2(1). Insert "unlawfully" before "takes" in the second line.

Sections 223.3 and 223.4. Insert "purposely" before "obtains" in the first lines. The lettered paragraphs are numbered instead of lettered.

Section 223.6. Insert "purposely" before "receives" in the first line. Also, the definition of "dealer" is to be expanded to include pawnbrokers.

Section 223.7. Insert "purposely" before "obtains" in the first line, "transportation" before "telephone" in the fifth line, and "knowingly" before "diverts" in the third line of Subsection (2).

Section 223.8. Insert "purposely" before "obtains" in the first line, and "to be reserved" before "in equivalent amount" in the fourth line.

Sections 224.5, 224.6, 224.7. Lettered paragraphs are to be numbered. In Section 224.6, insert "by the issuer" after "authorized" in Subsection (3), and substitute "or other evidence of" in place of "purporting to evidence" in the definition of "credit card".

Section 224.8. The word "partner" is to be transposed from paragraph (d) to paragraph (a) of Subsection (1).

Section 224.14. Insert "or purporting to affect" after "affecting".

Section 230.3. In the last paragraph of the note on "Status of Section", change "1955" to "1959".

Section 240.0(8). Insert ", other than a judicial proceeding," before "the outcome" in line two.

Section 240.1(3). Insert "legal" before "duty" in the second line.

Section 240.2(1). Insert "known legal" before "duty" at the end of the second line of paragraph (c).
In paragraph (d) substitute "with purpose" for "designed".

Section 241.7. Lettered paragraphs are to be numbered.

Section 242.2. Change "bodily harm" to "bodily injury".

Section 242.3. Lettered paragraphs are to be numbered.

Section 242.6(4)(a). The word "actor" is substituted for "detainee".

Section 250.4. Lettered paragraphs are to be numbered. A new paragraph (4) is inserted before the paragraph presently designated as (d), to read as follows: "subjects another to an offensive touching; or". In paragraph (d), renumbered (5), change "harmful" to "alarming".

Section 250.11. Delete the word "petty" before "misdemeanor" in the first line.

Section 250.12. Insert "incident" before "to" in last line of Subsection (2)(a).

Section 251.2(1). Correct spelling of "petty" in line two of Subsection (1).

THE REPORTERS

The American Law Institute

MODEL PENAL CODE

Proposed Official Draft

Submitted by the Council to the Members for Discussion at the Thirty-ninth Annual Meeting on May 23, 24, 25 and 26, 1962.

May 4, 1962

The Executive Office
THE AMERICAN LAW INSTITUTE
4025 Chestnut Street
Philadelphia, Pa. 19104

© 1962 by THE AMERICAN LAW INSTITUTE

THE AMERICAN LAW INSTITUTE

Chairman of the Council
HARRISON TWEED

President
NORRIS DARRELL

1st Vice-President
WILLIAM A. SCHNADER

2nd Vice-President
JOHN G. BUCHANAN

Treasurer
BERNARD G. SEGAL

Director
HERBERT F. GOODRICH

Assistant Director
PAUL A. WOLKIN

COUNCIL

Dillon Anderson	Houston	Texas
Francis M. Bird	Atlanta	Georgia
John G. Buchanan	Pittsburgh	Pennsylvania
Charles Bunn	Charlottesville	Virginia
Howard F. Burns	Cleveland	Ohio
Herbert W. Clark	San Francisco	California
Homer D. Crotty	Los Angeles	California
R. Ammi Cutter	Boston	Massachusetts
Norris Darrell	New York	New York
Edward J. Dimock	New York	New York
Arthur Dixon	Chicago	Illinois
Gerald F. Flood	Philadelphia	Pennsylvania
Henry J. Friendly	New York	New York
Erwin N. Griswold	Cambridge	Massachusetts
H. Eastman Hackney	Pittsburgh	Pennsylvania
Albert J. Harno	Springfield	Illinois
William V. Hodges	Denver	Colorado
Joseph C. Hutcheson, Jr.	Houston	Texas
Laurance M. Hyde	Jefferson City	Missouri
William J. Jameson	Billings	Montana
Joseph F. Johnston	Birmingham	Alabama
William B. Lockhart	Minneapolis	Minnesota
Ross L. Malone	Roswell	New Mexico
William L. Marbury	Baltimore	Maryland
Carl McGowan	Chicago	Illinois
Charles M. Merrill	San Francisco	California
Robert N. Miller	Washington	District of Columbia
Timothy N. Pfeiffer	New York	New York
Frederick D. G. Ribble	Charlottesville	Virginia
Eugene V. Rostow	New Haven	Connecticut
Walter V. Schaefer	Chicago	Illinois
William A. Schnader	Philadelphia	Pennsylvania
Bernard G. Segal	Philadelphia	Pennsylvania
Eugene B. Strassburger	Pittsburgh	Pennsylvania
Harrison Tweed	New York	New York
John W. Wade	Nashville	Tennessee
Raymond S. Wilkins	Boston	Massachusetts
Charles H. Willard	New York	New York
Laurens Williams	Washington	District of Columbia
Samuel Williston (*Emeritus*)	Cambridge	Massachusetts
John Minor Wisdom	New Orleans	Louisiana
Charles E. Wyzanski, Jr.	Boston	Massachusetts

REPORTORIAL STAFF

Reporters

HERBERT WECHSLER, *Chief Reporter*, Columbia University School of Law, New York, N. Y.

LOUIS B. SCHWARTZ, University of Pennsylvania Law School, Philadelphia, Pa.

Associate Reporters

MORRIS PLOSCOWE, New York, N. Y.
 (Tentative Draft No. 2, Articles 6, 7, 301)
PAUL W. TAPPAN, New York University, New York, N. Y.
 (Sentencing and Treatment of Offenders; Organization of Correction)

Special Consultants

FRANCIS A. ALLEN, University of Chicago Law School, Chicago, Ill.
 (Sections 2.07, 3.07 and 6.04)
SANFORD BATES, Pennington, N. J.
 (Sentencing and Treatment of Offenders; Organization of Correction)
REX A. COLLINGS, JR., University of California School of Law, Berkeley, Cal.
 (Articles 210, 211, 212, 250 and 251)
FRANK P. GRAD, Columbia University School of Law, New York, N. Y.
 (Sentencing and Treatment of Offenders; Organization of Correction)
MANFRED S. GUTTMACHER, M.D., Baltimore, Md. (Article 4)
WILLIAM K. JONES, Columbia University School of Law, New York, N. Y.
 (Article 5)
ROBERT E. KNOWLTON, Rutgers University Law School, Newark, N. J.
 (Articles 213, 223, 224 and 241)
HAROLD KORN, New York, N. Y. (Article 5)
MONRAD G. PAULSEN, Columbia University School of Law, New York, N. Y.
 (Sections 2.08, 2.09, 2.10 and 2.13)
FRANK J. REMINGTON, University of Wisconsin School of Law, Madison, Wis.
 (Sections 1.03, 1.06-1.11)
THORSTEN SELLIN, University of Pennsylvania, Philadelphia, Pa.
 (Tentative Draft No. 3; The Death Penalty)
LOUIS H. SWARTZ, New York, N. Y.
 (Article 4; Sentencing and Treatment of Offenders)
GLANVILLE WILLIAMS, Jesus College, Cambridge University, England
 (Article 3)

Research Associates (1953-1962)

PAUL BERGER (1953)
RUSSELL E. BROOKS (1961-2)
YALE KAMISAR (1953)
LEE KOZOL (1956-7)
PAULA MARKOWITZ (1957-8)
ARTHUR R. PEARCE (1954-5)

CURTIS R. REITZ (1954-5)
ARTHUR ROSETT (1958-9)
RUTH SCHWARTZMAN (1953-5)
DONNA J. SHELLABERGER (1954-7)
MAX SINGER (1956-7)

CRIMINAL LAW ADVISORY COMMITTEE

FRANCIS A. ALLEN, Professor of Law, University of Chicago Law School, Chicago, Ill.

SANFORD BATES, Consultant in Administration, formerly Commissioner, Department of Institutions and Agencies, State of New Jersey, Pennington, N. J.

DALE E. BENNETT, Professor of Law, Louisiana State University Law School, Baton Rouge, La.

JAMES V. BENNETT, Director, Bureau of Prisons, Department of Justice, Washington, D. C.

CURTIS BOK, Justice, Supreme Court of Pennsylvania, Philadelphia, Pa.

CHARLES D. BREITEL, Justice, New York Supreme Court, New York, N. Y.

ERNEST W. BURGESS, Professor of Sociology, University of Chicago, Chicago, Ill.

LEONARD S. COTTRELL, Russell Sage Foundation, New York, N. Y.

SAMUEL DASH, Formerly District Attorney of Philadelphia, Philadelphia, Pa.

GEORGE H. DESSION, Professor of Law, Yale Law School, New Haven, Conn. (Deceased 1955).

EDWARD J. DIMOCK, Judge, United States District Court, Southern District of N. Y., New York, N. Y.

RICHARD C. DONNELLY, Professor of Law, Yale Law School, New Haven, Conn.

GERALD F. FLOOD, Judge, Superior Court of Pennsylvania, Philadelphia, Pa.

LAWRENCE Z. FREEDMAN, M.D., Professor of Psychiatry, University of Chicago, Chicago, Ill.

STANLEY H. FULD, Judge, New York Court of Appeals, New York, N. Y. (to 1961).

SHELDON GLUECK, Professor of Law, Law School of Harvard University, Cambridge, Mass.

MANFRED S. GUTTMACHER, M.D., Chief Medical Officer, Supreme Bench of Baltimore, Baltimore, Md.

LEARNED HAND, Judge, United States Court of Appeals, Second Circuit, New York, N. Y. (Deceased 1961).

ALBERT J. HARNO, Springfield, Ill.

HENRY M. HART, Professor of Law, Law School of Harvard University, Cambridge, Mass.

KENNETH D. JOHNSON, Dean, New York School of Social Work, New York, N. Y. (Deceased 1958).

FLORENCE M. KELLEY, Presiding Justice, Domestic Relations Court, New York City, New York, N. Y.

THOMAS D. MCBRIDE, Former Justice, Supreme Court of Pennsylvania, Philadelphia, Pa.

JEROME MICHAEL, Professor of Law, Columbia University School of Law, New York, N. Y. (Deceased 1953).

LLOYD OHLIN, Professor, New York School of Social Work, New York, N. Y.

RUSSELL G. OSWALD, Chairman, New York State Board of Parole, Albany, N. Y.

WINFRED OVERHOLSER, M.D., Superintendent, St. Elizabeth's Hospital, Federal Security Agency, Washington, D. C.

JOHN J. PARKER, Chief Judge, United States Court of Appeals, Fourth Circuit, Charlotte, N. C. (Deceased 1958).

TIMOTHY N. PFEIFFER, New York, N. Y.

ORIE L. PHILLIPS, Judge (Ret.), United States Court of Appeals, Tenth Circuit, Denver, Colo.

MORRIS PLOSCOWE, New York, N. Y.

FRANK J. REMINGTON, Professor of Law, University of Wisconsin Law School, Madison, Wis.

JOSEPH SARAFITE, Judge, Court of General Sessions, New York, N. Y.

THORSTEN SELLIN, Professor of Sociology, University of Pennsylvania, Philadelphia, Pa.

ARTHUR H. SHERRY, Professor of Law, University of California School of Law, Berkeley, Cal.

JOSEPH SLOANE, Judge, Court of Common Pleas, Philadelphia, Pa.

FLOYD E. THOMPSON, Chicago, Ill. (Deceased 1960).

LIONEL TRILLING, Professor of English, Columbia University, New York, N. Y. (To 1959).

WILL C. TURNBLADH, St. Paul, Minnesota.

JOHN BARKER WAITE, Professor Emeritus of Law, University of Michigan Law School, Ann Arbor, Mich.

EX OFFICIO.

NORRIS DARRELL, New York, N. Y.
President, The American Law Institute
HERBERT F. GOODRICH, Philadelphia, Pa.
Director, The American Law Institute

ADVISERS TO THE COUNCIL

* EDWARD J. DIMOCK, New York, N. Y.
* GERALD F. FLOOD, Philadelphia, Pa.
* LEARNED HAND, New York, N. Y. (Deceased, 1961).
* ALBERT J. HARNO, Springfield, Ill.
* TIMOTHY N. PFEIFFER, New York, N. Y.
  CHARLES E. WYZANSKI, Boston, Mass.

---

* Served also as Adviser to the Reporters.

FOREWORD

This Proposed Official Draft marks the end of our work on the Model Penal Code. Please note that while this book contains all the sections of the Code, part of the material is not before us at this meeting because it was submitted and approved last year. Last year's submission included Section 1.02 "Purposes; Principles of Construction", and Section 1.04 "Classes of Crimes; Violations." It included Article 4 called "Responsibility." This material ran from Section 4.01 to Section 4.10 inclusive. Then the material covered Article 6 "Authorized Disposition of Offenders" and Article 7 "Authority of Court in Sentencing."

Last year's draft also had one section numbered 201.6 "Sentence of Death for Murder; Further Proceedings to Determine Sentence." Following last year's meeting some changes were made in this section, now numbered 210.6.

The 1961 submission then continued with Part III, "Treatment and Correction." It took up Article 301 "Suspension of Sentence; Probation;" Article 302 "Fines;" Article 303 "Short-Term Imprisonment;" Article 304 "Long-Term Imprisonment;" Article 305 "Release on Parole;" and Article 306 "Loss and Restoration of Rights Incident to Conviction or Imprisonment."

The book then concluded with Part IV "Organization of Correction." This included Article 401 "Department of Correction;" Article 402 "Board of Parole;" Article 403 "Administration of Institutions;" Article 404 "Division of Parole" with an alternative; and Article 405 "Division of Probation."

The above described material having been approved by vote of the Institute is in this book this year so that upon the approval of the remainder of the sections and the modified section from last year, we shall have an Official text of the Code. What remains to be done is the bringing of the comments down to date and such revision as is necessary. But if approval is given at the 1962 session of the Institute, we shall have a completed Model Penal Code.

Finis Opus Coronat!

HEREBERT F. GOODRICH,
Director,
The American Law Institute.

TABLE OF CONTENTS

MODEL PENAL CODE

PART I. GENERAL PROVISIONS

ARTICLE 1. PRELIMINARY

Section		Page
1.01.	Title and Effective Date	1
1.02.	Purposes; Principles of Construction	2
1.03.	Territorial Applicability	4
1.04.	Classes of Crimes; Violations	6
1.05.	All Offenses Defined by Statute; Application of General Provisions of the Code	8
1.06.	Time Limitations	9
1.07.	Method of Prosecution When Conduct Constitutes More Than One Offense	11
1.08.	When Prosecution Barred by Former Prosecution for the Same Offense	14
1.09.	When Prosecution Barred by Former Prosecution for Different Offense	16
1.10.	Former Prosecution in Another Jurisdiction: When a Bar	18
1.11.	Former Prosecution Before Court Lacking Jurisdiction or When Fraudently Procured by the Defendant	19
1.12.	Proof Beyond a Reasonable Doubt; Affirmative Defenses; Burden of Proving Fact When Not an Element of an Offense; Presumptions	20
1.13.	General Definitions	22

ARTICLE 2. GENERAL PRINCIPLES OF LIABILITY

2.01.	Requirement of Voluntary Act; Omission as Basis of Liability; Possession as an Act	24

(ix)

TABLE OF CONTENTS (Continued)

Section		Page
2.02.	General Requirements of Culpability	25
2.03.	Causal Relationship Between Conduct and Result; Divergence Between Result Designed or Contemplated and Actual Result or Between Probable and Actual Result	28
2.04	Ignorance or Mistake	30
2.05	When Culpability Requirements Are Inapplicable to Violations and to Offenses Defined by Other Statutes; Effect of Absolute Liability in Reducing Grade of Offense to Violation	31
2.06.	Liability for Conduct of Another; Complicity	32
2.07.	Liability of Corporations, Unincorporated Associations and Persons Acting, or Under a Duty to Act, in Their Behalf	35
2.08	Intoxication	38
2.09.	Duress	40
2.10.	Military Orders	41
2.11.	Consent	41
2.12.	De Minimis Infractions	42
2.13.	Entrapment	43

ARTICLE 3. GENERAL PRINCIPLES OF JUSTIFICATION

3.01.	Justification an Affirmative Defense; Civil Remedies Unaffected	45
3.02.	Justification Generally: Choice of Evils	45
3.03.	Execution of Public Duty	46
3.04.	Use of Force in Self-Protection	47
3.05.	Use of Force for the Protection of Other Persons	50
3.06.	Use of Force for the Protection of Property	51
3.07.	Use of Force in Law Enforcement	56
3.08.	Use of Force by Persons With Special Responsibility for Care, Discipline or Safety of Others	59
3.09.	Mistake of Law as to Unlawfulness of Force or Legality of Arrest; Reckless or Negligent Use of Otherwise Justifiable Force; Reckless or Negligent Injury or Risk of Injury to Innocent Persons	62
3.10.	Justification in Property Crimes	63
3.11.	Definitions	64

TABLE OF CONTENTS (Continued)

ARTICLE 4. RESPONSIBILITY

Section		Page
4.01.	Mental Disease or Defect Excluding Responsibility	66
4.02.	Evidence of Mental Disease or Defect Admissible When Relevant to Element of the Offense; [Mental Disease or Defect Impairing Capacity as Ground for Mitigation of Punishment in Capital Cases]	67
4.03.	Mental Disease or Defect Excluding Responsibility Is Affirmative Defense; Requirement of Notice; Form of Verdict and Judgment When Finding of Irresponsibility Is made	67
4.04.	Mental Disease or Defect Excluding Fitness to Proceed	68
4.05.	Psychiatric Examination of Defendant With Respect to Mental Disease or Defect	69
4.06	Determination of Fitness to Proceed; Effect of Finding of Unfitness; Proceedings if Fitness Is Regained [; Post-Commitment Hearings]	70
4.07.	Determination of Irresponsibility on Basis of Report; Access to Defendant by Psychiatrist of His Own Choice; Form of Expert Testimony When Issue of Responsibility Is Tried	73
4.08.	Legal Effect of Acquittal on the Ground of Mental Disease or Defect Excluding Responsibility; Commitment; Release or Discharge	75
4.09.	Statements for Purposes of Examination or Treatment Inadmissible Except on Issue of Mental Condition	78
4.10.	Immaturity Excluding Criminal Conviction; Transfer of Proceedings to Juvenile Court	79

ARTICLE 5. INCHOATE CRIMES

5.01.	Criminal Attempt	81
5.02.	Criminal Solicitation	83
5.03.	Criminal Conspiracy	83
5.04.	Incapacity, Irresponsibility or Immunity of Party to Solicitation or Conspiracy	86
5.05.	Grading of Criminal Attempt, Solicitation and Conspiracy; Mitigation in Cases of Lesser Danger; Multiple Convictions Barred	87
5.06.	Possessing Instruments of Crime; Weapons	88
5.07.	Prohibited Offensive Weapons	89

TABLE OF CONTENTS (Continued)

ARTICLE 6. AUTHORIZED DISPOSITION OF OFFENDERS

Section		Page
6.01.	Degrees of Felonies	91
6.02.	Sentence in Accordance With Code; Authorized Dispositions	91
6.03.	Fines	93
6.04.	Penalties Against Corporations and Unincorporated Associations; Forfeiture of Corporate Charter or Revocation of Certificate Authorizing Foreign Corporation to Do Business in the State	94
6.05.	Young Adult Offenders	95
6.06.	Sentence of Imprisonment for Felony; Ordinary Terms	97
6.06.	(Alternate) Sentence of Imprisonment for Felony; Ordinary Terms	98
6.07.	Sentence of Imprisonment for Felony; Extended Terms	99
6.08.	Sentence of Imprisonment for Misdemeanors and Petty Misdemeanors; Ordinary Terms	100
6.09.	Sentence of Imprisonment for Misdemeanors and Petty Misdemeanors; Extended Terms	100
6.10.	First Release of All Offenders on Parole; Sentence of Imprisonment Includes Separate Parole Term; Length of Parole Term; Length of Recommitment and Reparole After Revocation of Parole; Final Unconditional Release	102
6.11.	Place of Imprisonment	103
6.12.	Reduction of Conviction by Court to Lessor Degree of Felony or to Misdemeanor	104
6.13.	Civil Commitment in Lieu of Prosecution or of Sentence	104

ARTICLE 7. AUTHORITY OF COURT IN SENTENCING

7.01.	Criteria for Withholding Sentence of Imprisonment and for Placing Defendant on Probation	106
7.02.	Criteria for Imposing Fines	108
7.03.	Criteria for Sentence of Extended Term of Imprisonment; Felonies	109
7.04.	Criteria for Sentence of Extended Term of Imprisonment; Misdemeanors and Petty Misdemeanors	111

TABLE OF CONTENTS (Continued)

Section		Page
7.05.	Former Conviction in Another Jurisdiction; Definition and Proof of Conviction; Sentence Taking Into Account Admitted Crimes Bars Subsequent Conviction for Such Crimes	113
7.06.	Multiple Sentences; Concurrent and Consecutive Terms	114
7.07.	Procedure on Sentence; Pre-sentence Investigation and Report; Remand for Psychiatric Examination; Transmission of Records to Department of Correction	117
7.08.	Commitment for Observation; Sentence of Imprisonment for Felony Deemed Tentative for Period of One Year; Re-sentence on Petition of Commissioner of Correction	120
7.09.	Credit for Time of Detention Prior to Sentence; Credit for Imprisonment Under Earlier Sentence for the Same Crime	122

PART II. DEFINITION OF SPECIFIC CRIMES

OFFENSES AGAINST EXISTENCE OR STABILITY OF THE STATE

Reporter's Note 123

OFFENSES INVOLVING DANGER TO THE PERSON

ARTICLE 210. CRIMINAL HOMICIDE

210.0.	Definitions	124
210.1.	Criminal Homicide	125
210.2.	Murder	125
210.3.	Manslaughter	126
210.4.	Negligent Homicide	126
210.5.	Causing or Aiding Suicide	127
210.6.	Sentence of Death for Murder; Further Proceedings to Determine Sentence	128

ARTICLE 211. ASSAULT; RECKLESS ENDANGERING; THREATS

211.0.	Definitions	134
211.2.	Recklessly Endangering Another Person	135
211.3.	Terroristic Threats	136

(xiii)

TABLE OF CONTENTS (Continued)

ARTICLE 212. KIDNAPPING AND RELATED OFFENSES; COERCION

Section		Page
212.0.	Definitions	137
212.1.	Kidnapping	137
212.2.	Felonious Restraint	138
212.3.	False Imprisonment	138
212.4.	Interference with Custody	139
212.5.	Criminal Coercion	140

ARTICLE 213. SEXUAL OFFENSES

213.0.	Definitions	142
213.1.	Rape and Related Offenses	142
213.2.	Deviate Sexual Intercourse by Force or Imposition	144
213.3.	Corruption of Minors and Seduction	146
213.4.	Sexual Assault	147
213.5.	Indecent Exposure	149
213.6.	Provisions Generally Applicable to Article 213	149

OFFENSES AGAINST PROPERTY

ARTICLE 220. ARSON, CRIMINAL MISCHIEF, AND OTHER PROPERTY DESTRUCTION

220.1.	Arson and Related Offenses	152
220.2.	Causing or Risking Catastrophe	153
220.3.	Criminal Mischief	154

ARTICLE 221. BURGLARY AND OTHER CRIMINAL INTRUSION

221.0.	Definitions	156
221.1.	Burglary	156
221.2.	Criminal Trespass	158

ARTICLE 222. ROBBERY

222.1.	Robbery	161

TABLE OF CONTENTS (Continued)

ARTICLE 223. THEFT AND RELATED OFFENSES

Section		Page
223.0.	Definitions	162
223.1.	Consolidation of Theft Offenses; Grading; Provisions Applicable to Theft Generally	164
223.2.	Theft by Unlawful Taking or Disposition	167
223.3.	Theft by Deception	168
223.4.	Theft by Extortion	169
223.5.	Theft of Property Lost, Mislaid or Delivered by Mistake	170
223.6.	Receiving Stolen Property	170
223.7.	Theft of Services	172
223.8.	Theft by Failure to Make Required Disposition of Funds Received	172
223.9.	Unauthorized Use of Automobiles and Other Vehicles	173

ARTICLE 224. FORGERY AND FRAUDULENT PRACTICES

224.0.	Definitions	175
224.1.	Forgery	175
224.2.	Simulating Objects of Antiquity, Rarity, Etc.	177
224.3.	Fraudulent Destruction, Removal or Concealment of Recordable Instruments	177
224.4.	Tampering With Records	178
224.5.	Bad Checks	178
224.6.	Credit Cards	178
224.7.	Deceptive Business Practices	179
224.8.	Commercial Bribery and Breach of Duty to Act Disinterestedly	181
224.9.	Rigging Publicly Exhibited Contest	182
224.10.	Defrauding Secured Creditors	183
224.11.	Fraud in Insolvency	183
224.12.	Receiving Deposits in a Failing Financial Institution	184
224.13.	Misapplication of Entrusted Property and Property of Government or Financial Institution	185
224.14.	Securing Execution of Documents by Deception	185

TABLE OF CONTENTS (Continued)

OFFENSES AGAINST THE FAMILY

ARTICLE 230. OFFENSES AGAINST THE FAMILY

Section		Page
230.1.	Bigamy and Polygamy	187
230.2.	Incest	188
230.3.	Abortion	189
230.4.	Endangering Welfare of Children	192
230.5.	Persistent Non-Support	193

OFFENSES AGAINST PUBLIC ADMINISTRATION

ARTICLE 240. BRIBERY AND CORRUPT INFLUENCE

240.0.	Definitions	194
240.1.	Bribery in Official and Political Matters	195
240.2.	Threats and Other Improper Influence in Official and Political Matters	197
240.3.	Compensation for Past Official Action	198
240.4.	Retaliation for Past Official Action	199
240.5.	Gifts to Public Servants by Persons Subject to Their Jurisdiction	199
240.6.	Compensating Public Servant for Assisting Private Interests in Relation to Matters Before Him	201
240.7.	Selling Political Endorsement; Special Influence	202

ARTICLE 241. PERJURY AND OTHER FALSIFICATION IN OFFICIAL MATTERS

241.0.	Definitions	204
241.1.	Perjury	204
241.2.	False Swearing	206
241.3.	Unsworn Falsification to Authorities	207
241.4.	False Alarms to Agencies of Public Safety	208
241.5.	False Reports to Law Enforcement Authorities	208

TABLE OF CONTENTS (Continued)

Section		Page
241.6.	Tampering With Witnesses and Informants; Retaliation Against Them	209
241.7.	Tampering With or Fabricating Physical Evidence	210
241.8.	Tampering With Public Records or Information	211
241.9.	Impersonating a Public Servant	211

ARTICLE 242. OBSTRUCTING GOVERNMENTAL OPERATIONS; ESCAPES

242.0.	Definitions	213
242.1.	Obstructing Administration of Law or Other Governmental Function	213
242.2.	Resisting Arrest or Other Law Enforcement	213
242.3.	Hindering Apprehension or Prosecution	214
242.4.	Aiding Consummation of Crime	215
242.5.	Compounding	215
242.6.	Escape	216
242.7.	Implements for Escape; Other Contraband	218
242.8.	Bail Jumping; Default in Required Appearance	219

ARTICLE 243. ABUSE OF OFFICE

243.0.	Definitions	220
243.1.	Official Oppression	220
243.2.	Speculating or Wagering on Official Action or Information	220

OFFENSES AGAINST PUBLIC ORDER AND DECENCY

ARTICLE 250. RIOT, DISORDERLY CONDUCT, AND RELATED OFFENSES

250.1.	Riot; Failure to Disperse	222
250.2.	Disorderly Conduct	223
250.3.	False Public Alarms	224
250.4.	Harassment	224
250.5.	Public Drunkenness; Drug Incapacitation	225

TABLE OF CONTENTS (Continued)

Section		Page
250.6.	Loitering or Prowling	226
250.7.	Obstructing Highways and Other Public Passages	227
250.8.	Disrupting Meetings and Processions	228
250.9.	Desecration of Venerated Objects	229
250.10.	Abuse of Corpse	229
250.11.	Cruelty to Animals	230
250.12.	Violation of Privacy	230

ARTICLE 251. PUBLIC INDECENCY

251.1.	Open Lewdness	233
251.2.	Prostitution and Related Offenses	233
251.3.	Loitering to Solicit Deviate Sexual Relations	236
251.4.	Obscenity	237

ADDITIONAL ARTICLES

Reporter's Note 241

PART III. TREATMENT AND CORRECTION

ARTICLE 301. SUSPENSION OF SENTENCE; PROBATION

301.1.	Conditions of Suspension or Probation	242
301.2.	Period of Suspension or Probation; Modification of Conditions; Discharge of Defendant	244
301.3.	Summons or Arrest of Defendant Under Suspended Sentence or on Probation; Commitment Without Bail; Revocation and Resentence	245
301.4.	Notice and Hearing on Revocation or Modification of Conditions of Suspension or Probation	246
301.5.	Order Removing Disqualification or Disability Based on Conviction	247
301.6.	Suspension or Probation Is Final Judgment for Other Purposes	248

ARTICLE 302. FINES

302.1.	Time and Method of Payment; Disposition of Funds	249
302.2.	Consequences of Non-Payment; Imprisonment for Contumacious Non-Payment; Summary Collection	249
302.3.	Revocation of Fine	251

TABLE OF CONTENTS (Continued)

ARTICLE 303. SHORT-TERM IMPRISONMENT

Section		Page
303.1.	State and Local Institutions for Short-Term Imprisonment; Review of Adequacy; Joint Use of Institutions; Approval of Plan of New Institutions	252
303.2.	Records of Prisoners; Classification; Transfer	254
303.3.	Segregation of Prisoners; Segregation and Transfer of Prisoners With Physical or Mental Diseases or Defects	255
303.4.	Medical Care; Food and Clothing	258
303.5.	Program of Rehabilitation	259
303.6.	Discipline and Control	260
303.7.	Employment and Labor of Prisoners	261
303.8.	Reduction of Term for Good Behavior	263
303.9.	Privilege of Leaving Institution for Work and Other Purposes; Conditions; Application of Earnings	264
303.10.	Release from Institutions	266

ARTICLE 304. LONG-TERM IMPRISONMENT

304.1.	Reception Center; Reception Classification Boards; Reception Classification and Reclassification; Transfer of Prisoners	267
304.2.	Institutions; Review of Adequacy; Use of Institutions of Another Jurisdiction	269
304.3.	Central Prisoner File; Treatment, Classification and Reclassification in Institutions	271
304.4.	Segregation and Transfer of Prisoners With Physical or Mental Diseases or Defects	274
304.5.	Medical Care, Food and Clothing	276
304.6.	Program of Rehabilitation	277
304.7.	Discipline and Control	277
304.8.	Employment and Labor of Prisoners	279
304.9.	Compassionate Leave; Pre-Parole Furlough	282
304.10.	Release from Institutions	283

TABLE OF CONTENTS (Continued)

ARTICLE 305. RELEASE ON PAROLE

Section		Page
305.1.	Reduction of Prison Term for Good Behavior	284
305.2.	Reduction of Parole Term for Good Behavior	284
305.3.	Award of Reduction of Term for Good Behavior	285
305.4.	Forfeiture, Withholding, and Restoration of Reduction of Term for Good Behavior	286
305.5.	Report of Reductions Granted, Forfeited and Restored	286
305.6.	Parole Eligibility and Hearing	287
305.7.	Preparation for Hearing; Assistance to Prisoner	288
305.8.	Decision of Board of Parole; Reconsideration	288
305.9.	Criteria for Determining Date of First Release on Parole	289
305.10.	Data to Be Considered in Determining Parole Release	292
305.11.	Eligibility for Discharge from Parole	293
305.12.	Termination of Supervision; Discharge from Parole	293
305.13.	Conditions of Parole	294
305.14.	Parole Residence Facilities	295
305.15.	Revocation of Parole for Violation of Condition; Hearing	296
305.16.	Sanctions Short of Revocation for Violation of Condition of Parole	297
305.17.	Duration of Re-imprisonment and Re-parole after Revocation	299
305.18.	Parole to Detainers	300
305.19.	Finality of Determinations With Respect to Reduction of Terms for Good Behavior and Parole	301

ARTICLE 306. LOSS AND RESTORATION OF RIGHTS INCIDENT TO CONVICTION OR IMPRISONMENT

306.1.	Basis of Disqualification or Disability	303
306.2.	Forfeiture of Public Office	304
306.3.	Voting and Jury Service	304
306.4.	Testimonial Capacity; Testimony of Prisoners	305
306.5.	Appointment of Agent, Attorney-in-Fact or Trustee for Prisoner	306
306.6.	Order Removing Disqualifications or Disabilities; Vacation of Conviction; Effect of Order of Removal or Vacation	306

TABLE OF CONTENTS (Continued)

PART IV. ORGANIZATION OF CORRECTION

ARTICLE 401. DEPARTMENT OF CORRECTION

Section		Page
401.1.	Department of Correction; Creation; Responsibilities	309
401.2.	Director of Correction; Appointment; Powers and Duties	310
401.3.	Organization of Department of Correction	312
401.4.	Division of Treatment Services; Deputy Director for Treatment Services	313
401.5.	Division of Custodial Services; Deputy Director for Custodial Services	314
401.6.	Division of Young Adult Correction; Deputy Director for Young Adult Correction	315
401.7.	Division of Prison Industries; Deputy Director for Prison Industries	316
401.8.	Division of Fiscal Control; Deputy Director for Fiscal Control	317
401.9.	Division of Research and Training; Deputy Director for Research and Training	318
401.10.	Commission of Correction and Community Services; Organization; Functions	319
401.11.	Visitation and Inspection of Institutions	321
401.12.	Appointment and Promotion of Employees; Department Under Civil Service Law [Merit System]	323

ARTICLE 402. BOARD OF PAROLE

402.1.	Board of Parole; Composition and Tenure	324
402.2.	Powers and Duties of the Board of Parole	325
402.3.	Young Adult Division of Board of Parole	326

ARTICLE 403. ADMINISTRATION OF INSTITUTIONS

403.1.	Appointment of Personnel	328
403.2.	Powers and Duties of Wardens and Other Administrative Heads of State and Local Institutions	329
403.3.	Separation of Female Prisoners	331

TABLE OF CONTENTS (Continued)

ARTICLE 404. DIVISION OF PAROLE

Section		Page
404.1.	Division of Parole; Parole Administrator	332
404.2.	Powers and Duties of the Parole Administrator	333
404.3.	Field Parole Service; Organization and Duties	334

ALTERNATIVE ARTICLE 404. DIVISION OF PROBATION AND PAROLE

404.1.	Division of Probation and Parole; Probation and Parole Administrator	337
404.2.	Powers and Duties of the Probation and Parole Administrator	337
404.3.	Field Probation and Parole Service; Organization and Duties	339

ARTICLE 405. DIVISION OF PROBATION

405.1.	Division of Probation; Probation Administrator	342
405.2.	Powers and Duties of the Probation Administrator	343
405.3.	Extension of Probation Field Services by Division of Probation	344
405.4.	Field Probation Service; Organization and Duties	344

PART I. GENERAL PROVISIONS

ARTICLE 1. PRELIMINARY

Section 1.01. Title and Effective Date.

(1) This Act is called the Penal and Correctional Code and may be cited as P.C.C. It shall become effective on

(2) Except as provided in Subsections (3) and (4) of this Section, the Code does not apply to offenses committed prior to its effective date and prosecutions for such offenses shall be governed by the prior law, which is continued in effect for that purpose, as if this Code were not in force. For the purposes of this Section, an offense was committed prior to the effective date of the Code if any of the elements of the offense occurred prior thereto.

(3) In any case pending on or after the effective date of the Code, involving an offense committed prior to such date:

(a) procedural provisions of the Code shall govern, insofar as they are justly applicable and their application does not introduce confusion or delay;

(b) provisions of the Code according a defense or mitigation shall apply, with the consent of the defendant;

(c) the Court, with the consent of the defendant, may impose sentence under the provisions of the Code applicable to the offense and the offender.

(4) Provisions of the Code governing the treatment and the release or discharge of prisoners, probationers and pa-

§ 1.02

rolees shall apply to persons under sentence for offenses committed prior to the effective date of the Code, except that the minimum or maximum period of their detention or supervision shall in no case be increased.

STATUS OF SECTION

Presented to the Institute in Tentative Draft No. 2 and considered at the May 1954 meeting.

Reprinted in Tentative Draft No. 4.

Minor verbal changes have been made.

For Commentary, see Tentative Draft No. 2, p. 2.

Section 1.02. Purposes; Principles of Construction.

(1) The general purposes of the provisions governing the definition of offenses are:

(a) to forbid and prevent conduct that unjustifiably and inexcusably inflicts or threatens substantial harm to individual or public interests;

(b) to subject to public control persons whose conduct indicates that they are disposed to commit crimes;

(c) to safeguard conduct that is without fault from condemnation as criminal;

(d) to give fair warning of the nature of the conduct declared to constitute an offense;

(e) to differentiate on reasonable grounds between serious and minor offenses.

(2) The general purposes of the provisions governing the sentencing and treatment of offenders are:

(a) to prevent the commission of offenses;

(b) to promote the correction and rehabilitation of offenders;

(c) to safeguard offenders against excessive, disproportionate or arbitrary punishment;

(d) to give fair warning of the nature of the sentences that may be imposed on conviction of an offense;

(e) to differentiate among offenders with a view to a just individualization in their treatment;

(f) to define, coordinate and harmonize the powers, duties and functions of the courts and of administrative officers and agencies responsible for dealing with offenders;

(g) to advance the use of generally accepted scientific methods and knowledge in the sentencing and treatment of offenders;

(h) to integrate responsibility for the administration of the correctional system in a State Department of Correction [or other single department or agency].

(3) The provisions of the Code shall be construed according to the fair import of their terms but when the language is susceptible of differing constructions it shall be interpreted to further the general purposes stated in this Section and the special purposes of the particular provision involved. The discretionary powers conferred by the Code shall be exercised in accordance with the criteria stated in the Code and, insofar as such criteria are not decisive, to further the general purposes stated in this Section.

STATUS OF SECTION

Presented to the Institute in Tentative Draft No. 2 and considered at the May 1954 meeting.

Reprinted in Tentative Draft No. 4.

Resubmitted to the Institute, with minor verbal changes, in Proposed Final Draft No. 1 and approved at the May 1961 meeting.

For Commentary, see Tentative Draft No. 2, p. 4.

Section 1.03. Territorial Applicability.

(1) Except as otherwise provided in this Section, a person may be convicted under the law of this State of an offense committed by his own conduct or the conduct of another for which he is legally accountable if:

(a) either the conduct which is an element of the offense or the result which is such an element occurs within this State; or

(b) conduct occurring outside the State is sufficient under the law of this State to constitute an attempt to commit an offense within the State; or

(c) conduct occurring outside the State is sufficient under the law of this State to constitute a conspiracy to commit an offense within the State and an overt act in furtherance of such conspiracy occurs within the State; or

(d) conduct occurring within the State establishes complicity in the commission of, or an attempt, solicitation or conspiracy to commit, an offense in another jurisdiction which also is an offense under the law of this State; or

(e) the offense consists of the omission to perform a legal duty imposed by the law of this State with respect to domicile, residence or a relationship to a person, thing or transaction in the State; or

(f) the offense is based on a statute of this State which expressly prohibits conduct outside the State, when the conduct bears a reasonable relation to a legitimate interest of this State and the actor knows or should know that his conduct is likely to affect that interest.

(2) Subsection (1)(a) does not apply when either causing a specified result or a purpose to cause or danger of causing such a result is an element of an offense and the result occurs or is designed or likely to occur only in another jurisdiction where the conduct charged would not constitute an offense, unless a legislative purpose plainly appears to declare the conduct criminal regardless of the place of the result.

(3) Subsection (1)(a) does not apply when causing a particular result is an element of an offense and the result is caused by conduct occurring outside the State which would not constitute an offense if the result had occurred there, unless the actor purposely or knowingly caused the result within the State.

(4) When the offense is homicide, either the death of the victim or the bodily impact causing death constitutes a "result," within the meaning of Subsection (1)(a) and if the body of a homicide victim is found within the State, it is presumed that such result occurred within the State.

(5) This State includes the land and water and the air space above such land and water with respect to which the State has legislative jurisdiction.

STATUS OF SECTION

Presented to the Institute in Tentative Draft No. 5 and considered at the May 1956 meeting.

The Section has been completely revised in point of form and modified in point of substance in accordance with suggestions at the meeting.

The major substantive changes appear in Subsections (2) and (3), dealing with the cases where conduct in this State causes a result in another or conduct in another causes a result in this. In both cases a qualified legal effect is given to the law of the other State, insofar as it may treat the conduct as non-criminal.

Subsection (1)(f) responds to a suggestion that the Code articulate the general considerations that might justify a State in dealing with conduct occurring wholly outside its borders, when no element of the offense occurs within the State.

For Commentary, see Tentative Draft No. 5, p. 3.

Section 1.04. Classes of Crimes; Violations.

(1) **An offense defined by this Code or by any other statute of this State, for which a sentence of [death or of] imprisonment is authorized, constitutes a crime. Crimes are classified as felonies, misdemeanors or petty misdemeanors.**

(2) **A crime is a felony if it is so designated in this Code or if persons convicted thereof may be sentenced [to death or] to imprisonment for a term which, apart from an extended term, is in excess of one year.**

(3) **A crime is a misdemeanor if it is so designated in this Code or in a statute other than this Code enacted subsequent thereto.**

(4) **A crime is a petty misdemeanor if it is so designated in this Code or in a statute other than this Code enacted subsequent thereto or if it is defined by a statute other than this Code which now provides that persons convicted thereof may be sentenced to imprisonment for a term of which the maximum is less than one year.**

(5) **An offense defined by this Code or by any other statute of this State constitutes a violation if it is so designated in this Code or in the law defining the offense or if no other sentence than a fine, or fine and forfeiture or other civil penalty is authorized upon conviction or if it is defined by a statute other than this Code which now provides that the offense shall not constitute a crime. A violation does not**

constitute a crime and conviction of a violation shall not give rise to any disability or legal disadvantage based on conviction of a criminal offense.

(6) Any offense declared by law to constitute a crime, without specification of the grade thereof or of the sentence authorized upon conviction, is a misdemeanor.

(7) An offense defined by any statute of this State other than this Code shall be classified as provided in this Section and the sentence that may be imposed upon conviction thereof shall hereafter be governed by this Code.

STATUS OF SECTION

Formerly numbered 1.05.

Presented to the Institute in Tentative Draft No. 2 and Proposed Final Draft No. 1 and considered at the May 1954 and May 1961 meetings.

Reprinted in Tentative Draft No. 4.

Subsections (3) and (4) have been revised. As previously drafted they provided that a crime is a misdemeanor if persons convicted thereof may be sentenced to imprisonment for a term which, apart from an extended term, is in excess of thirty days but not more than a year and that it is a petty misdemeanor if persons convicted thereof may be sentenced to imprisonment for a term which, apart from an extended term, does not exceed thirty days. While these are the sentences authorized by the Code for misdemeanors and petty misdemeanors respectively (see Section 6.08), the formulations would have had the effect of increasing to one year the permissible sentence for crimes defined by statutes other than the Code which now provide for maximum sentences of more than thirty days but well under a year, e.g., three or six months. There is no reason to believe that such an increase is desirable and it would present jurisdictional problems in many states. The safer formulation is, accordingly, to downgrade such offenses for the purposes of sentence to the petty misdemeanor level, relying on a local judgment to make such exceptions to this general provision as may be thought wise in dealing with particular offenses. Those offenses which the legislature wishes to be misdemeanors and so denominates subsequent to the enactment of the Code will, of course, be so classified for purposes of sentence under Subsection (3).

Subsection (5) has been revised to grade as violations those offenses defined by statutes other than the Code which the legislature has provided shall not constitute crimes. The effect of this provision is to limit the maximum sentence for such an offense to a fine, excluding both probation and imprisonment. See Section 6.02 (4). This reflects the purpose of the Code to employ penal sanctions only with respect to conduct warranting the moral condemnation implicit in the concept of a crime.

Subsection (7) has been added to make clear that the intent of the provision is to superimpose the grading and sentencing plan of the Code upon offenses defined by statutes other than the Code, superseding their own sentencing provisions.

For Commentary, see Tentative Draft No. 2, p. 7.

Section 1.05. All Offenses Defined by Statute; Application of General Provisions of the Code.

(1) No conduct constitutes an offense unless it is a crime or violation under this Code or another statute of this State.

(2) The provisions of Part I of the Code are applicable to offenses defined by other statutes, unless the Code otherwise provides.

(3) This Section does not affect the power of a court to punish for contempt or to employ any sanction authorized by law for the enforcement of an order or a civil judgment or decree.

STATUS OF SECTION

Presented to the Institute in Tentative Draft No. 4 and considered at the May 1955 meeting.

For Commentary, see Tentative Draft No. 4, p. 106.

Section 1.06. Time Limitations.

(1) A prosecution for murder may be commenced at any time.

(2) Except as otherwise provided in this Section, prosecutions for other offenses are subject to the following periods of limitation:

    (a) a prosecution for a felony of the first degree must be commenced within six years after it is committed;

    (b) a prosecution for any other felony must be commenced within three years after it is committed;

    (c) a prosecution for a misdemeanor must be commenced within two years after it is committed;

    (d) a prosecution for a petty misdemeanor or a violation must be commenced within six months after it is committed.

(3) If the period prescribed in Subsection (2) has expired, a prosecution may nevertheless be commenced for:

    (a) any offense a material element of which is either fraud or a breach of fiduciary obligation within one year after discovery of the offense by an aggrieved party or by a person who has legal duty to represent an aggrieved party and who is himself not a party to the offense, but in no case shall this provision extend the period of limitation otherwise applicable by more than three years; and

    (b) any offense based upon misconduct in office by a public officer or employee at any time when the defendant is in public office or employment or within two years thereafter, but in no case shall this provision extend the period of limitation otherwise applicable by more than three years.

(4) An offense is committed either when every element occurs, or, if a legislative purpose to prohibit a continuing course of conduct plainly appears, at the time when the course of conduct or the defendant's complicity therein is terminated. Time starts to run on the day after the offense is committed.

(5) A prosecution is commenced either when an indictment is found [or an information filed] or when a warrant or other process is issued, provided that such warrant or process is executed without unreasonable delay.

(6) The period of limitation does not run:

(a) during any time when the accused is continuously absent from the State or has no reasonably ascertainable place of abode or work within the State, but in no case shall this provision extend the period of limitation otherwise applicable by more than three years; or

(b) during any time when a prosecution against the accused for the same conduct is pending in this State.

STATUS OF SECTION

Formerly numbered 1.07.

Presented to the Institute in Tentative Draft No. 5 and considered at the May 1956 meeting.

Subsection (3)(a) has been revised. It formerly provided that the supplementary period began to run upon discovery of the offense "by an aggrieved party or by a person who has legal capacity to represent an aggrieved party or a legal duty to report such offense." The category of persons with a duty to report was deemed to be too vague.

Subsection (3)(b) also made the period begin to run upon discovery. Both the Advisory Committee and the Council deemed it wiser in the case of public officers and employees to give effect to the continuation of their office or employment, as is now the law in many states.

Paragraph (6)(a) has been changed, in accordance with the view of the majority of the Institute, to provide that continuous absence from the State is itself sufficient to toll the statute. The Section formerly required a "purpose to avoid detection, apprehension or prosecution." The words "has no reasonably ascertainable place of abode or work" within the State have been substituted for "is absent from his usual place of abode," since the object is to reach the person who is hiding.

Other verbal changes have been made.

For Commentary, see Tentative Draft No. 5, p. 16.

Section 1.07. Method of Prosecution When Conduct Constitutes More Than One Offense.

(1) **Prosecution for Multiple Offenses; Limitation on Convictions.** When the same conduct of a defendant may establish the commission of more than one offense, the defendant may be prosecuted for each such offense. He may not, however, be convicted of more than one offense if:

(a) one offense is included in the other, as defined in Subsection (4) of this Section; or

(b) one offense consists only of a conspiracy or other form of preparation to commit the other; or

(c) inconsistent findings of fact are required to establish the commission of the offenses; or

(d) the offenses differ only in that one is defined to prohibit a designated kind of conduct generally and the other to prohibit a specific instance of such conduct; or

(e) the offense is defined as a continuing course of conduct and the defendant's course of conduct was uninterrupted, unless the law provides that specific periods of such conduct constitute separate offenses.

§ 1.07

(2) **Limitation on Separate Trials for Multiple Offenses.** Except as provided in Subsection (3) of this Section, a defendant shall not be subject to separate trials for multiple offenses based on the same conduct or arising from the same criminal episode, if such offenses are known to the appropriate prosecuting officer at the time of the commencement of the first trial and are within the jurisdiction of a single court.

(3) **Authority of Court to Order Separate Trials.** When a defendant is charged with two or more offenses based on the same conduct or arising from the same criminal episode, the Court, on application of the prosecuting attorney or of the defendant, may order any such charge to be tried separately, if it is satisfied that justice so requires.

(4) **Conviction of Included Offense Permitted.** A defendant may be convicted of an offense included in an offense charged in the indictment [or the information]. An offense is so included when:

(a) it is established by proof of the same or less than all the facts required to establish the commission of the offense charged; or

(b) it consists of an attempt or solicitation to commit the offense charged or to commit an offense otherwise included therein; or

(c) it differs from the offense charged only in the respect that a less serious injury or risk of injury to the same person, property or public interest or a lesser kind of culpability suffices to establish its commission.

(5) **Submission of Included Offense to Jury.** The Court shall not be obligated to charge the jury with respect to an included offense unless there is a rational basis for a verdict

acquitting the defendant of the offense charged and convicting him of the included offense.

STATUS OF SECTION

Formerly numbered 1.08.

Presented to the Institute in Tentative Draft No. 5 and considered at the May 1956 meeting.

Subsection (2) has been revised. The former title was "Requirement of Single Prosecution." This has been changed to make clear that the purpose of the provision is to limit separate trials but not to require a single indictment or information. The title of Subsection (3) has also been changed to avoid the same implication.

As previously drafted Subsection (2) required joinder of multiple charges when:

"(a) the offenses are based on the same conduct; or

"(b) the offenses are based on a series of acts or omissions motivated by a purpose to accomplish a single criminal objective, and necessary or incidental to accomplishment of that objective; or

"(c) the offenses are based on a series of acts or omissions motivated by a common purpose or plan and which result in the repeated commission of the same offense or affect the same person or the same persons or the property thereof."

While the Advisory Committee favored broadening this formulation to include all offenses "based on a course of conduct having a common criminal purpose or plan or involving repeated commission of the same kind of offense," the Council was of the opinion that both the original draft and this proposed substitute were too inclusive in their scope. The present submission, limiting the requirement to multiple offenses "based on the same conduct or arising from the same criminal episode" is designed to meet the Council's view.

Subsection (4)(b) has been revised to make solicitation as well as attempt an included offense.

Subsection (5) has been changed by the addition of the language "be obligated to" following "The Court shall not." The purpose of the change is to allow a court to submit an illogical included offense if the court believes that it is proper to do so. The majority of the Institute supported this change at the May 1956 meeting.

For Commentary, see Tentative Draft No. 5, p. 31.

Section 1.08. When Prosecution Barred by Former Prosecution for the Same Offense.

When a prosecution is for a violation of the same provision of the statutes and is based upon the same facts as a former prosecution, it is barred by such former prosecution under the following circumstances:

(1) The former prosecution resulted in an acquittal.* There is an acquittal if the prosecution resulted in a finding of not guilty by the trier of fact or in a determination that there was insufficient evidence to warrant a conviction. A finding of guilty of a lesser included offense is an acquittal of the greater inclusive offense, although the conviction is subsequently set aside.

(2) The former prosecution was terminated, after the information had been filed or the indictment found, by a final order or judgment for the defendant, which has not been set aside, reversed, or vacated and which necessarily required a determination inconsistent with a fact or a legal proposition that must be established for conviction of the offense.

(3) The former prosecution resulted in a conviction. There is a conviction if the prosecution resulted in a judgment of conviction which has not been reversed or vacated, a verdict of guilty which has not been set aside and which is capable of supporting a judgment, or a plea of guilty accepted by the Court. In the latter two cases failure to enter judgment must be for a reason other than a motion of the defendant.

---

* States like Connecticut and Wisconsin which give the prosecution a broad right of appeal will want to add a clause at this point substantially as follows: "unless such acquittal has been set aside because of an error of law prejudicial to the prosecution."

(4) The former prosecution was improperly terminated. Except as provided in this Subsection, there is an improper termination of a prosecution if the termination is for reasons not amounting to an acquittal, and it takes place after the first witness is sworn but before verdict. Termination under any of the following circumstances is not improper:

(a) The defendant consents to the termination or waives, by motion to dismiss or otherwise, his right to object to the termination.

(b) The trial court finds that the termination is necessary because:

(1) it is physically impossible to proceed with the trial in conformity with law; or

(2) there is a legal defect in the proceedings which would make any judgment entered upon a verdict reversible as a matter of law; or

(3) prejudicial conduct, in or outside the courtroom, makes it impossible to proceed with the trial without injustice to either the defendant or the State; or

(4) the jury is unable to agree upon a verdict; or

(5) false statements of a juror on voire dire prevent a fair trial.

STATUS OF SECTION

Formerly numbered 1.09.

Presented to the Institute in Tentative Draft No. 5 and considered at the May 1956 meeting.

Since the consideration of this Section by the Institute, the United States Supreme Court has held that under the double jeopardy clause of the Fifth Amendment a defendant charged with first degree and convicted of second degree murder, who obtains a reversal on appeal, may not again be tried for murder in the first degree. *Green v. United*

States, 355 U.S. 184 (1957). Though this result may not be binding on the states under the Fourteenth Amendment, the Council voted to adopt it in the Code, reversing the position previously taken in Subsection (1).

Minor verbal changes have been made.

For Commentary, see Tentative Draft No. 5, p. 45.

Section 1.09. When Prosecution Barred by Former Prosecution for Different Offense.

Although a prosecution is for a violation of a different provision of the statutes than a former prosecution or is based on different facts, it is barred by such former prosecution under the following circumstances:

(1) The former prosecution resulted in an acquittal* or in a conviction as defined in Section 1.08 and the subsequent prosecution is for:

    (a) any offense of which the defendant could have been convicted on the first prosecution; or

    (b) any offense for which the defendant should have been tried on the first prosecution under Section 1.07, unless the Court ordered a separate trial of the charge of such offense; or

    (c) the same conduct, unless (i) the offense of which the defendant was formerly convicted or acquitted and the offense for which he is subsequently prosecuted each requires proof of a fact not required by the other and the law defining each of such offenses is intended to prevent a substantially different harm or evil, or (ii) the second offense was not consummated when the former trial began.

---

* See footnote, supra, Sec. 1.08(1).

(2) The former prosecution was terminated, after the information was filed or the indictment found, by an acquittal or by a final order or judgment for the defendant which has not been set aside, reversed or vacated and which acquittal, final order or judgment necessarily required a determination inconsistent with a fact which must be established for conviction of the second offense.

(3) The former prosecution was improperly terminated, as improper termination is defined in Section 1.08, and the subsequent prosecution is for an offense of which the defendant could have been convicted had the former prosecution not been improperly terminated.

STATUS OF SECTION

Formerly numbered 1.10.

Presented to the Institute in Tentative Draft No. 5 and considered at the May 1956 meeting.

Verbal changes have been made in Subsection (1)(b).

Subsection (1)(c) is changed by adding the requirement that a subsequent offense be one intended by the legislature to prevent a "substantially different harm or evil." This language is taken from the definition of "material element" in Section 1.13. The prior draft merely restated the so-called "Blockburger rule," which allows a second prosecution if each offense requires proof of a fact not required by the other. Mechanically applied, as it has often been, the "Blockburger rule" results in subsequent prosecutions for essentially the same offense. See Fisher, *Double Jeopardy, Two Sovereignties and the Intruding Constitution*, 28 U. of Chi. L. Rev. 591 (1961). To a large extent this will be prevented by the compulsory joinder provision of Section 1.07. But there still is need for dealing with those instances where a severance is allowed by the trial judge. In such a case the subsequent prosecution must meet the requirement of the "Blockburger rule" plus the requirement that each offense be "intended to prevent a substantially different harm or evil."

A similar change is made in Section 1.10.

For Commentary, see Tentative Draft No. 5, p. 55.

Section 1.10. Former Prosecution in Another Jurisdiction: When a Bar.

When conduct constitutes an offense within the concurrent jurisdiction of this State and of the United States or another State, a prosecution in any such other jurisdiction is a bar to a subsequent prosecution in this State under the following circumstances:

(1) The first prosecution resulted in an acquittal or in a conviction as defined in Section 1.08 and the subsequent prosecution is based on the same conduct, unless (a) the offense of which the defendant was formerly convicted or acquitted and the offense for which he is subsequently prosecuted each requires proof of a fact not required by the other and the law defining each of such offenses is intended to prevent a substantially different harm or evil or (b) the second offense was not consummated when the former trial began; or

(2) The former prosecution was terminated, after the information was filed or the indictment found, by an acquittal or by a final order or judgment for the defendant which has not been set aside, reversed or vacated and which acquittal, final order or judgment necessarily required a determination inconsistent with a fact which must be established for conviction of the offense of which the defendant is subsequently prosecuted.

STATUS OF SECTION

Formerly numbered 1.11.

Presented to the Institute in Tentative Draft No. 5 and considered at the May 1956 meeting.

Subsection (1) is changed to add the requirement that a subsequent offense be one intended by the legislature to present a "substantially different harm or evil." The prior draft merely restated the so-called "Blockburger rule," which allows a second prosecution if each offense requires proof of a fact not required by the other. Mechanically applied, as it has often been, the "Blockburger rule" results in subsequent prosecutions for essentially the same offense. To prevent this the requirement that each be "intended to prevent a substantially different harm or evil" was added.

For Commentary, see Tentative Draft No. 5, p. 60.

Section 1.11. Former Prosecution Before Court Lacking Jurisdiction or When Fraudulently Procured by the Defendant.

A prosecution is not a bar within the meaning of Sections 1.08, 1.09 and 1.10 under any of the following circumstances:

(1) The former prosecution was before a court which lacked jurisdiction over the defendant or the offense; or

(2) The former prosecution was procured by the defendant without the knowledge of the appropriate prosecuting officer and with the purpose of avoiding the sentence which might otherwise be imposed; or

(3) The former prosecution resulted in a judgment of conviction which was held invalid in a subsequent proceeding on a writ of habeas corpus, coram nobis or similar process.

STATUS OF SECTION

Formerly numbered 1.12.

Presented to the Institute in Tentative Draft No. 5 and considered at the May 1956 meeting.

For Commentary, see Tentative Draft No. 5, p. 64.

§ 1.12

Section 1.12. Proof Beyond a Reasonable Doubt; Affirmative Defenses; Burden of Proving Fact When Not an Element of an Offense; Presumptions.

(1) No person may be convicted of an offense unless each element of such offense is proved beyond a reasonable doubt. In the absence of such proof, the innocence of the defendant is assumed.

(2) Subsection (1) of this Section does not:

(a) require the disproof of an affirmative defense unless and until there is evidence supporting such defense; or

(b) apply to any defense which the Code or another statute plainly requires the defendant to prove by a preponderance of evidence.

(3) A ground of defense is affirmative, within the meaning of Subsection (2)(a) of this Section, when:

(a) it arises under a section of the Code which so provides; or

(b) it relates to an offense defined by a statute other than the Code and such statute so provides; or

(c) it involves a matter of excuse or justification peculiarly within the knowledge of the defendant on which he can fairly be required to adduce supporting evidence.

(4) When the application of the Code depends upon the finding of a fact which is not an element of an offense, unless the Code otherwise provides:

(a) the burden of proving the fact is on the prosecution or defendant, depending on whose interest or contention will be furthered if the finding should be made; and

(b) the fact must be proved to the satisfaction of the Court or jury, as the case may be.

(5) When the Code establishes a presumption with respect to any fact which is an element of an offense, it has the following consequences:

(a) when there is evidence of the facts which give rise to the presumption, the issue of the existence of the presumed fact must be submitted to the jury, unless the Court is satisfied that the evidence as a whole clearly negatives the presumed fact; and

(b) when the issue of the existence of the presumed fact is submitted to the jury, the Court shall charge that while the presumed fact must, on all the evidence, be proved beyond a reasonable doubt, the law declares that the jury may regard the facts giving rise to the presumption as sufficient evidence of the presumed fact.

(6) A presumption not established by the Code or inconsistent with it has the consequences otherwise accorded it by law.

STATUS OF SECTION

Formerly numbered 1.12.

Presented to the Institute in Tentative Draft No. 4 and considered at the May 1955 meeting.

The alternative formulation of Subsection (5) has been eliminated from the text but will be presented in the Commentary.

For Commentary, see Tentative Draft No. 4, p. 108.

Section 1.13. General Definitions.

In this Code, unless a different meaning plainly is required:

(1) "statute" includes the Constitution and a local law or ordinance of a political subdivision of the State;

(2) "act" or "action" means a bodily movement whether voluntary or involuntary;

(3) "voluntary" has the meaning specified in Section 2.01;

(4) "omission" means a failure to act;

(5) "conduct" means an action or omission and its accompanying state of mind, or, where relevant, a series of acts and omissions;

(6) "actor" includes, where relevant, a person guilty of an omission;

(7) "acted" includes, where relevant, "omitted to act";

(8) "person," "he" and "actor" include any natural person and, where relevant, a corporation or an unincorporated association;

(9) "element of an offense" means (i) such conduct or (ii) such attendant circumstances or (iii) such a result of conduct as

(a) is included in the description of the forbidden conduct in the definition of the offense; or

(b) establishes the required kind of culpability; or

(c) negatives an excuse or justification for such conduct; or

(d) negatives a defense under the statute of limitations; or

(e) establishes jurisdiction or venue;

(10) "material element of an offense" means an element that does not relate exclusively to the statute of limitations, jurisdiction, venue or to any other matter similarly unconnected with (i) the harm or evil, incident to conduct, sought to be prevented by the law defining the offense, or (ii) the existence of a justification or excuse for such conduct;

(11) "purposely" has the meaning specified in Section 2.02 and equivalent terms such as "with purpose," "designed" or "with design" have the same meaning;

(12) "intentionally" or "with intent" means purposely;

(13) "knowingly" has the meaning specified in Section 2.02 and equivalent terms such as "knowing" or "with knowledge" have the same meaning;

(14) "recklessly" has the meaning specified in Section 2.02 and equivalent terms such as "recklessness" or "with recklessness" have the same meaning;

(15) "negligently" has the meaning specified in Section 2.02 and equivalent terms such as "negligence" or "with negligence" have the same meaning;

(16) "reasonably believes" or "reasonable belief" designates a belief which the actor is not reckless or negligent in holding.

STATUS OF SECTION

Formerly numbered 1.14.

Presented to the Institute in Tentative Draft No. 4 and considered at the May 1955 meeting.

The title has been changed by the addition of "General."

Subsections (11) to (16) have been added.

For Commentary, see Tentative Draft No. 4, p. 118.

ARTICLE 2. GENERAL PRINCIPLES OF LIABILITY

Section 2.01. Requirement of Voluntary Act; Omission as Basis of Liability; Possession as an Act.

(1) A person is not guilty of an offense unless his liability is based on conduct which includes a voluntary act or the omission to perform an act of which he is physically capable.

(2) The following are not voluntary acts within the meaning of this Section:

    (a) a reflex or convulsion;

    (b) a bodily movement during unconsciousness or sleep;

    (c) conduct during hypnosis or resulting from hypnotic suggestion;

    (d) a bodily movement that otherwise is not a product of the effort or determination of the actor, either conscious or habitual.

(3) Liability for the commission of an offense may not be based on an omission unaccompanied by action unless:

    (a) the omission is expressly made sufficient by the law defining the offense; or

    (b) a duty to perform the omitted act is otherwise imposed by law.

(4) Possession is an act, within the meaning of this Section, if the possessor knowingly procured or received the thing possessed or was aware of his control thereof for a sufficient period to have been able to terminate his possession.

STATUS OF SECTION

Presented to the Institute in Tentative Draft No. 4 and considered at the May 1955 meeting.

Pursuant to a suggestion at the meeting, the last words of Subsection (1) have been changed from "an act which it was physically possible to perform" to "of which he is physically capable."

In Subsection (2)(b) "coma" as an alternative to "unconsciousness" has been eliminated.

For Commentary, see Tentative Draft No. 4, p. 119.

Section 2.02. General Requirements of Culpability.

(1) <u>Minimum Requirements of Culpability</u>. Except as provided in Section 2.05, a person is not guilty of an offense unless he acted purposely, knowingly, recklessly or negligently, as the law may require, with respect to each material element of the offense.

(2) <u>Kinds of Culpability Defined</u>.

(a) <u>Purposely</u>.

A person acts purposely with respect to a material element of an offense when:

(i) if the element involves the nature of his conduct or a result thereof, it is his conscious object to engage in conduct of that nature or to cause such a result; and

(ii) if the element involves the attendant circumstances, he is aware of the existence of such circumstances or he believes or hopes that they exist.

(b) <u>Knowingly</u>.

A person acts knowingly with respect to a material element of an offense when:

(i) if the element involves the nature of his conduct or the attendant circumstances, he is aware that his conduct is of that nature or that such circumstances exist; and

(ii) if the element involves a result of his conduct, he is aware that it is practically certain that his conduct will cause such a result.

(c) Recklessly.

A person acts recklessly with respect to a material element of an offense when he consciously disregards a substantial and unjustifiable risk that the material element exists or will result from his conduct. The risk must be of such a nature and degree that, considering the nature and purpose of the actor's conduct and the circumstances known to him, its disregard involves a gross deviation from the standard of conduct that a law-abiding person would observe in the actor's situation.

(d) Negligently.

A person acts negligently with respect to a material element of an offense when he should be aware of a substantial and unjustifiable risk that the material element exists or will result from his conduct. The risk must be of such a nature and degree that the actor's failure to perceive it, considering the nature and purpose of his conduct and the circumstances known to him, involves a gross deviation from the standard of care that a reasonable person would observe in the actor's situation.

(3) Culpability Required Unless Otherwise Provided. When the culpability sufficient to establish a material element of an offense is not prescribed by law, such element

is established if a person acts purposely, knowingly or recklessly with respect thereto.

(4) Prescribed Culpability Requirement Applies to All Material Elements. When the law defining an offense prescribes the kind of culpability that is sufficient for the commission of an offense, without distinguishing among the material elements thereof, such provision shall apply to all the material elements of the offense, unless a contrary purpose plainly appears.

(5) Substitutes for Negligence, Recklessness and Knowledge. When the law provides that negligence suffices to establish an element of an offense, such element also is established if a person acts purposely, knowingly or recklessly. When recklessness suffices to establish an element, such element also is established if a person acts purposely or knowingly. When acting knowingly suffices to establish an element, such element also is established if a person acts purposely.

(6) Requirement of Purpose Satisfied if Purpose Is Conditional. When a particular purpose is an element of an offense, the element is established although such purpose is conditional, unless the condition negatives the harm or evil sought to be prevented by the law defining the offense.

(7) Requirement of Knowledge Satisfied by Knowledge of High Probability. When knowledge of the existence of a particular fact is an element of an offense, such knowledge is established if a person is aware of a high probability of its existence, unless he actually believes that it does not exist.

(8) Requirement of Wilfulness Satisfied by Acting Knowingly. A requirement that an offense be committed wilfully is satisfied if a person acts knowingly with respect to the material elements of the offense, unless a purpose to impose further requirements appears.

(9) Culpability as to Illegality of Conduct. Neither knowledge nor recklessness or negligence as to whether conduct constitutes an offense or as to the existence, meaning or application of the law determining the elements of an offense is an element of such offense, unless the definition of the offense or the Code so provides.

(10) Culpability as Determinant of Grade of Offense. When the grade or degree of an offense depends on whether the offense is committed purposely, knowingly, recklessly or negligently, its grade or degree shall be the lowest for which the determinative kind of culpability is established with respect to any material element of the offense.

STATUS OF SECTION

Presented to the Institute in Tentative Draft No. 4 and considered at the May 1955 meeting.

Verbal changes have been made.

For Commentary, see Tentative Draft No. 4, p. 123.

Section 2.03. Causal Relationship Between Conduct and Result; Divergence Between Result Designed or Contemplated and Actual Result or Between Probable and Actual Result.

(1) Conduct is the cause of a result when:

(a) it is an antecedent but for which the result in question would not have occurred; and

(b) the relationship between the conduct and result satisfies any additional causal requirements imposed by the Code or by the law defining the offense.

(2) When purposely or knowingly causing a particular result is an element of an offense, the element is not established if the actual result is not within the purpose or the contemplation of the actor unless:

(a) the actual result differs from that designed or contemplated, as the case may be, only in the respect that a different person or different property is injured or affected or that the injury or harm designed or contemplated would have been more serious or more extensive than that caused; or

(b) the actual result involves the same kind of injury or harm as that designed or contemplated and is not too remote or accidental in its occurrence to have a [just] bearing on the actor's liability or on the gravity of his offense.

(3) When recklessly or negligently causing a particular result is an element of an offense, the element is not established if the actual result is not within the risk of which the actor is aware or, in the case of negligence, of which he should be aware unless:

(a) the actual result differs from the probable result only in the respect that a different person or different property is injured or affected or that the probable injury or harm would have been more serious or more extensive than that caused; or

(b) the actual result involves the same kind of injury or harm as the probable result and is not too remote or accidental in its occurrence to have a [just] bearing on the actor's liability or on the gravity of his offense.

(4) When causing a particular result is a material element of an offense for which absolute liability is imposed by law, the element is not established unless the actual result is a probable consequence of the actor's conduct.

STATUS OF SECTION

Presented to the Institute in Tentative Draft No. 4 and considered at the May 1955 meeting.

In Subsections (2)(b) and (3)(b) the words "remote or" have been added before "accidental," the word "just" has been bracketed as optional and the alternatives in the previous draft have been eliminated.

Subsection (4) has been added in response to criticism of the draft's reliance upon but-for cause alone in cases of strict liability. See H. L. A. Hart and Honoré, Causation in the Law (1959) p. 361; Mueller, "Causing Criminal Harm" in Essays in Criminal Science (1960) pp. 169, 185.

For Commentary, see Tentative Draft No. 4, p. 132.

Section 2.04. Ignorance or Mistake.

(1) Ignorance or mistake as to a matter of fact or law is a defense if:

(a) the ignorance or mistake negatives the purpose, knowledge, belief, recklessness or negligence required to establish a material element of the offense; or

(b) the law provides that the state of mind established by such ignorance or mistake constitutes a defense.

(2) Although ignorance or mistake would otherwise afford a defense to the offense charged, the defense is not available if the defendant would be guilty of another offense had the situation been as he supposed. In such case, however, the ignorance or mistake of the defendant shall reduce the grade and degree of the offense of which he may be convicted to those of the offense of which he would be guilty had the situation been as he supposed.

(3) A belief that conduct does not legally constitute an offense is a defense to a prosecution for that offense based upon such conduct when:

    (a) the statute or other enactment defining the offense is not known to the actor and has not been published or otherwise reasonably made available prior to the conduct alleged; or

    (b) he acts in reasonable reliance upon an official statement of the law, afterward determined to be invalid or erroneous, contained in (i) a statute or other enactment; (ii) a judicial decision, opinion or judgment; (iii) an administrative order or grant of permission; or (iv) an official interpretation of the public officer or body charged by law with responsibility for the interpretation, administration or enforcement of the law defining the offense.

(4) The defendant must prove a defense arising under Subsection (3) of this Section by a preponderance of evidence.

STATUS OF SECTION

Presented to the Institute in Tentative Draft No. 4 and considered at the May 1955 meeting.

Subsection (2) is, in substance, Alternative (2) of the former draft, which both the Advisory Committee and the Council deemed the preferable treatment of the problem of the actor who submits as a defense to the crime charged a mistake which, had the facts been as he thought, would have involved commission of another crime.

For Commentary, see Tentative Draft No. 4, p. 135.

Section 2.05. When Culpability Requirements Are Inapplicable to Violations and to Offenses Defined by Other Statutes; Effect of Absolute Liability in Reducing Grade of Offense to Violation.

(1) The requirements of culpability prescribed by Sections 2.01 and 2.02 do not apply to:

§ 2.06

(a) offenses which constitute violations, unless the requirement involved is included in the definition of the offense or the Court determines that its application is consistent with effective enforcement of the law defining the offense; or

(b) offenses defined by statutes other than the Code, insofar as a legislative purpose to impose absolute liability for such offenses or with respect to any material element thereof plainly appears.

(2) Notwithstanding any other provision of existing law and unless a subsequent statute otherwise provides:

(a) when absolute liability is imposed with respect to any material element of an offense defined by a statute other than the Code and a conviction is based upon such liability, the offense constitutes a violation; and

(b) although absolute liability is imposed by law with respect to one or more of the material elements of an offense defined by a statute other than the Code, the culpable commission of the offense may be charged and proved, in which event negligence with respect to such elements constitutes sufficient culpability and the classification of the offense and the sentence that may be imposed therefor upon conviction are determined by Section 1.04 and Article 6 of the Code.

STATUS OF SECTION

Presented to the Institute and considered at the May 1955 meeting.

Verbal changes have been made.

For Commentary, see Tentative Draft No. 4, p. 140.

Section 2.06. Liability for Conduct of Another; Complicity.

(1) A person is guilty of an offense if it is committed by his own conduct or by the conduct of another person for which he is legally accountable, or both.

(2) A person is legally accountable for the conduct of another person when:

(a) acting with the kind of culpability that is sufficient for the commission of the offense, he causes an innocent or irresponsible person to engage in such conduct; or

(b) he is made accountable for the conduct of such other person by the Code or by the law defining the offense; or

(c) he is an accomplice of such other person in the commission of the offense.

(3) A person is an accomplice of another person in the commission of an offense if:

(a) with the purpose of promoting or facilitating the commission of the offense, he

(i) solicits such other person to commit it; or

(ii) aids or agrees or attempts to aid such other person in planning or committing it; or

(iii) having a legal duty to prevent the commission of the offense, fails to make proper effort so to do; or

(b) his conduct is expressly declared by law to establish his complicity.

(4) When causing a particular result is an element of an offense, an accomplice in the conduct causing such result is an accomplice in the commission of that offense, if he acts with the kind of culpability, if any, with respect to that result that is sufficient for the commission of the offense.

(5) A person who is legally incapable of committing a particular offense himself may be guilty thereof if it is

committed by the conduct of another person for which he is legally accountable, unless such liability is inconsistent with the purpose of the provision establishing his incapacity.

(6) Unless otherwise provided by the Code or by the law defining the offense, a person is not an accomplice in an offense committed by another person if:

(a) he is a victim of that offense; or

(b) the offense is so defined that his conduct is inevitably incident to its commission; or

(c) he terminates his complicity prior to the commission of the offense and

(i) wholly deprives it of effectiveness in the commission of the offense; or

(ii) gives timely warning to the law enforcement authorities or otherwise makes proper effort to prevent the commission of the offense.

(7) An accomplice may be convicted on proof of the commission of the offense and of his complicity therein, though the person claimed to have committed the offense has not been prosecuted or convicted or has been convicted of a different offense or degree of offense or has an immunity to prosecution or conviction or has been acquitted.

STATUS OF SECTION

Formerly numbered 2.04.

Presented to the Institute in Tentative Draft No. 1 and Tentative Draft No. 4 and considered at the May 1953 and 1955 meetings.

Subsection (3)(a)(i) has been changed from "commanded, requested, encouraged or provoked" to "solicits." Criminal solicitation is defined in Section 5.02. Provocation, as distinguished from command, request or encouragement, is eliminated pursuant to suggestion from the floor at the May 1953 meeting.

Subsection (3)(b) of the previous drafts, basing complicity on "knowingly substantially" facilitating the commission of the offense, has been omitted pursuant to vote of the Institute at the May 1953 meeting.

Subsection (4) has been revised in form and Subsection (5) has been added.

In Subsection (7) the words "or an immunity to prosecution or conviction" have been added.

Other verbal changes have been made.

For Commentary, see Tentative Draft No. 1, p. 13.

Section 2.07. Liability of Corporations, Unincorporated Associations and Persons Acting, or Under a Duty to Act, in Their Behalf.

(1) A corporation may be convicted of the commission of an offense if:

(a) the offense is a violation or the offense is defined by a statute other than the Code in which a legislative purpose to impose liability on corporations plainly appears and the conduct is performed by an agent of the corporation acting in behalf of the corporation within the scope of his office or employment, except that if the law defining the offense designates the agents for whose conduct the corporation is accountable or the circumstances under which it is accountable, such provisions shall apply; or

(b) the offense consists of an omission to discharge a specific duty of affirmative performance imposed on corporations by law; or

(c) the commission of the offense was authorized, requested, commanded, performed or recklessly tolerated by the board of directors or by a high managerial agent acting in behalf of the corporation within the scope of his office or employment.

(2) When absolute liability is imposed for the commission of an offense, a legislative purpose to impose liability

on a corporation shall be assumed, unless the contrary plainly appears.

(3) An unincorporated association may be convicted of the commission of an offense if:

(a) the offense is defined by a statute other than the Code which expressly provides for the liability of such an association and the conduct is performed by an agent of the association acting in behalf of the association within the scope of his office or employment, except that if the law defining the offense designates the agents for whose conduct the association is accountable or the circumstances under which it is accountable, such provisions shall apply; or

(b) the offense consists of an omission to discharge a specific duty of affirmative performance imposed on associations by law.

(4) As used in this Section:

(a) "corporation" does not include an entity organized as or by a governmental agency for the execution of a governmental program;

(b) "agent" means any director, officer, servant, employee or other person authorized to act in behalf of the corporation or association and, in the case of an unincorporated association, a member of such association;

(c) "high managerial agent" means an officer of a corporation or an unincorporated association, or, in the case of a partnership, a partner, or any other agent of a corporation or association having duties of such responsibility that his conduct may fairly be assumed to represent the policy of the corporation or association.

(5) In any prosecution of a corporation or an unincorporated association for the commission of an offense included within the terms of Subsection (1)(a) or Subsection (3)(a) of this Section, other than an offense for which absolute liability has been imposed, it shall be a defense if the defendant proves by a preponderance of evidence that the high managerial agent having supervisory responsibility over the subject matter of the offense employed due diligence to prevent its commission. This paragraph shall not apply if it is plainly inconsistent with the legislative purpose in defining the particular offense.

(6)(a) A person is legally accountable for any conduct he performs or causes to be performed in the name of the corporation or an unincorporated association or in its behalf to the same extent as if it were performed in his own name or behalf.

(b) Whenever a duty to act is imposed by law upon a corporation or an unincorporated association, any agent of the corporation or association having primary responsibility for the discharge of the duty is legally accountable for a reckless omission to perform the required act to the same extent as if the duty were imposed by law directly upon himself.

(c) When a person is convicted of an offense by reason of his legal accountability for the conduct of a corporation or an unincorporated association, he is subject to the sentence authorized by law when a natural person is convicted of an offense of the grade and the degree involved.

STATUS OF SECTION

Presented to the Institute in Tentative Drafts No. 4 and 5 and considered at the May 1956 meeting.

The following revisions have been made:

1. Subsections (1)(b) and (3)(b) have been limited to cases where the offense consists of an omission "to discharge a specific duty

of affirmative performance imposed" on corporations or associations by law. The reference to a "specific" duty is designed to make clear that the provisions do not govern in such a case as negligent homicide, where the duty violated is one that the law imposes generally, as distinguished, for example, from a duty to file a report of a kind that the corporation or association is specifically required to file.

2. The scope of corporate liability has been extended by Subsection (1)(c) to cases where the commission of the offense is "recklessly tolerated" by the board of directors or by a high managerial agent.

3. Former Subsection (3)(c) envisaged that the liability of unincorporated associations might be declared for some specific offenses defined by the Code. On reconsideration of the question, no adequate basis appeared for selecting such offenses and the Subsection was accordingly eliminated. A general provision, analogous to that applied to corporations by Subsection (1)(c), raises far too many controversial questions to be feasibly included in the Code. It will, however, be considered in the Commentary.

4. Subsection (4)(a) has been added to exclude the governmental corporation from the scope of the Section, in the view that corporate liability is generally pointless in such cases.

5. The last sentence of Subsection (5) has been revised so that the defense will be available unless "plainly" inconsistent with the legislative purpose in defining the particular offense.

6. Subsection (6)(b) has been limited to cases where the individual is at least "reckless" in his failure to perform the required act for the corporation or association.

Other verbal changes have been made.

For Commentary, see Tentative Draft No. 4, p. 146.

Section 2.08. Intoxication.

(1) Except as provided in Subsection (4) of this Section, intoxication of the actor is not a defense unless it negatives an element of the offense.

(2) When recklessness establishes an element of the offense, if the actor, due to self-induced intoxication, is unaware of a risk of which he would have been aware had he been sober, such unawareness is immaterial.

(3) Intoxication does not, in itself, constitute mental disease within the meaning of Section 4.01.

(4) Intoxication which (a) is not self-induced or (b) is pathological is an affirmative defense if by reason of such intoxication the actor at the time of his conduct lacks substantial capacity either to appreciate its criminality [wrongfulness] or to conform his conduct to the requirements of law.

(5) <u>Definitions</u>. In this Section unless a different meaning plainly is required:

(a) "intoxication" means a disturbance of mental or physical capacities resulting from the introduction of substances into the body;

(b) "self-induced intoxication" means intoxication caused by substances which the actor knowingly introduces into his body, the tendency of which to cause intoxication he knows or ought to know, unless he introduces them pursuant to medical advice or under such circumstances as would afford a defense to a charge of crime;

(c) "pathological intoxication" means intoxication grossly excessive in degree, given the amount of the intoxicant, to which the actor does not know he is susceptible.

STATUS OF SECTION

Presented to the Institute in Tentative Draft No. 9 and considered at the May 1959 meeting.

The word "wrongfulness" has been inserted in Subsection (4) in brackets to conform to the option provided in the criteria of responsibility in Section 4.01.

In the last line of Subsection (5)(b), the words "such duress as would afford a defense to a charge of crime" have been changed to "such circumstances." The prime purpose of the change is to make applicable the choice of evils defense of Section 3.02. This was contemplated by the former draft, as in all cases of duress (see Section 2.09(4)), but might not be perceived upon the language.

The definition of "pathological intoxication" has been changed in response to a suggestion at the Institute meeting to make clear that the actor must not know of his susceptibility to the excessive reaction. With this change, there seems no reason to require that the reaction be "caused by an abnormal bodily condition," as provided by the former draft.

For Commentary, see Tentative Draft No. 9, p. 2.

Section 2.09. Duress.

(1) It is an affirmative defense that the actor engaged in the conduct charged to constitute an offense because he was coerced to do so by the use of, or a threat to use, unlawful force against his person or the person of another, which a person of reasonable firmness in his situation would have been unable to resist.

(2) The defense provided by this Section is unavailable if the actor recklessly placed himself in a situation in which it was probable that he would be subjected to duress. The defense is also unavailable if he was negligent in placing himself in such a situation, whenever negligence suffices to establish culpability for the offense charged.

(3) It is not a defense that a woman acted on the command of her husband, unless she acted under such coercion as would establish a defense under this Section. [The presumption that a woman, acting in the presence of her husband, is coerced is abolished.]

(4) When the conduct of the actor would otherwise be justifiable under Section 3.02, this Section does not preclude such defense.

STATUS OF SECTION

Presented to the Institute in Tentative Draft No. 10 and considered at the May 1960 meeting.

The words "for the offense charged" have been added at the end of Subsection (2).

For Commentary, see Tentative Draft No. 10, p. 2.

Section 2.10. Military Orders.

It is an affirmative defense that the actor, in engaging in the conduct charged to constitute an offense, does no more than execute an order of his superior in the armed services which he does not know to be unlawful.

STATUS OF SECTION

Approved by the Advisory Committee and the Council at their March 1962 meetings.

The present Manual limits the defense in military law to cases where the actor "did not know and could not reasonably be expected to know that the act ordered was illegal." U.S. Dept. of the Army, Field Manual: The Law of Land Warfare 182 (1956). Military courts are admonished, however, to "take into consideration the fact that obedience to lawful orders is the duty of every member of the armed forces; that the latter cannot be expected, in conditions of war discipline, to weigh scrupulously the legal merits of the orders received," etc. In a prosecution in a civil court, it seems unrealistic to inquire whether a defendant who did not know an order was illegal could "reasonably be expected" to have known it. This limitation on the defense is accordingly abandoned in the view that when that question is in issue it is preferable that it should be litigated in a military court.

Section 2.11. Consent.

(1) *In General.* The consent of the victim to conduct charged to constitute an offense or to the result thereof is a defense if such consent negatives an element of the offense or precludes the infliction of the harm or evil sought to be prevented by the law defining the offense.

(2) *Consent to Bodily Harm.* When conduct is charged to constitute an offense because it causes or threatens bodily harm, consent to such conduct or to the infliction of such harm is a defense if:

   (a) the bodily harm consented to or threatened by the conduct consented to is not serious; or

(b) the conduct and the harm are reasonably foreseeable hazards of joint participation in a lawful athletic contest or competitive sport; or

(c) the consent establishes a justification for the conduct under Article 3 of the Code.

(3) **Ineffective Consent.** Unless otherwise provided by the Code or by the law defining the offense, assent does not constitute consent if:

(a) it is given by a person who is legally incompetent to authorize the conduct charged to constitute the offense; or

(b) it is given by a person who by reason of youth, mental disease or defect or intoxication is manifestly unable or known by the actor to be unable to make a reasonable judgment as to the nature or harmfulness of the conduct charged to constitute the offense; or

(c) it is given by a person whose improvident consent is sought to be prevented by the law defining the offense; or

(d) it is induced by force, duress or deception of a kind sought to be prevented by the law defining the offense.

STATUS OF SECTION

Approved by the Advisory Committee and the Council at their March 1962 meetings.

Section 2.12. De Minimis Infractions.

The Court shall dismiss a prosecution if, having regard to the nature of the conduct charged to constitute an offense and the nature of the attendant circumstances, it finds that the defendant's conduct:

(1) was within a customary license or tolerance, neither expressly negatived by the person whose interest was infringed nor inconsistent with the purpose of the law defining the offense; or

(2) did not actually cause or threaten the harm or evil sought to be prevented by the law defining the offense or did so only to an extent too trivial to warrant the condemnation of conviction; or

(3) presents such other extenuations that it cannot reasonably be regarded as envisaged by the legislature in forbidding the offense.

The Court shall not dismiss a prosecution under Subsection (3) of this Section without filing a written statement of its reasons.

STATUS OF SECTION

Approved by the Advisory Committee and the Council at their March 1962 meetings.

Section 2.13. Entrapment.

(1) A public law enforcement official or a person acting in cooperation with such an official perpetrates an entrapment if for the purpose of obtaining evidence of the commission of an offense, he induces or encourages another person to engage in conduct constituting such offense by either:

(a) making knowingly false representations designed to induce the belief that such conduct is not prohibited; or

(b) employing methods of persuasion or inducement which create a substantial risk that such an offense will be committed by persons other than those who are ready to commit it.

§ 2.13

(2) Except as provided in Subsection (3) of this Section, a person prosecuted for an offense shall be acquitted if he proves by a preponderance of evidence that his conduct occurred in response to an entrapment. The issue of entrapment shall be tried by the Court in the absence of the jury.

(3) The defense afforded by this Section is unavailable when causing or threatening bodily injury is an element of the offense charged and the prosecution is based on conduct causing or threatening such injury to a person other than the person perpetrating the entrapment.

STATUS OF SECTION

Formerly numbered 2.10.

Presented to the Institute in Tentative Draft No. 9 and considered at the May 1959 meeting.

Subsection (1) is the previous alternative formulation, which was adopted by vote of the Institute. The only change made is the substitution of the word "induces" for "solicits," deemed preferable since "solicits" is a word of art defined in Section 5.02.

In Subsection (2) the words "by a preponderance of evidence" were added.

Subsection (3) has been amended pursuant to a suggestion at the Institute meeting to require that causing or threatening bodily injury be an element of the offense charged for the defense of entrapment to be unavailable. It was feared that otherwise the defense might be excluded in such cases as sale of narcotics, where it is most important that it be preserved.

For Commentary, see Tentative Draft No. 9, p. 14.

ARTICLE 3. GENERAL PRINCIPLES OF JUSTIFICATION

Section 3.01. Justification an Affirmative Defense; Civil Remedies Unaffected. 1

(1) In any prosecution based on conduct which is justifiable under this Article, justification is an affirmative defense.

(2) The fact that conduct is justifiable under this Article does not abolish or impair any remedy for such conduct which is available in any civil action.

STATUS OF SECTION

Presented to the Institute in Tentative Draft No. 8 and considered at the May 1958 meeting.

For Commentary, see Tentative Draft No. 8, p. 4.

Section 3.02. Justification Generally: Choice of Evils.

(1) Conduct which the actor believes to be necessary to avoid a harm or evil to himself or to another is justifiable, provided that:

(a) the harm or evil sought to be avoided by such conduct is greater than that sought to be prevented by the law defining the offense charged; and

(b) neither the Code nor other law defining the offense provides exceptions or defenses dealing with the specific situation involved; and

(c) a legislative purpose to exclude the justification claimed does not otherwise plainly appear.

(2) When the actor was reckless or negligent in bringing about the situation requiring a choice of harms or evils or in appraising the necessity for his conduct, the justifica-

tion afforded by this Section is unavailable in a prosecution for any offense for which recklessness or negligence, as the case may be, suffices to establish culpability.

STATUS OF SECTION

Presented to the Institute in Tentative Draft No. 8 and considered at the May 1958 meeting.

The words "harm or" have been inserted before "evil," in the interest of stylistic uniformity.

For Commentary, see Tentative Draft No. 8, p. 5.

Section 3.03. Execution of Public Duty.

(1) Except as provided in Subsection (2) of this Section, conduct is justifiable when it is required or authorized by:

 (a) the law defining the duties or functions of a public officer or the assistance to be rendered to such officer in the performance of his duties; or

 (b) the law governing the execution of legal process; or

 (c) the judgment or order of a competent court or tribunal; or

 (d) the law governing the armed services or the lawful conduct of war; or

 (e) any other provision of law imposing a public duty.

(2) The other sections of this Article apply to:

 (a) the use of force upon or toward the person of another for any of the purposes dealt with in such sections; and

(b) the use of deadly force for any purpose, unless the use of such force is otherwise expressly authorized by law or occurs in the lawful conduct of war.

(3) The justification afforded by Subsection (1) of this Section applies:

(a) when the actor believes his conduct to be required or authorized by the judgment or direction of a competent court or tribunal or in the lawful execution of legal process, notwithstanding lack of jurisdiction of the court or defect in the legal process; and

(b) when the actor believes his conduct to be required or authorized to assist a public officer in the performance of his duties, notwithstanding that the officer exceeded his legal authority.

STATUS OF SECTION

Presented to the Institute in Tentative Draft No. 8 and considered at the May 1958 meeting.

The words "or tribunal" have been added in Subsection (1)(c), pursuant to suggestion at the meeting of the Institute.

For Commentary, see Tentative Draft No. 8, p. 11.

Section 3.04. Use of Force in Self-Protection.

(1) <u>Use of Force Justifiable for Protection of the Person.</u> Subject to the provisions of this Section and of Section 3.09, the use of force upon or toward another person is justifiable when the actor believes that such force is immediately necessary for the purpose of protecting himself against the use of unlawful force by such other person on the present occasion.

(2) <u>Limitations on Justifying Necessity for Use of Force.</u>

(a) The use of force is not justifiable under this Section:

(i) to resist an arrest which the actor knows is being made by a peace officer, although the arrest is unlawful; or

(ii) to resist force used by the occupier or possessor of property or by another person on his behalf, where the actor knows that the person using the force is doing so under a claim of right to protect the property, except that this limitation shall not apply if:

(1) the actor is a public officer acting in the performance of his duties or a person lawfully assisting him therein or a person making or assisting in a lawful arrest; or

(2) the actor has been unlawfully dispossessed of the property and is making a re-entry or recaption justified by Section 3.06; or

(3) the actor believes that such force is necessary to protect himself against death or serious bodily harm.

(b) The use of deadly force is not justifiable under this Section unless the actor believes that such force is necessary to protect himself against death, serious bodily harm, kidnapping or sexual intercourse compelled by force or threat; nor is it justifiable if:

(i) the actor, with the purpose of causing death or serious bodily harm, provoked the use of force against himself in the same encounter; or

(ii) the actor knows that he can avoid the necessity of using such force with complete safety by retreating or by surrendering possession of a thing to a person asserting a claim of right thereto or by complying with a demand that he abstain from any action which he has no duty to take, except that:

(1) the actor is not obliged to retreat from his dwelling or place of work, unless he was the initial aggressor or is assailed in his place of work by another person whose place of work the actor knows it to be; and

(2) a public officer justified in using force in the performance of his duties or a person justified in using force in his assistance or a person justified in using force in making an arrest or preventing an escape is not obliged to desist from efforts to perform such duty, effect such arrest or prevent such escape because of resistance or threatened resistance by or on behalf of the person against whom such action is directed.

(c) Except as required by paragraphs (a) and (b) of this Subsection, a person employing protective force may estimate the necessity thereof under the circumstances as he believes them to be when the force is used, without retreating, surrendering possession, doing any other act which he has no legal duty to do or abstaining from any lawful action.

(3) *Use of Confinement as Protective Force.* The justification afforded by this Section extends to the use of confinement as protective force only if the actor takes all reasonable measures to terminate the confinement as soon as he knows that he safely can, unless the person confined has been arrested on a charge of crime.

STATUS OF SECTION

Presented to the Institute in Tentative Draft No. 8 and considered at the May 1958 meeting.

The Institute voted not to require retreat from the actor's dwelling when he is assailed by another person whose dwelling it also is and Subsection (2)(b)(ii)(1) has been modified accordingly.

§ 3.05   50   Model Penal Code

A verbal correction approved by the Institute has been made in Subsection (2)(a)(ii)(2). See Proceedings (1958) p. 256.

In Subsection (2)(b) "kidnapping" has been substituted for "kidnapping by violence" and "sexual intercourse by force or threat" for "rape or sodomy by force or intimidation."

For Commentary, see Tentative Draft No. 8, p. 14.

Section 3.05. Use of Force for the Protection of Other Persons.

(1) Subject to the provisions of this Section and of Section 3.09, the use of force upon or toward the person of another is justifiable to protect a third person when:

  (a) the actor would be justified under Section 3.04 in using such force to protect himself against the injury he believes to be threatened to the person whom he seeks to protect; and

  (b) under the circumstances as the actor believes them to be, the person whom he seeks to protect would be justified in using such protective force; and

  (c) the actor believes that his intervention is necessary for the protection of such other person.

(2) Notwithstanding Subsection (1) of this Section:

  (a) when the actor would be obliged under Section 3.04 to retreat, to surrender the possession of a thing or to comply with a demand before using force in self-protection, he is not obliged to do so before using force for the protection of another person, unless he knows that he can thereby secure the complete safety of such other person; and

  (b) when the person whom the actor seeks to protect would be obliged under Section 3.04 to retreat, to surrender the possession of a thing or to comply with a demand if he knew that he could obtain complete safety by so doing, the actor is obliged to try to cause him to to do so before using force in his protection if the actor knows that he can obtain complete safety in that way; and

(c) neither the actor nor the person whom he seeks to protect is obliged to retreat when in the other's dwelling or place of work to any greater extent than in his own.

STATUS OF SECTION

Presented to the Institute in Tentative Draft No. 8 and considered at the May 1958 meeting.

For Commentary, see Tentative Draft No. 8, p. 31.

Section 3.06. Use of Force for the Protection of Property.

(1) **Use of Force Justifiable for Protection of Property.** Subject to the provisions of this Section and of Section 3.09, the use of force upon or toward the person of another is justifiable when the actor believes that such force is immediately necessary:

(a) to prevent or terminate an unlawful entry or other trespass upon land or a trespass against or the unlawful carrying away of tangible, movable property, provided that such land or movable property is, or is believed by the actor to be, in his possession or in the possession of another person for whose protection he acts; or

(b) to effect an entry or re-entry upon land or to retake tangible movable property, provided that the actor believes that he or the person by whose authority he acts or a person from whom he or such other person derives title was unlawfully dispossessed of such land or movable property and is entitled to possession, and provided, further, that:

(i) the force is used immediately or on fresh purusit after such dispossession; or

(ii) the actor believes that the person against whom he uses force has no claim of right to the possession of the property and, in the case of land, the circumstances, as the actor believes them to be, are of such urgency that it would be an exceptional hardship to postpone the entry or re-entry until a court order is obtained.

(2) <u>Meaning of Possession</u>. For the purposes of Subsection (1) of this Section:

(a) a person who has parted with the custody of property to another who refuses to restore it to him is no longer in possession, unless the property is movable and was and still is located on land in his possession;

(b) a person who has been dispossessed of land does not regain possession thereof merely by setting foot thereon;

(c) a person who has a license to use or occupy real property is deemed to be in possession thereof except against the licensor acting under claim of right.

(3) <u>Limitations on Justifiable Use of Force</u>.

(a) <u>Request to Desist</u>. The use of force is justifiable under this Section only if the actor first requests the person against whom such force is used to desist from his interference with the property, unless the actor believes that:

(i) such request would be useless; or

(ii) it would be dangerous to himself or another person to make the request; or

(iii) substantial harm will be done to the physical condition of the property which is sought to be protected before the request can effectively be made.

(b) <u>Exclusion of Trespasser.</u> The use of force to prevent or terminate a trespass is not justifiable under this Section if the actor knows that the exclusion of the trespasser will expose him to substantial danger of serious bodily harm.

(c) <u>Resistance of Lawful Re-entry or Recaption.</u> The use of force to prevent an entry or re-entry upon land or the recaption of movable property is not justifiable under this Section, although the actor believes that such re-entry or recaption is unlawful, if:

(i) the re-entry or recaption is made by or on behalf of a person who was actually dispossessed of the property; and

(ii) it is otherwise justifiable under paragraph (1)(b) of this Section.

(d) <u>Use of Deadly Force.</u> The use of deadly force is not justifiable under this Section unless the actor believes that:

(i) the person against whom the force is used is attempting to dispossess him of his dwelling otherwise than under a claim of right to its possession; or

(ii) the person against whom the force is used is attempting to commit or consummate arson, burglary, robbery or other felonious theft or property destruction and either:

(1) has employed or threatened deadly force against or in the presence of the actor; or

(2) the use of force other than deadly force to prevent the commission or the consummation of the crime would expose the actor or another in his presence to substantial danger of serious bodily harm.

(4) **Use of Confinement as Protective Force.** The justification afforded by this Section extends to the use of confinement as protective force only if the actor takes all reasonable measures to terminate the confinement as soon as he knows that he can do so with safety to the property, unless the person confined has been arrested on a charge of crime.

(5) **Use of Device to Protect Property.** The justification afforded by this Section extends to the use of a device for the purpose of protecting property only if:

(a) the device is not designed to cause or known to create a substantial risk of causing death or serious bodily harm; and

(b) the use of the particular device to protect the property from entry or trespass is reasonable under the circumstances, as the actor believes them to be; and

(c) the device is one customarily used for such a purpose or reasonable care is taken to make known to probable intruders the fact that it is used.

(6) **Use of Force to Pass Wrongful Obstructor.** The use of force to pass a person whom the actor believes to be purposely or knowingly and unjustifiably obstructing the actor from going to a place to which he may lawfully go is justifiable, provided that:

(a) the actor believes that the person against whom he uses force has no claim of right to obstruct the actor; and

Art. 3 55 § 3.06

(b) the actor is not being obstructed from entry or movement on land which he knows to be in the possession or custody of the person obstructing him, or in the possession or custody of another person by whose authority the obstructor acts, unless the circumstances, as the actor believes them to be, are of such urgency that it would not be reasonable to postpone the entry or movement on such land until a court order is obtained; and

(c) the force used is not greater than would be justifiable if the person obstructing the actor were using force against him to prevent his passage.

STATUS OF SECTION

Presented to the Institute in Tentative Draft No. 8 and considered at the May 1958 meeting.

Resubmitted to the Council in revised form and considered at the December 1958 meeting.

The revision involves substantial formal changes for the sake of clarity, developed with the aid of Mr. Sinclair Hatch, who very properly was critical of the original submission on this ground. See Proceedings (1958) p. 300.

The major substantive change inheres in the addition of Subsection (3)(d)(ii), in the effort to execute the mandate of the Institute that the justification for the use of deadly force to protect property be expanded to encompass the most serious and violent situations, which the Reporter was requested to define. The Council approved the formulation as a fair expression of the wishes of the Institute.

The provision as now drafted is broader than the analogous privilege in any of the three most recent codes. See Louisiana Code § 14.20 ("violent or forcible felony involving danger to life or of great bodily harm"); Wisconsin Criminal Code 939.49(1) ("It is not reasonable to intentionally use force intended or likely to cause death or great bodily harm for the sole purpose of defense of one's property"); Illinois Criminal Code §§ 7-3, 2-8 ("forcible felony" defined as "treason, murder, voluntary manslaughter, rape, robbery, burglary, arson, kidnapping, aggravated battery and any other felony which involves the use or threat of physical force or violence against any individual"). It is, however, clear that the Institute wished to

§ 3.07   Model Penal Code

go beyond the use of deadly force for the prevention of the violent crime, if violence was used or threatened and the force is used to prevent escape with the fruits, and also where the actor apprehends that use of lesser force would expose him to danger. Hence, the formulation cannot well be any narrower than that presented here, without defeating these desires.

For Commentary, see Tentative Draft No. 8, p. 36.

Section 3.07. Use of Force in Law Enforcement.

(1) <u>Use of Force Justifiable to Effect an Arrest.</u> Subject to the provisions of this Section and of Section 3.09, the use of force upon or toward the person of another is justifiable when the actor is making or assisting in making an arrest and the actor believes that such force is immediately necessary to effect a lawful arrest.

(2) <u>Limitations on the Use of Force.</u>

    (a) The use of force is not justifiable under this Section unless:

        (i) the actor makes known the purpose of the arrest or believes that it is otherwise known by or cannot reasonably be made known to the person to be arrested; and

        (ii) when the arrest is made under a warrant, the warrant is valid or believed by the actor to be valid.

    (b) The use of deadly force is not justifiable under this Section unless:

        (i) the arrest is for a felony; and

        (ii) the person effecting the arrest is authorized to act as a peace officer or is assisting a person whom he believes to be authorized to act as a peace officer; and

(iii) the actor believes that the force employed creates no substantial risk of injury to innocent persons; and

(iv) the actor believes that:

(1) the crime for which the arrest is made involved conduct including the use or threatened use of deadly force; or

(2) there is a substantial risk that the person to be arrested will cause death or serious bodily harm if his apprehension is delayed.

(3) <u>Use of Force to Prevent Escape from Custody</u>. The use of force to prevent the escape of an arrested person from custody is justifiable when the force could justifiably have been employed to effect the arrest under which the person is in custody, except that a guard or other person authorized to act as a peace officer is justified in using any force, including deadly force, which he believes to be immediately necessary to prevent the escape of a person from a jail, prison, or other institution for the detention of persons charged with or convicted of a crime.

(4) <u>Use of Force by Private Person Assisting an Unlawful Arrest</u>.

(a) A private person who is summoned by a peace officer to assist in effecting an unlawful arrest, is justified in using any force which he would be justified in using if the arrest were lawful, provided that he does not believe the arrest is unlawful.

(b) A private person who assists another private person in effecting an unlawful arrest, or who, not being summoned, assists a peace officer in effecting an unlawful arrest, is justified in using any force which he would be justified in using if the arrest were lawful, provided that (i) he believes the arrest is lawful, and (ii) the arrest would be lawful if the facts were as he believes them to be.

(5) **Use of Force to Prevent Suicide or the Commission of a Crime.**

(a) The use of force upon or toward the person of another is justifiable when the actor believes that such force is immediately necessary to prevent such other person from committing suicide, inflicting serious bodily harm upon himself, committing or consummating the commission of a crime involving or threatening bodily harm, damage to or loss of property or a breach of the peace, except that:

(i) any limitations imposed by the other provisions of this Article on the justifiable use of force in self-protection, for the protection of others, the protection of property, the effectuation of an arrest or the prevention of an escape from custody shall apply notwithstanding the criminality of the conduct against which such force is used; and

(ii) the use of deadly force is not in any event justifiable under this Subsection unless:

(1) the actor believes that there is a substantial risk that the person whom he seeks to prevent from committing a crime will cause death or serious bodily harm to another unless the commission or the consummation of the crime is prevented and that the use of such force presents no substantial risk of injury to innocent persons; or

(2) the actor believes that the use of such force is necessary to suppress a riot or mutiny after the rioters or mutineers have been or-

dered to disperse and warned, in any particular manner that the law may require, that such force will be used if they do not obey.

(b) The justification afforded by this Subsection extends to the use of confinement as preventive force only if the actor takes all reasonable measures to terminate the confinement as soon as he knows that he safely can, unless the person confined has been arrested on a charge of crime.

STATUS OF SECTION

Presented to the Institute in Tentative Draft No. 8 and considered at the May 1958 meeting.

Resubmitted to the Council in revised form and considered at the December 1958 meeting.

The revision is designed to carry out the mandate of the Institute upon two points: (1) to extend the privilege of using deadly force to effect an arrest to a person assisting a peace officer rather than limit that privilege to officers (see Subsection (2)(b)(ii)); and (2) to extend the privilege to cases where the actor believes that the crime for which the arrest is made involved conduct including the use or threatened use of deadly force (see Subsection (2)(b)(iv)(1)).

For Commentary, see Tentative Draft No. 8, p. 52.

Section 3.08. Use of Force by Persons with Special Responsibility for Care, Discipline or Safety of Others.

The use of force upon or toward the person of another is justifiable if:

(1) the actor is the parent or guardian or other person similarly responsible for the general care and supervision of a minor or a person acting at the request of such parent, guardian or other responsible person and:

(a) the force is used for the purpose of safeguarding or promoting the welfare of the minor, including the prevention or punishment of his misconduct; and

(b) the force used is not designed to cause or known to create a substantial risk of causing death, serious bodily harm, disfigurement, extreme pain or mental distress or gross degradation; or

(2) the actor is a teacher or a person otherwise entrusted with the care or supervision for a special purpose of a minor and:

(a) the actor believes that the force used is necessary to further such special purpose, including the maintenance of reasonable discipline in a school, class or other group, and that the use of such force is consistent with the welfare of the minor; and

(b) the degree of force, if it had been used by the parent or guardian of the minor, would not be unjustifiable under Subsection (1)(b) of this Section; or

(3) the actor is the guardian or other person similarly responsible for the general care and supervision of an incompetent person; and:

(a) the force is used for the purpose of safeguarding or promoting the welfare of the incompetent person, including the prevention of his misconduct, or, when such incompetent person is in a hospital or other institution for his care and custody, for the maintenance of reasonable discipline in such institution; and

(b) the force used is not designed to cause or known to create a substantial risk of causing death, serious bodily harm, disfigurement, extreme or unnecessary pain, mental distress, or humiliation; or

(4) the actor is a doctor or other therapist or a person assisting him at his direction, and:

(a) the force is used for the purpose of administering a recognized form of treatment which the actor believes to be adapted to promoting the physical or mental health of the patient; and

(b) the treatment is administered with the consent of the patient or, if the patient is a minor or an incompetent person, with the consent of his parent or guardian or other person legally competent to consent in his behalf, or the treatment is administered in an emergency when the actor believes that no one competent to consent can be consulted and that a reasonable person, wishing to safeguard the welfare of the patient, would consent; or

(5) the actor is a warden or other authorized official of a correctional institution, and:

(a) he believes that the force used is necessary for the purpose of enforcing the lawful rules or procedures of the institution, unless his belief in the lawfulness of the rule or procedure sought to be enforced is erroneous and his error is due to ignorance or mistake as to the provisions of the Code, any other provision of the criminal law or the law governing the administration of the institution; and

(b) the nature or degree of force used is not forbidden by Article 303 or 304 of the Code; and

(c) if deadly force is used, its use is otherwise justifiable under this Article; or

(6) the actor is a person responsible for the safety of a vessel or an aircraft or a person acting at his direction, and

(a) he believes that the force used is necessary to prevent interference with the operation of the vessel or aircraft or obstruction of the execution of a lawful order, unless his belief in the lawfulness of the order is erroneous and his error is due to ignorance or mistake as to the law defining his authority; and

(b) if deadly force is used, its use is otherwise justifiable under this Article; or

(7) the actor is a person who is authorized or required by law to maintain order or decorum in a vehicle, train or other carrier or in a place where others are assembled, and:

(a) he believes that the force used is necessary for such purpose; and

(b) the force used is not designed to cause or known to create a substantial risk of causing death, bodily harm, or extreme mental distress.

STATUS OF SECTION

Presented to the Institute in Tentative Draft No. 8 and considered at the May 1958 meeting.

Subsection (5)(c) has been added.

Minor verbal changes have been made.

For Commentary, see Tentative Draft No. 8, p. 71.

Section 3.09. Mistake of Law as to Unlawfulness of Force or Legality of Arrest; Reckless or Negligent Use of Otherwise Justifiable Force; Reckless or Negligent Injury or Risk of Injury to Innocent Persons.

(1) The justification afforded by Sections 3.04 to 3.07, inclusive, is unavailable when:

(a) the actor's belief in the unlawfulness of the force or conduct against which he employs protective force or his belief in the lawfulness of an arrest which he endeavors to effect by force is erroneous; and

(b) his error is due to ignorance or mistake as to the provisions of the Code, any other provision of the criminal law or the law governing the legality of an arrest or search.

(2) When the actor believes that the use of force upon or toward the person of another is necessary for any of the purposes for which such belief would establish a justification under Sections 3.03 to 3.08 but the actor is reckless or negligent in having such belief or in acquiring or failing to acquire any knowledge or belief which is material to the justifiability of his use of force, the justification afforded by those Sections is unavailable in a prosecution for an offense for which recklessness or negligence, as the case may be, suffices to establish culpability.

(3) When the actor is justified under Sections 3.03 to 3.08 in using force upon or toward the person of another but he recklessly or negligently injures or creates a risk of injury to innocent persons, the justification afforded by those Sections is unavailable in a prosecution for such recklessness or negligence towards innocent persons.

STATUS OF SECTION

Presented to the Institute in Tentative Draft No. 8 and considered at the May 1958 meeting.

For Commentary, see Tentative Draft No. 8, p. 76.

Section 3.10. Justification in Property Crimes.

Conduct involving the appropriation, seizure or destruction of, damage to, intrusion on or interference with property is justifiable under circumstances which would establish a defense of privilege in a civil action based thereon, unless:

§ 3.11

(1) the Code or the law defining the offense deals with the specific situation involved; or

(2) a legislative purpose to exclude the justification claimed otherwise plainly appears.

STATUS OF SECTION

Presented to the Institute in Tentative Draft No. 8 and considered at the May 1958 meeting.

For Commentary, see Tentative Draft No. 8, p. 1.

Section 3.11. Definitions.

In this Article, unless a different meaning plainly is required:

(1) "unlawful force" means force, including confinement, which is employed without the consent of the person against whom it is directed and the employment of which constitutes an offense or actionable tort or would constitute such offense or tort except for a defense (such as the absence of intent, negligence, or mental capacity; duress; youth; or diplomatic status) not amounting to a privilege to use the force. Assent constitutes consent, within the meaning of this Section, whether or not it otherwise is legally effective, except assent to the infliction of death or serious bodily harm.

(2) "deadly force" means force which the actor uses with the purpose of causing or which he knows to create a substantial risk of causing death or serious bodily harm. Purposely firing a firearm in the direction of another person or at a vehicle in which another person is believed to be constitutes deadly force. A threat to cause death or serious bodily harm, by the production of a weapon or otherwise, so long as the actor's purpose is limited to creating an apprehension that he will use

deadly force if necessary, does not constitute deadly force;

(3) "dwelling" means any building or structure, though movable or temporary, or a portion thereof, which is for the time being the actor's home or place of lodging.

STATUS OF SECTION

Formerly numbered 3.12.

Presented to the Institute in Tentative Draft No. 8 and considered at the May 1958 meeting.

The last sentence of Subsection (1) is new, the prior formulation having left unsettled when assent in fact to otherwise unlawful force should preclude resort to defensive force.

Since assent may be withdrawn, and since some resort to defensive force is privileged to prevent crime under Section 3.07(5), without reference to the defense against "unlawful force," it seems sufficient to exclude only the case where the assent is given to the infliction of death or serious bodily harm. A third person would thus be authorized to use deadly force to prevent death or serious bodily harm, even though the victim had assented, but not, for example, to prevent sexual intercourse with an incompetent, though lesser force might be employed to prevent the crime.

For Commentary, see Tentative Draft No. 8, p. 28.

ARTICLE 4. RESPONSIBILITY

Section 4.01. Mental Disease or Defect Excluding Responsibility.

(1) A person is not responsible for criminal conduct if at the time of such conduct as a result of mental disease or defect he lacks substantial capacity either to appreciate the criminality [wrongfulness] of his conduct or to conform his conduct to the requirements of law.

(2) As used in this Article, the terms "mental disease or defect" do not include an abnormality manifested only by repeated criminal or otherwise anti-social conduct.

STATUS OF SECTION

Presented to the Institute in Tentative Draft No. 4 for consideration at the May 1955 meeting.

The Section was resubmitted in Proposed Final Draft No. 1 with two modifications: (1) the insertion of the bracketed word "wrongfulness" after "criminality," to indicate an option in the choice of words; and (2) the insertion of the words "As used in this Article" at the beginning of Subsection (2).

The first change was designed to indicate that the Institute does not disapprove the modification of the formulation by a number of groups that have considered it, including the Governor's Committee on the Insanity Defense in New York State.

The second modification was designed to avoid the misunderstanding, which has occasionally arisen, that the Code seeks to legislate concerning medical terminology rather than merely to resolve a specific set of legal problems dealt with in this Article.

In this form the Section was reconsidered and approved at the May 1961 meeting of the Institute.

For Commentary, see Tentative Draft No. 4, p. 156.

Section 4.02. Evidence of Mental Disease or Defect Admissible When Relevant to Element of the Offense; [Mental Disease or Defect Impairing Capacity as Ground for Mitigation of Punishment in Capital Cases].

(1) Evidence that the defendant suffered from a mental disease or defect is admissible whenever it is relevant to prove that the defendant did or did not have a state of mind which is an element of the offense.

[(2) Whenever the jury or the Court is authorized to determine or to recommend whether or not the defendant shall be sentenced to death or imprisonment upon conviction, evidence that the capacity of the defendant to appreciate the criminality [wrongfulness] of his conduct or to conform his conduct to the requirements of law was impaired as a result of mental disease or defect is admissible in favor of sentence of imprisonment.]

STATUS OF SECTION

Presented to the Institute in Tentative Draft No. 4 for consideration at the May 1955 meeting.

Resubmitted to the Institute, with minor verbal changes, in Proposed Final Draft No. 1 and approved at the May 1961 meeting.

Subsection (2), in brackets, is relevant for those jurisdictions which retain the death penalty.

For Commentary, see Tentative Draft No. 4, p. 193.

Section 4.03. Mental Disease or Defect Excluding Responsibility Is Affirmative Defense; Requirement of Notice; Form of Verdict and Judgment When Finding of Irresponsibility Is Made.

(1) Mental disease or defect excluding responsibility is an affirmative defense.

§ 4.04

(2) Evidence of mental disease or defect excluding responsibility is not admissible unless the defendant, at the time of entering his plea of not guilty or within ten days thereafter or at such later time as the Court may for good cause permit, files a written notice of his purpose to rely on such defense.

(3) When the defendant is acquitted on the ground of mental disease or defect excluding responsibility, the verdict and the judgment shall so state.

STATUS OF SECTION

Presented to the Institute in Tentative Draft No. 4 for consideration at the May 1955 meeting.

An alternative provision requiring the defendant to establish the defense by a preponderance of the evidence was eliminated by vote of the Institute at the May 1955 meeting.

Resubmitted to the Institute, with minor verbal changes, in Proposed Final Draft No. 1 and approved at the May 1961 meeting.

For Commentary, see Tentative Draft No. 4, p. 193.

Section 4.04. Mental Disease or Defect Excluding Fitness to Proceed.

No person who as a result of mental disease or defect lacks capacity to understand the proceedings against him or to assist in his own defense shall be tried, convicted or sentenced for the commission of an offense so long as such incapacity endures.

STATUS OF SECTION

Presented to the Institute in Tentative Draft No. 4 for consideration at the May 1955 meeting.

Resubmitted to the Institute in Proposed Final Draft No. 1 and approved at the May 1961 meeting.

For Commentary, see Tentative Draft No. 4, p. 194.

Section 4.05. Psychiatric Examination of Defendant with Respect to Mental Disease or Defect.

(1) Whenever the defendant has filed a notice of intention to rely on the defense of mental disease or defect excluding responsibility, or there is reason to doubt his fitness to proceed, or reason to believe that mental disease or defect of the defendant will otherwise become an issue in the cause, the Court shall appoint at least one qualified psychiatrist or shall request the Superintendent of the   Hospital to designate at least one qualified psychiatrist, which designation may be or include himself, to examine and report upon the mental condition of the defendant. The Court may order the defendant to be committed to a hospital or other suitable facility for the purpose of the examination for a period of not exceeding sixty days or such longer period as the Court determines to be necessary for the purpose and may direct that a qualified psychiatrist retained by the defendant be permitted to witness and participate in the examination.

(2) In such examination any method may be employed which is accepted by the medical profession for the examination of those alleged to be suffering from mental disease or defect.

(3) The report of the examination shall include the following: (a) a description of the nature of the examination; (b) a diagnosis of the mental condition of the defendant; (c) if the defendant suffers from a mental disease or defect, an opinion as to his capacity to understand the proceedings against him and to assist in his own defense; (d) when a notice of intention to rely on the defense of irresponsibility has been filed, an opinion as to the extent, if any, to which the capacity of the defendant to appreciate the criminality [wrongfulness] of his conduct or to conform his conduct to the requirements of law was impaired at the time of the

criminal conduct charged; and (e) when directed by the Court, an opinion as to the capacity of the defendant to have a particular state of mind which is an element of the offense charged.

If the examination can not be conducted by reason of the unwillingness of the defendant to participate therein, the report shall so state and shall include, if possible, an opinion as to whether such unwillingness of the defendant was the result of mental disease or defect.

The report of the examination shall be filed [in triplicate] with the clerk of the Court, who shall cause copies to be delivered to the district attorney and to counsel for the defendant.

STATUS OF SECTION

Presented to the Institute in Tentative Draft No. 4 for consideration at the May 1955 meeting.

In Subsection (2) the word "alleged" was substituted for the word "thought" in response to a suggestion made at the meeting of the Institute in May 1955.

Resubmitted to the Institute, with minor verbal changes, in Proposed Final Draft No. 1 and approved at the May 1961 meeting.

For Commentary, see Tentative Draft No. 4, p. 195.

Section 4.06. Determination of Fitness to Proceed; Effect of Finding of Unfitness; Proceedings if Fitness is Regained [; Post-Commitment Hearing].

(1) When the defendant's fitness to proceed is drawn in question, the issue shall be determined by the Court. If neither the prosecuting attorney nor counsel for the defendant contests the finding of the report filed pursuant to Section 4.05, the Court may make the determination on the basis of such report. If the finding is contested, the Court shall hold a hearing on the issue. If the report is received in evidence upon such hearing, the party who contests the finding thereof shall have the right to summon and to cross-examine

the psychiatrists who joined in the report and to offer evidence upon the issue.

(2) If the Court determines that the defendant lacks fitness to proceed, the proceeding against him shall be suspended, except as provided in Subsection (3) [Subsections (3) and (4)] of this Section, and the Court shall commit him to the custody of the Commissioner of Mental Hygiene [Public Health or Correction] to be placed in an appropriate institution of the Department of Mental Hygiene [Public Health or Correction] for so long as such unfitness shall endure. When the Court, on its own motion or upon the application of the Commissioner of Mental Hygiene [Public Health or Correction] or the prosecuting attorney, determines, after a hearing if a hearing is requested, that the defendant has regained fitness to proceed, the proceeding shall be resumed. If, however, the Court is of the view that so much time has elapsed since the commitment of the defendant that it would be unjust to resume the criminal proceeding, the Court may dismiss the charge and may order the defendant to be discharged or, subject to the law governing the civil commitment of persons suffering from mental disease or defect, order the defendant to be committed to an appropriate institution of the Department of Mental Hygiene [Public Health].

(3) The fact that the defendant is unfit to proceed does not preclude any legal objection to the prosecution which is susceptible of fair determination prior to trial and without the personal participation of the defendant.

[Alternative: (3) At any time within ninety days after commitment as provided in Subsection (2) of this Section, or at any later time with permission of the Court granted for good cause, the defendant or his counsel or the Commissioner of Mental Hygiene [Public Health or Correction] may apply for a special post-commitment hearing. If the application is made by or on behalf of a defendant not represented

§ 4.06

by counsel, he shall be afforded a reasonable opportunity to obtain counsel, and if he lacks funds to do so, counsel shall be assigned by the Court. The application shall be granted only if the counsel for the defendant satisfies the Court by affidavit or otherwise that as an attorney he has reasonable grounds for a good faith belief that his client has, on the facts and the law, a defense to the charge other than mental disease or defect excluding responsibility.

[(4) If the motion for a special post-commitment hearing is granted, the hearing shall be by the Court without a jury. No evidence shall be offered at the hearing by either party on the issue of mental disease or defect as a defense to, or in mitigation of, the crime charged. After hearing, the Court may in an appropriate case quash the indictment or other charge, or find it to be defective or insufficient, or determine that it is not proved beyond a reasonable doubt by the evidence, or otherwise terminate the proceedings on the evidence or the law. In any such case, unless all defects in the proceedings are promptly cured, the Court shall terminate the commitment ordered under Subsection (2) of this Section and order the defendant to be discharged or, subject to the law governing the civil commitment of persons suffering from mental disease or defect, order the defendant to be committed to an appropriate institution of the Department of Mental Hygiene [Public Health].]

STATUS OF SECTION

Presented to the Institute in Tentative Draft No. 4 for consideration at the May 1955 meeting.

In the second sentence of Subsection (2), brackets around "or the district attorney" were eliminated by vote of the Institute at the May 1955 meeting. In the same sentence the requirement of a hearing has been qualified by adding the words "if a hearing is requested."

Resubmitted to the Institute in Proposed Final Draft No. 1 and considered at the May 1961 meeting.

In the second sentence of Subsection (2), the words "on its own motion or" have been added. The Subsection has also been revised to make clear that if the criminal proceeding has been dismissed, any further commitment of the defendant is "subject to the law governing the civil commitment of persons suffering from mental disease or defect."

The term "district attorney" has been changed to "prosecuting attorney."

Subsection (3) was added on the ground that the defendant's unfitness to proceed should not preclude his counsel from making any legal objection to the prosecution which is susceptible of fair determination prior to trial and without the personal participation of the defendant. This provision is aimed at motions ordinarily determined at the pre-trial stage, rather than at the trial. The words "his counsel from making" and "if he elects to do so" have been eliminated in response to a suggestion made at the meeting of the Institute in May 1961.

Alternative Subsections (3) and (4), in brackets, are included in response to a motion made at the meeting of the Institute in May 1961 asking that the Reporter submit an alternative providing for a post-commitment hearing patterned after the proposal made by the Massachusetts Judicial Council in its Thirty-Sixth Report 22-24, 27-28 (1960).

For Commentary, see Tentative Draft No. 4, p. 197.

Section 4.07. Determination of Irresponsibility on Basis of Report; Access to Defendant by Psychiatrist of His Own Choice; Form of Expert Testimony When Issue of Responsibility Is Tried.

(1) If the report filed pursuant to Section 4.05 finds that the defendant at the time of the criminal conduct charged suffered from a mental disease or defect which substantially impaired his capacity to appreciate the criminality [wrongfulness] of his conduct or to conform his conduct to the requirements of law, and the Court, after a hearing if a hearing is requested by the prosecuting attorney or the defendant, is satisfied that such impairment was sufficient to exclude responsibility, the Court on motion of the defendant shall enter judgment of acquittal on the ground of mental disease or defect excluding responsibility.

(2) When, notwithstanding the report filed pursuant to Section 4.05, the defendant wishes to be examined by a

qualified psychiatrist or other expert of his own choice, such examiner shall be permitted to have reasonable access to the defendant for the purposes of such examination.

(3) Upon the trial, the psychiatrists who reported pursuant to Section 4.05 may be called as witnesses by the prosecution, the defendant or the Court. If the issue is being tried before a jury, the jury may be informed that the psychiatrists were designated by the Court or by the Superintendent of the   Hospital at the request of the Court, as the case may be. If called by the Court, the witness shall be subject to cross-examination by the prosecution and by the defendant. Both the prosecution and the defendant may summon any other qualified psychiatrist or other expert to testify, but no one who has not examined the defendant shall be competent to testify to an expert opinion with respect to the mental condition or responsibility of the defendant, as distinguished from the validity of the procedure followed by, or the general scientific propositions stated by, another witness.

(4) When a psychiatrist or other expert who has examined the defendant testifies concerning his mental condition, he shall be permitted to make a statement as to the nature of his examination, his diagnosis of the mental condition of the defendant at the time of the commission of the offense charged and his opinion as to the extent, if any, to which the capacity of the defendant to appreciate the criminality [wrongfulness] of his conduct or to conform his conduct to the requirements of law or to have a particular state of mind which is an element of the offense charged was impaired as a result of mental disease or defect at that time. He shall be permitted to make any explanation reasonably serving to clarify his diagnosis and opinion and may be cross-examined as to any matter bearing on his competency or credibility or the validity of his diagnosis or opinion.

Art. 4 § 4.08

STATUS OF SECTION

Presented to the Institute in Tentative Draft No. 4 for consideration at the May 1955 meeting.

Subsection (1) was revised to make the right to a hearing explicit.

The words "or other expert" were inserted in Subsections (2), (3) and (4) to take account of the possibility that others than psychiatrists may qualify as experts, such as psychologists in cases of mental deficiency.

Resubmitted to the Institute in Proposed Final Draft No. 1 and approved at the May 1961 meeting.

In Subsection (1) the words "on motion of the defendant" have been inserted after "the Court" in response to a suggestion made at the meeting of the Institute in May 1961.

The term "district attorney" has been changed to "prosecuting attorney," and other verbal changes have been made.

For Commentary, see Tentative Draft No. 4, p. 198.

Section 4.08. Legal Effect of Acquittal on the Ground of Mental Disease or Defect Excluding Responsibility; Commitment; Release or Discharge.

(1) When a defendant is acquitted on the ground of mental disease or defect excluding responsibility, the Court shall order him to be committed to the custody of the Commissioner of Mental Hygiene [Public Health] to be placed in an appropriate institution for custody, care and treatment.

(2) If the Commissioner of Mental Hygiene [Public Health] is of the view that a person committed to his custody, pursuant to paragraph (1) of this Section, may be discharged or released on condition without danger to himself or to others, he shall make application for the discharge or release of such person in a report to the Court by which such person was committed and shall transmit a copy of such application and report to the prosecuting attorney of the county [parish] from which the defendant was committed. The Court shall thereupon appoint at least two qualified psychiatrists to examine such person and to report within sixty days, or such longer period as the Court determines to be necessary for the purpose, their opinion as to his mental condition. To facilitate such examination and the proceedings thereon, the Court may cause such person to be confined in any institution located near the place where the Court sits, which may hereafter be designated by the Commissioner of Mental Hygiene [Public Health] as suitable for the temporary detention of irresponsible persons.

(3) If the Court is satisfied by the report filed pursuant to paragraph (2) of this Section and such testimony of the reporting psychiatrists as the Court deems necessary that the committed person may be discharged or released on condition without danger to himself or others, the Court shall order his discharge or his release on such conditions as the Court determines to be necessary. If the Court is not so satisfied, it shall promptly order a hearing to determine whether such person may safely be discharged or released. Any such hearing shall be deemed a civil proceeding and the burden shall be upon the committed person to prove that he may safely be discharged or released. According to the determination of the Court upon the hearing, the committed person shall thereupon be discharged or released on such conditions as the Court determines to be necessary, or shall be recommitted to the custody of the Commissioner of Mental Hygiene [Public Health], subject to discharge or release only in accordance with the procedure prescribed above for a first hearing.

(4) If, within [five] years after the conditional release of a committed person, the Court shall determine, after hearing evidence, that the conditions of release have not been fulfilled and that for the safety of such person or for the safety of others his conditional release should be revoked, the Court shall forthwith order him to be recommitted to

Art. 4 § 4.08

the Commissioner of Mental Hygiene [Public Health], subject to discharge or release only in accordance with the procedure prescribed above for a first hearing.

(5) A committed person may make application for his discharge or release to the Court by which he was committed, and the procedure to be followed upon such application shall be the same as that prescribed above in the case of an application by the Commissioner of Mental Hygiene [Public Health]. However, no such application by a committed person need be considered until he has been confined for a period of not less than [six months] from the date of the order of commitment, and if the determination of the Court be adverse to the application, such person shall not be permitted to file a further application until [one year] has elapsed from the date of any preceding hearing on an application for his release or discharge.

STATUS OF SECTION

Presented to the Institute in Tentative Draft No. 4 for consideration at the May 1955 meeting.

References in Subsections (2), (3) and (4) to "release on probation" were changed to "release on condition," following the form of this Section as adopted in New York. N.Y. Laws 1960 Ch. 550, amending CODE OF CRIM. PROC. § 454.

In Subsection (4) the initial words "within [five] years" were inserted, following the New York statute. The period during which the individual released on condition ought to remain subject to recommitment under the provisions of this Section surely should be limited, though there is room for difference of opinion as to how long the period should be. The suggestion of five years is, therefore, bracketed.

Resubmitted to the Institute, with these and other verbal changes, in Proposed Final Draft No. 1 and approved at the May 1961 meeting.

The term "district attorney" has been changed to "prosecuting attorney."

In Subsection (5) brackets have been placed around the words "six months" and "one year," in the view that such time limits are arbitrary.

For Commentary, see Tentative Draft No. 4, p. 199.

Section 4.09. Statements for Purposes of Examination or Treatment Inadmissible Except on Issue of Mental Condition.

A statement made by a person subjected to psychiatric examination or treatment pursuant to Sections 4.05, 4.06 or 4.08 for the purposes of such examination or treatment shall not be admissible in evidence against him in any criminal proceeding on any issue other than that of his mental condition but it shall be admissible upon that issue, whether or not it would otherwise be deemed a privileged communication [, unless such statement constitutes an admission of guilt of the crime charged].

STATUS OF SECTION

Presented to the Institute in Tentative Draft No. 4 for consideration at the May 1955 meeting.

In the original formulation the word "criminal" in the phrase "against him in any criminal proceeding," was bracketed, to make it optional whether the privilege should be extended to civil proceedings. The brackets were eliminated by vote of the Institute.

Resubmitted to the Institute in Proposed Final Draft No. 1 and approved at the May 1961 meeting.

The words in brackets were suggested by the version of this section enacted in Massachusetts. MASS. GEN. LAWS Ch. 233, Section 23B, added by Mass. Acts 1958 Ch. 256.

As submitted to the Institute in Proposed Final Draft No. 1, the bracketed provision referred to "a confession." Even apart from the bracketed provision, a confession of guilt made in the course of psychiatric examination or treatment pursuant to Sections 4.05, 4.06 or 4.08 would be inadmissible except on the issue of defendant's mental condition. There is a problem, however, of the ability of members of a jury to follow an instruction that they should consider such a confession on the issue of mental condition only, and should not consider it with respect to the other issues bearing on guilt. The bracketed provision is designed to meet this problem, and to protect the provisions for psychiatric examination of the defendant by court-appointed experts from objection based on the defendant's privilege against self-incrimination.

The words "an admission" have been substituted for the words "a confession" in response to a suggestion made at the meeting of the Institute in May 1961, a change designed to avoid technical distinctions drawn from other rules of evidence.

For Commentary, see Tentative Draft No. 4, p. 201.

Section 4.10. Immaturity Excluding Criminal Conviction; Transfer of Proceedings to Juvenile Court.

(1) A person shall not be tried for or convicted of an offense if:

    (a) at the time of the conduct charged to constitute the offense he was less than sixteen years of age [, in which case the Juvenile Court shall have exclusive jurisdiction*]; or

    (b) at the time of the conduct charged to constitute the offense he was sixteen or seventeen years of age, unless:

        (i) the Juvenile Court has no jurisdiction over him, or,

        (ii) the Juvenile Court has entered an order waiving jurisdiction and consenting to the institution of criminal proceedings against him.

(2) No court shall have jurisdiction to try or convict a person of an offense if criminal proceedings against him are barred by Subsection (1) of this Section. When it appears that a person charged with the commission of an offense may be of such an age that criminal proceedings may be barred under Subsection (1) of this Section, the Court shall hold a hearing thereon, and the burden shall be on the prosecution to establish to the satisfaction of the Court that the criminal proceeding is not barred upon such grounds. If

---

* The bracketed words are unnecessary if the Juvenile Court Act so provides or is amended accordingly.

§ 4.10

the Court determines that the proceeding is barred, custody of the person charged shall be surrendered to the Juvenile Court, and the case, including all papers and processes relating thereto, shall be transferred.

STATUS OF SECTION

Presented to the Institute in Tentative Draft No. 7 for consideration at the May 1957 meeting.

Resubmitted to the Institute in Proposed Final Draft No. 1 and approved at the May 1961 meeting.

For Commentary, see Tentative Draft No. 7, p. 6.

ARTICLE 5. INCHOATE CRIMES

Section 5.01. Criminal Attempt.

(1) <u>Definition of Attempt</u>. A person is guilty of an attempt to commit a crime if, acting with the kind of culpability otherwise required for commission of the crime, he:

    (a) purposely engages in conduct which would constitute the crime if the attendant circumstances were as he believes them to be; or

    (b) when causing a particular result is an element of the crime, does or omits to do anything with the purpose of causing or with the belief that it will cause such result without further conduct on his part; or

    (c) purposely does or omits to do anything which, under the circumstances as he believes them to be, is an act or omission constituting a substantial step in a course of conduct planned to culminate in his commission of the crime.

(2) <u>Conduct Which May Be Held Substantial Step Under Subsection (1)(c)</u>. Conduct shall not be held to constitute a substantial step under Subsection (1)(c) of this Section unless it is strongly corroborative of the actor's criminal purpose. Without negativing the sufficiency of other conduct, the following, if strongly corroborative of the actor's criminal purpose, shall not be held insufficient as a matter of law:

    (a) lying in wait, searching for or following the contemplated victim of the crime;

    (b) enticing or seeking to entice the contemplated victim of the crime to go to the place contemplated for its commission;

(c) reconnoitering the place contemplated for the commission of the crime;

(d) unlawful entry of a structure, vehicle or enclosure in which it is contemplated that the crime will be committed;

(e) possession of materials to be employed in the commission of the crime, which are specially designed for such unlawful use or which can serve no lawful purpose of the actor under the circumstances;

(f) possession, collection or fabrication of materials to be employed in the commission of the crime, at or near the place contemplated for its commission, where such possession, collection or fabrication serves no lawful purpose of the actor under the circumstances;

(g) soliciting an innocent agent to engage in conduct constituting an element of the crime.

(3) **Conduct Designed to Aid Another in Commission of a Crime.** A person who engages in conduct designed to aid another to commit a crime which would establish his complicity under Section 2.06 if the crime were committed by such other person, is guilty of an attempt to commit the crime, although the crime is not committed or attempted by such other person.

(4) **Renunciation of Criminal Purpose.** When the actor's conduct would otherwise constitute an attempt under Subsection (1)(b) or (1)(c) of this Section, it is an affirmative defense that he abandoned his effort to commit the crime or otherwise prevented its commission, under circumstances manifesting a complete and voluntary renunciation of his criminal purpose. The establishment of such defense does not, however, affect the liability of an accomplice who did not join in such abandonment or prevention.

Within the meaning of this Article, renunciation of criminal purpose is not voluntary if it is motivated, in whole or in part, by circumstances, not present or apparent at the inception of the actor's course of conduct, which increase the probability of detection or apprehension or which make more difficult the accomplishment of the criminal purpose. Renunciation is not complete if it is motivated by a decision to postpone the criminal conduct until a more advantageous time or to transfer the criminal effort to another but similar objective or victim.

Section 5.02. Criminal Solicitation.

(1) Definition of Solicitation. A person is guilty of solicitation to commit a crime if with the purpose of promoting or facilitating its commission he commands, encourages or requests another person to engage in specific conduct which would constitute such crime or an attempt to commit such crime or which would establish his complicity in its commission or attempted commission.

(2) Uncommunicated Solicitation. It is immaterial under Subsection (1) of this Section that the actor fails to communicate with the person he solicits to commit a crime if his conduct was designed to effect such communication.

(3) Renunciation of Criminal Purpose. It is an affirmative defense that the actor, after soliciting another person to commit a crime, persuaded him not to do so or otherwise prevented the commission of the crime, under circumstances manifesting a complete and voluntary renunciation of his criminal purpose.

Section 5.03. Criminal Conspiracy.

(1) Definition of Conspiracy. A person is guilty of conspiracy with another person or persons to commit a crime if with the purpose of promoting or facilitating its commission he:

(a) agrees with such other person or persons that they or one or more of them will engage in conduct which constitutes such crime or an attempt or solicitation to commit such crime; or

(b) agrees to aid such other person or persons in the planning or commission of such crime or of an attempt or solicitation to commit such crime.

(2) Scope of Conspiratorial Relationship. If a person guilty of conspiracy, as defined by Subsection (1) of this Section, knows that a person with whom he conspires to commit a crime has conspired with another person or persons to commit the same crime, he is guilty of conspiring with such other person or persons, whether or not he knows their identity, to commit such crime.

(3) Conspiracy With Multiple Criminal Objectives. If a person conspires to commit a number of crimes, he is guilty of only one conspiracy so long as such multiple crimes are the object of the same agreement or continuous conspiratorial relationship.

(4) Joinder and Venue in Conspiracy Prosecutions.

(a) Subject to the provisions of paragraph (b) of this Subsection, two or more persons charged with criminal conspiracy may be prosecuted jointly if:

(i) they are charged with conspiring with one another; or

(ii) the conspiracies alleged, whether they have the same or different parties, are so related that they constitute different aspects of a scheme of organized criminal conduct.

(b) In any joint prosecution under paragraph (a) of this Subsection:

(i) no defendant shall be charged with a conspiracy in any county [parish or district] other than one in which he entered into such conspiracy or in which an overt act pursuant to such conspiracy was done by him or by a person with whom he conspired; and

(ii) neither the liability of any defendant nor the admissibility against him of evidence of acts or declarations of another shall be enlarged by such joinder; and

(iii) the Court shall order a severance or take a special verdict as to any defendant who so requests, if it deems it necessary or appropriate to promote the fair determination of his guilt or innocence, and shall take any other proper measures to protect the fairness of the trial.

(5) Overt Act. No person may be convicted of conspiracy to commit a crime, other than a felony of the first or second degree, unless an overt act in pursuance of such conspiracy is alleged and proved to have been done by him or by a person with whom he conspired.

(6) Renunciation of Criminal Purpose. It is an affirmative defense that the actor, after conspiring to commit a crime, thwarted the success of the conspiracy, under circumstances manifesting a complete and voluntary renunciation of his criminal purpose.

(7) Duration of Conspiracy. For purposes of Section 1.06 (4):

(a) conspiracy is a continuing course of conduct which terminates when the crime or crimes which are its object are committed or the agreement that they be committed is abandoned by the defendant and by those with whom he conspired; and

(b) such abandonment is presumed if neither the defendant nor anyone with whom he conspired does any overt act in pursuance of the conspiracy during the applicable period of limitation; and

(c) if an individual abandons the agreement, the conspiracy is terminated as to him only if and when he advises those with whom he conspired of his abandonment or he informs the law enforcement authorities of the existence of the conspiracy and of his participation therein.

Section 5.04. Incapacity, Irresponsibility or Immunity of Party to Solicitation or Conspiracy.

(1) Except as provided in Subsection (2) of this Section, it is immaterial to the liability of a person who solicits or conspires with another to commit a crime that:

(a) he or the person whom he solicits or with whom he conspires does not occupy a particular position or have a particular characteristic which is an element of such crime, if he believes that one of them does; or

(b) the person whom he solicits or with whom he conspires is irresponsible or has an immunity to prosecution or conviction for the commission of the crime.

(2) It is a defense to a charge of solicitation or conspiracy to commit a crime that if the criminal object were achieved, the actor would not be guilty of a crime under the law defining the offense or as an accomplice under Section 2.06(5) or 2.06(6)(a) or (b).

Section 5.05. Grading of Criminal Attempt, Solicitation and Conspiracy; Mitigation in Cases of Lesser Danger; Multiple Convictions Barred.

(1) <u>Grading</u>. Except as otherwise provided in this Section, attempt, solicitation and conspiracy are crimes of the same grade and degree as the most serious offense which is attempted or solicited or is an object of the conspiracy. An attempt, solicitation or conspiracy to commit a [capital crime or a] felony of the first degree is a felony of the second degree.

(2) <u>Mitigation</u>. If the particular conduct charged to constitute a criminal attempt, solicitation or conspiracy is so inherently unlikely to result or culminate in the commission of a crime that neither such conduct nor the actor presents a public danger warranting the grading of such offense under this Section, the Court shall exercise its power under Section 6.12 to enter judgment and impose sentence for a crime of lower grade or degree or, in extreme cases, may dismiss the prosecution.

(3) <u>Multiple Convictions</u>. A person may not be convicted of more than one offense defined by this Article for conduct designed to commit or to culminate in the commission of the same crime.

STATUS OF SECTIONS 5.01-5.05

Presented to the Institute in Tentative Draft No. 10 and considered at the May 1960 meeting.

Pursuant to suggestion at the meeting of the Institute, Subsections 5.01(4), 5.02(3) and 5.03(6) have been modified to require that renunciation of criminal purpose, when adduced as a defense, be "complete" and "voluntary." These terms are defined for purposes of the entire Article in the second paragraph of 5.01(4), which is new.

Minor verbal changes have been made.

For Commentary, see Tentative Draft No. 10, p. 24.

Section 5.06. Possessing Instruments of Crime; Weapons.

(1) Criminal Instruments Generally. A person commits a misdemeanor if he possesses any instrument of crime with purpose to employ it criminally. "Instrument of crime" means:

(a) anything specially made or specially adapted for criminal use; or

(b) anything commonly used for criminal purposes and possessed by the actor under circumstances which do not negative unlawful purpose.

(2) Presumption of Criminal Purpose from Possession of Weapon. If a person possesses a firearm or other weapon on or about his person, in a vehicle occupied by him, or otherwise readily available for use, it shall be presumed that he had the purpose to employ it criminally, unless:

(a) the weapon is possessed in the actor's home or place of business;

(b) the actor is licensed or otherwise authorized by law to possess such weapon; or

(c) the weapon is a type commonly used in lawful sport.

"Weapon" means anything readily capable of lethal use and possessed under circumstances not manifestly appropriate for lawful uses which it may have; the term includes a firearm which is not loaded or lacks a clip or other component to render it immediately operable, and components which can readily be assembled into a weapon.

(3) Presumptions as to Possession of Criminal Instruments in Automobiles. Where a weapon or other instrument of crime is found in an automobile, it shall be presumed to

be in the possession of the occupant if there is but one. If there is more than one occupant, it shall be presumed to be in the possession of all, except under the following circumstances:

> (a) where it is found upon the person of one of the occupants;
>
> (b) where the automobile is not a stolen one and the weapon or instrument is found out of view in a glove compartment, car trunk, or other enclosed customary depository, in which case it shall be presumed to be in the possession of the occupant or occupants who own or have authority to operate the automobile;
>
> (c) in the case of a taxicab, a weapon or instrument found in the passengers' portion of the vehicle shall be presumed to be in the possession of all the passengers, if there are any, and, if not, in the possession of the driver.

STATUS OF SECTION

Presented to the Institute in Tentative Draft No. 13, and considered at the May 1961 meeting.

The Institute voted against including a bracketed subsection (4) which appeared in Tentative Draft No. 13. That subsection would have penalized possession of concealed revolvers and pistols, with certain exceptions, regardless of criminal purpose.

Verbal changes have been made.

Section 5.07. Prohibited Offensive Weapons.

A person commits a misdemeanor if, except as authorized by law, he makes, repairs, sells, or otherwise deals in, uses, or possesses any offensive weapon. "Offensive weapon" means any bomb, machine gun, sawed-off shotgun, firearm specially made or specially adapted for concealment or silent discharge, any blackjack, sandbag, metal knuckles, dagger, or other implement for the infliction of serious bodily harm which serves no common lawful purpose. It is a defense under this Section for the defendant to prove by a preponderance of evidence that he possessed or dealt with the weapon solely as a curio or in a dramatic performance, or that he possessed it briefly in consequence of having found it or taken it from an aggressor, or under circumstances similarly negativing any purpose or likelihood that the weapon would be used unlawfully. The presumptions provided in Section 5.06(3) are applicable to prosecutions under this Section.

STATUS OF SECTION

Presented to the Institute in Tentative Draft No. 13, and considered at the May 1961 meeting.

ARTICLE 6. AUTHORIZED DISPOSITION OF OFFENDERS

Section 6.01. Degrees of Felonies.

(1) Felonies defined by this Code are classified, for the purpose of sentence, into three degrees, as follows:

    (a) felonies of the first degree;

    (b) felonies of the second degree;

    (c) felonies of the third degree.

A felony is of the first or second degree when it is so designated by the Code. A crime declared to be a felony, without specification of degree, is of the third degree.

(2) Notwithstanding any other provision of law, a felony defined by any statute of this State other than this Code shall constitute for the purpose of sentence a felony of the third degree.

STATUS OF SECTION

Presented to the Institute in Tentative Draft No. 2 and considered at the May 1954 meeting.

Reprinted in Tentative Draft No. 4.

Resubmitted to the Institute in Proposed Final Draft No. 1 and approved at the May 1961 meeting.

For Commentary, see Tentative Draft No. 2, p. 10.

Section 6.02. Sentence in Accordance with Code; Authorized Dispositions.

(1) No person convicted of an offense shall be sentenced otherwise than in accordance with this Article.

[(2) The Court shall sentence a person who has been convicted of murder to death or imprisonment, in accordance with Section 210.6.]

§ 6.02

(3) Except as provided in Subsection (2) of this Section and subject to the applicable provisions of the Code, the Court may suspend the imposition of sentence on a person who has been convicted of a crime, may order him to be committed in lieu of sentence, in accordance with Section 6.13, or may sentence him as follows:

(a) to pay a fine authorized by Section 6.03; or

(b) to be placed on probation [, and, in the case of a person convicted of a felony or misdemeanor to imprisonment for a term fixed by the Court not exceeding thirty days to be served as a condition of probation]; or

(c) to imprisonment for a term authorized by Sections 6.05, 6.06, 6.07, 6.08, 6.09, or 7.06; or

(d) to fine and probation or fine and imprisonment, but not to probation and imprisonment [, except as authorized in paragraph (b) of this Subsection].

(4) The Court may suspend the imposition of sentence on a person who has been convicted of a violation or may sentence him to pay a fine authorized by Section 6.03.

(5) This Article does not deprive the Court of any authority conferred by law to decree a forfeiture of property, suspend or cancel a license, remove a person from office, or impose any other civil penalty. Such a judgment or order may be included in the sentence.

STATUS OF SECTION

Presented to the Institute in Tentative Draft No. 2 and considered at the May 1954 meeting.

Revised in light of Institute discussion and resubmitted in Tentative Draft No. 4 for consideration at the May 1955 meeting.

Subsection (2) was further revised in light of Institute action on Tentative Draft No. 9 at May 1959 meeting.

Subsection (3)(b) was further revised to include the optional authorization of a sentence combining probation and imprisonment for not exceeding thirty days, upon conviction of a felony or misdemeanor. While there is controversy as to the wisdom of combining probation and imprisonment, it was believed that a conservative provision of this kind may be considered necessary and unobjectionable in many jurisdictions. The case for such authority is strongest upon sentence for a misdemeanor, since supervised release from local institutions otherwise may be impossible, parole usually being unavailable.

Resubmitted to the Institute in Proposed Final Draft No. 1 and approved at the May 1961 meeting.

For Commentary, see Tentative Draft No. 2, p. 12.

Section 6.03. Fines.

A person who has been convicted of an offense may be sentenced to pay a fine not exceeding:

(1) $10,000, when the conviction is of a felony of the first or second degree;

(2) $5,000, when the conviction is of a felony of the third degree;

(3) $1,000, when the conviction is of a misdemeanor;

(4) $500, when the conviction is of a petty misdemeanor or a violation;

(5) any higher amount equal to double the pecuniary gain derived from the offense by the offender;

(6) any higher amount specifically authorized by statute.

STATUS OF SECTION

Presented to the Institute in Tentative Draft No. 2 and considered at the May 1954 meeting.

Reprinted in Tentative Draft No. 4.

Resubmitted to the Institute in Proposed Final Draft No. 1 and approved at the May 1961 meeting.

For Commentary, see Tentative Draft No. 2, p. 22.

Section 6.04. Penalties Against Corporations and Unincorporated Associations; Forfeiture of Corporate Charter or Revocation of Certificate Authorizing Foreign Corporation to Do Business in the State.

(1) The Court may suspend the sentence of a corporation or an unincorporated association which has been convicted of an offense or may sentence it to pay a fine authorized by Section 6.03.

(2) (a) The [prosecuting attorney] is authorized to institute civil proceedings in the appropriate court of general jurisdiction to forfeit the charter of a corporation organized under the laws of this State or to revoke the certificate authorizing a foreign corporation to conduct business in this State. The Court may order the charter forfeited or the certificate revoked upon finding (i) that the board of directors or a high managerial agent acting in behalf of the corporation has, in conducting the corporation's affairs, purposely engaged in a persistent course of criminal conduct and (ii) that for the prevention of future criminal conduct of the same character, the public interest requires the charter of the corporation to be forfeited and the corporation to be dissolved or the certificate to be revoked.

(b) When a corporation is convicted of a crime or a high managerial agent of a corporation, as defined in Section 2.07, is convicted of a crime committed in the conduct of the affairs of the corporation, the Court, in sentencing the corporation or the agent, may direct the [prosecuting attorney] to institute proceedings authorized by paragraph (a) of this Subsection.

(c) The proceedings authorized by paragraph (a) of this Subsection shall be conducted in accordance with the procedures authorized by law for the involuntary dissolution of a corporation or the revocation of the certificate authorizing a foreign corporation to conduct business in this State. Such proceedings shall be deemed additional to any other proceedings authorized by law for the purpose of forfeiting the charter of a corporation or revoking the certificate of a foreign corporation.

STATUS OF SECTION

Appeared in Tentative Draft No. 4 but not discussed at May 1955 meeting.

Reprinted in Tentative Draft No. 5 and considered by the Institute at the May 1956 meeting.

Subsection (2)(a)(i) was revised, in accordance with the instructions of the Institute, to require that persistent course of criminal conduct be by "board of directors or a high managerial agent" of the corporation. The words "for the prevention of future criminal conduct of the same character" in Subsection (2)(a)(ii) were inserted by the Council.

Resubmitted to the Institute in Proposed Final Draft No. 1 and approved at the May 1961 meeting.

For Commentary, see Tentative Draft No. 4, p. 202.

Section 6.05. Young Adult Offenders.

(1) Specialized Correctional Treatment. A young adult offender is a person convicted of a crime who, at the time of sentencing, is sixteen but less than twenty-two years of age. A young adult offender who is sentenced to a term of imprisonment which may exceed thirty days [alternatives: (1) ninety days; (2) one year] shall be committed to the custody of the Division of Young Adult Correction of the Department of Correction, and shall receive, as far as practicable, such special and individualized correctional and rehabilitative treatment as may be appropriate to his needs.

(2) Special Term. A young adult offender convicted of a felony may, in lieu of any other sentence of imprison-

ment authorized by this Article, be sentenced to a special term of imprisonment without a minimum and with a maximum of four years, regardless of the degree of the felony involved, if the Court is of the opinion that such special term is adequate for his correction and rehabilitation and will not jeopardize the protection of the public.

[(3) *Removal of Disabilities; Vacation of Conviction.*

(a) In sentencing a young adult offender to the special term provided by this Section or to any sentence other than one of imprisonment, the Court may order that so long as he is not convicted of another felony, the judgment shall not constitute a conviction for the purposes of any disqualification or disability imposed by law upon conviction of a crime.

(b) When any young adult offender is unconditionally discharged from probation or parole before the expiration of the maximum term thereof, the Court may enter an order vacating the judgment of conviction.]

[(4) *Commitment for Observation.* If, after pre-sentence investigation, the Court desires additional information concerning a young adult offender before imposing sentence, it may order that he be committed, for a period not exceeding ninety days, to the custody of the Division of Young Adult Correction of the Department of Correction for observation and study at an appropriate reception or classification center. Such Division of the Department of Correction and the [Young Adult Division of the] Board of Parole shall advise the Court of their findings and recommendations on or before the expiration of such ninety-day period.]

STATUS OF SECTION

Presented to the Institute in Tentative Draft No. 7 and considered at the May 1957 meeting.

Art. 6 97 § 6.06

Revised in accordance with the action of the Institute taken at the May 1957 meeting.

Resubmitted to the Institute in Proposed Final Draft No. 1 and approved at the May 1961 meeting.

Subsection (3) should be eliminated if Section 306.6, dealing with removal of disabilities generally, is adopted.

Subsection (4) should be eliminated if Subsection (1) of Section 7.08, dealing with commitments for observation generally, is adopted.

For Commentary, see Tentative Draft No. 7, p. 24.

Section 6.06. Sentence of Imprisonment for Felony; Ordinary Terms.

A person who has been convicted of a felony may be sentenced to imprisonment, as follows:

(1) in the case of a felony of the first degree, for a term the minimum of which shall be fixed by the Court at not less than one year nor more than ten years, and the maximum of which shall be life imprisonment;

(2) in the case of a felony of the second degree, for a term the minimum of which shall be fixed by the Court at not less than one year nor more than three years, and the maximum of which shall be ten years;

(3) in the case of a felony of the third degree, for a term the minimum of which shall be fixed by the Court at not less than one year nor more than two years, and the maximum of which shall be five years.

STATUS OF SECTION

Presented to the Institute in Tentative Draft No. 2 and considered at the May 1954 meeting.

Reprinted in revised form in Tentative Draft No. 4.

As presented to the Institute in Tentative Draft No. 2 the minimum term to be fixed by the Court for a felony of the first degree was "not less than one year nor more than twenty years." The Section was revised (Tentative Draft No. 4), with the approval of the Council

Alt. § 6.06

of the Institute, to provide a minimum to be fixed by the Court at "not less than one year nor more than ten years."

Resubmitted to the Institute in Proposed Final Draft No. 1 and approved at the May 1961 meeting.

For Commentary, see Tentative Draft No. 2, p. 24.

Alternate Section 6.06. Sentence of Imprisonment for Felony; Ordinary Terms.

A person who has been convicted of a felony may be sentenced to imprisonment, as follows:

(1) in the case of a felony of the first degree, for a term the minimum of which shall be fixed by the Court at not less than one year nor more than ten years, and the maximum at not more than twenty years or at life imprisonment;

(2) in the case of a felony of the second degree, for a term the minimum of which shall be fixed by the Court at not less than one year nor more than three years, and the maximum at not more than ten years;

(3) in the case of a felony of the third degree, for a term the minimum of which shall be fixed by the Court at not less than one year nor more than two years, and the maximum at not more than five years.

No sentence shall be imposed under this Section of which the minimum is longer than one-half the maximum, or, when the maximum is life imprisonment, longer than ten years.

STATUS OF ALTERNATE SECTION

This Section, under which the Court has the authority to fix the maximum (within the statutory limit), was approved by the Council of the Institute as an alternate to Section 6.06 at its March 1960 meeting. The final phrase "or, when the maximum is life imprisonment, longer than ten years" was added in Proposed Final Draft No. 1.

Submitted to the Institute in Proposed Final Draft No. 1 and approved by the Institute at the May 1961 meeting.

Section 6.07. Sentence of Imprisonment for Felony; Extended Terms.

In the cases designated in Section 7.03, a person who has been convicted of a felony may be sentenced to an extended term of imprisonment, as follows:

(1) in the case of a felony of the first degree, for a term the minimum of which shall be fixed by the Court at not less than five years nor more than ten years, and the maximum of which shall be life imprisonment;

(2) in the case of a felony of the second degree, for a term the minimum of which shall be fixed by the Court at not less than one year nor more than five years, and the maximum of which shall be fixed by the Court at not less than ten nor more than twenty years;

(3) in the case of a felony of the third degree, for a term the minimum of which shall be fixed by the Court at not less than one year nor more than three years, and the maximum of which shall be fixed by the Court at not less than five nor more than ten years.

STATUS OF SECTION

Presented to the Institute in Tentative Draft No. 2 and considered at the May 1954 meeting.

Reprinted in Tentative Draft No. 4.

As first presented to the Institute the minimum extended term to be fixed by the Court for a felony of the first degree was "not less than one year nor more than thirty years." The Section was revised, with the approval of the Council at its March 1957 meeting, to set the minimum to be fixed by the Court at "not less than five years nor more than ten years."

Resubmitted to the Institute in Proposed Final Draft No. 1 and approved at the May 1961 meeting.

For Commentary, see Tentative Draft No. 2, p. 24.

Section 6.08. Sentence of Imprisonment for Misdemeanors and Petty Misdemeanors; Ordinary Terms.

A person who has been convicted of a misdemeanor or a petty misdemeanor may be sentenced to imprisonment for a definite term which shall be fixed by the Court and shall not exceed one year in the case of a misdemeanor or thirty days in the case of a petty misdemeanor.

STATUS OF SECTION

Presented to the Institute in Tentative Draft No. 2 and considered at the May 1954 meeting.

Reprinted in Tentative Draft No. 4.

Section was revised to provide for a maximum term of imprisonment of thirty days (instead of three months) for persons convicted of petty misdemeanor.

Resubmitted to the Institute in Proposed Final Draft No. 1 and approved at the May 1961 meeting.

For Commentary, see Tentative Draft No. 2, p. 27.

Section 6.09. Sentence of Imprisonment for Misdemeanors and Petty Misdemeanors; Extended Terms.

(1) In the cases designated in Section 7.04, a person who has been convicted of a misdemeanor or a petty misdemeanor may be sentenced to an extended term of imprisonment, as follows:

(a) in the case of a misdemeanor, for a term the minimum of which shall be fixed by the Court at not more than one year and the maximum of which shall be three years;

(b) in the case of a petty misdemeanor, for a term the minimum of which shall be fixed by the Court at not more than six months and the maximum of which shall be two years.

(2) No such sentence for an extended term shall be imposed unless:

(a) the Director of Correction has certified that there is an institution in the Department of Correction, or in a county, city [or other appropriate political subdivision of the State] which is appropriate for the detention and correctional treatment of such misdemeanants or petty misdemeanants, and that such institution is available to receive such commitments; and

(b) the [Board of Parole] [Parole Administrator] has certified that the Board of Parole is able to visit such institution and to assume responsibility for the release of such prisoners on parole and for their parole supervision.

STATUS OF SECTION

Presented to the Institute in Tentative Draft No. 2 and considered at the May 1954 meeting.

Reprinted in Tentative Draft No. 4.

As first presented to the Institute the minimum extended term to be fixed by the Court for a misdemeanor was "not less than six months nor more than one year" and for a petty misdemeanor "not less than three months nor more than six months." The Section was revised, with the approval of the Council of the Institute at its March 1957 meeting, to eliminate the mandatory minima.

Subsection (2) was added.

Resubmitted to the Institute in Proposed Final Draft No. 1 and approved at the May 1961 meeting.

For Commentary, see Tentative Draft No. 2, p. 27.

§ 6.10

Section 6.10. First Release of All Offenders on Parole; Sentence of Imprisonment Includes Separate Parole Term; Length of Parole Term; Length of Recommitment and Reparole After Revocation of Parole; Final Unconditional Release.

(1) *First Release of All Offenders on Parole.* An offender sentenced to an indefinite term of imprisonment in excess of one year under Section 6.05, 6.06, 6.07, 6.09 or 7.06 shall be released conditionally on parole at or before the expiration of the maximum of such term, in accordance with Article 305.

(2) *Sentence of Imprisonment Includes Separate Parole Term; Length of Parole Term.* A sentence to an indefinite term of imprisonment in excess of one year under Section 6.05, 6.06, 6.07, 6.09 or 7.06 includes as a separate portion of the sentence a term of parole or of recommitment for violation of the conditions of parole which governs the duration of parole or recommitment after the offender's first conditional release on parole. The minimum of such term is one year and the maximum is five years, unless the sentence was imposed under Section 6.05(2) or Section 6.09, in which case the maximum is two years.

(3) *Length of Recommitment and Reparole After Revocation of Parole.* If an offender is recommitted upon revocation of his parole, the term of further imprisonment upon such recommitment and of any subsequent reparole or recommitment under the same sentence shall be fixed by the Board of Parole but shall not exceed in aggregate length the unserved balance of the maximum parole term provided by Subsection (2) of this Section.

(4) *Final Unconditional Release.* When the maximum of his parole term has expired or he has been sooner dis-

charged from parole under Section 305.12, an offender shall be deemed to have served his sentence and shall be released unconditionally.

STATUS OF SECTION

Formerly numbered 6.09A.

Presented to the Institute in Tentative Draft No. 5 and considered at the May 1956 meeting.

Substantially revised, with the approval of the Council at its March 1957 meeting, to make clear that only first release must be on parole and to change length of parole term to one to five years.

Subsection (2) was further revised so as to fix at two years the maximum parole term of persons sentenced to an extended term for misdemeanor or petty misdemeanor. The same change was made in the maximum parole term of persons sentenced as young adult offenders, reducing the maximum period of institutionalization and control to six years, as under the Federal Youth Corrections Act.

Resubmitted to the Institute in Proposed Final Draft No. 1 and approved at the May 1961 meeting.

Commentary that appears in Tentative Draft No. 5 at p. 72 has been revised to meet the criticism of parole administrators.

Section 6.11. Place of Imprisonment.

(1) When a person is sentenced to imprisonment for an indefinite term with a maximum in excess of one year, the Court shall commit him to the custody of the Department of Correction [or other single department or agency] for the term of his sentence and until released in accordance with law.

(2) When a person is sentenced to imprisonment for a definite term, the Court shall designate the institution or agency to which he is committed for the term of his sentence and until released in accordance with law.

§§ 6.12, 6.13

STATUS OF SECTION

Formerly numbered 6.10.

Presented to the Institute in Tentative Draft No. 2 for consideration at the May 1954 meeting.

Reprinted in Tentative Draft No. 4.

Resubmitted to the Institute, with verbal changes, in Proposed Final Draft No. 1 and approved at the May 1961 meeting.

For Commentary, see Tentative Draft No. 2, p. 28.

Section 6.12. Reduction of Conviction by Court to Lesser Degree of Felony or to Misdemeanor.

If, when a person has been convicted of a felony, the Court, having regard to the nature and circumstances of the crime and to the history and character of the defendant, is of the view that it would be unduly harsh to sentence the offender in accordance with the Code, the Court may enter judgment of conviction for a lesser degree of felony or for a misdemeanor and impose sentence accordingly.

STATUS OF SECTION

Formerly numbered 6.11.

Presented to the Institute in Tentative Draft No. 2 and considered at the May 1954 meeting.

Reprinted in Tentative Draft No. 4.

Resubmitted to the Institute in Proposed Final Draft No. 1 and approved at the May 1961 meeting.

For Commentary, see Tentative Draft No. 2, p. 28.

Section 6.13. Civil Commitment in Lieu of Prosecution or of Sentence.

(1) When a person prosecuted for a [felony of the third degree,] misdemeanor or petty misdemeanor is a chronic alcoholic, narcotic addict [or prostitute] or person

suffering from mental abnormality and the Court is authorized by law to order the civil commitment of such person to a hospital or other institution for medical, psychiatric or other rehabilitative treatment, the Court may order such commitment and dismiss the prosecution. The order of commitment may be made after conviction, in which event the Court may set aside the verdict or judgment of conviction and dismiss the prosecution.

(2) The Court shall not make an order under Subsection (1) of this Section unless it is of the view that it will substantially further the rehabilitation of the defendant and will not jeopardize the protection of the public:

STATUS OF SECTION

Formerly numbered 6.12.

Presented to the Institute in Tentative Draft No. 2 and considered at the May 1954 meeting.

Reprinted in Tentative Draft No. 4.

Resubmitted to the Institute in Proposed Final Draft No. 1 and approved at the May 1961 meeting.

This Section does not authorize civil commitment in any case but rather presupposes that authority for the commitment is otherwise conferred by law. Only in that event is the commitment authorized in lieu of sentence.

For Commentary, see Tentative Draft No. 2, p. 30.

ARTICLE 7. AUTHORITY OF COURT IN SENTENCING

Section 7.01. Criteria for Withholding Sentence of Imprisonment and for Placing Defendant on Probation.

(1) The Court shall deal with a person who has been convicted of a crime without imposing sentence of imprisonment unless, having regard to the nature and circumstances of the crime and the history, character and condition of the defendant, it is of the opinion that his imprisonment is necessary for protection of the public because:

(a) there is undue risk that during the period of a suspended sentence or probation the defendant will commit another crime; or

(b) the defendant is in need of correctional treatment that can be provided most effectively by his commitment to an institution; or

(c) a lesser sentence will depreciate the seriousness of the defendant's crime.

(2) The following grounds, while not controlling the discretion of the Court, shall be accorded weight in favor of withholding sentence of imprisonment:

(a) the defendant's criminal conduct neither caused nor threatened serious harm;

(b) the defendant did not contemplate that his criminal conduct would cause or threaten serious harm;

(c) the defendant acted under a strong provocation;

(d) there were substantial grounds tending to excuse or justify the defendant's criminal conduct, though failing to establish a defense;

(e) the victim of the defendant's criminal conduct induced or facilitated its commission;

(f) the defendant has compensated or will compensate the victim of his criminal conduct for the damage or injury that he sustained;

(g) the defendant has no history of prior delinquency or criminal activity or has led a law-abiding life for a substantial period of time before the commission of the present crime;

(h) the defendant's criminal conduct was the result of circumstances unlikely to recur;

(i) the character and attitudes of the defendant indicate that he is unlikely to commit another crime;

(j) the defendant is particularly likely to respond affirmatively to probationary treatment;

(k) the imprisonment of the defendant would entail excessive hardship to himself or his dependents.

(3) When a person who has been convicted of a crime is not sentenced to imprisonment, the Court shall place him on probation if he is in need of the supervision, guidance, assistance or direction that the probation service can provide.

STATUS OF SECTION

Presented to the Institute in Tentative Draft No. 2 and considered at the May 1954 meeting.

Reprinted in Tentative Draft No. 4.

The Section was substantially revised, with the approval of the Council at its March 1958 meeting, to express the principle that a probationary disposition is desirable unless there is a special reason for an institutional commitment.

Resubmitted to the Institute in Proposed Final Draft No. 1 and approved at the May 1961 meeting.

For Commentary, see Tentative Draft No. 2, p. 34.

Section 7.02. Criteria for Imposing Fines.

(1) The Court shall not sentence a defendant only to pay a fine, when any other disposition is authorized by law, unless having regard to the nature and circumstances of the crime and to the history and character of the defendant, it is of the opinion that the fine alone suffices for protection of the public.

(2) The Court shall not sentence a defendant to pay a fine in addition to a sentence of imprisonment or probation unless:

   (a) the defendant has derived a pecuniary gain from the crime; or

   (b) the Court is of opinion that a fine is specially adapted to deterrence of the crime involved or to the correction of the offender.

(3) The Court shall not sentence a defendant to pay a fine unless:

   (a) the defendant is or will be able to pay the fine; and

   (b) the fine will not prevent the defendant from making restitution or reparation to the victim of the crime.

(4) In determining the amount and method of payment of a fine, the Court shall take into account the financial resources of the defendant and the nature of the burden that its payment will impose.

STATUS OF SECTION

Presented to the Institute in Tentative Draft No. 2 and considered at the May 1954 meeting.

Reprinted in Tentative Draft No. 4.

Resubmitted to the Institute in Proposed Final Draft No. 1 and approved at the May 1961 meeting.

Verbal changes have been made.

For Commentary, see Tentative Draft No. 2, p. 36.

Section 7.03. Criteria for Sentence of Extended Term of Imprisonment; Felonies.

The Court may sentence a person who has been convicted of a felony to an extended term of imprisonment if it finds one or more of the grounds specified in this Section. The finding of the Court shall be incorporated in the record.

(1) The defendant is a persistent offender whose commitment for an extended term is necessary for protection of the public.

The Court shall not make such a finding unless the defendant is over twenty-one years of age and has previously been convicted of two felonies or of one felony and two misdemeanors, committed at different times when he was over [insert Juvenile Court age] years of age.

(2) The defendant is a professional criminal whose commitment for an extended term is necessary for protection of the public.

The Court shall not make such a finding unless the defendant is over twenty-one years of age and:

(a) the circumstances of the crime show that the defendant has knowingly devoted himself to criminal activity as a major source of livelihood; or

(b) the defendant has substantial income or resources not explained to be derived from a source other than criminal activity.

(3) The defendant is a dangerous, mentally abnormal person whose commitment for an extended term is necessary for protection of the public.

The Court shall not make such a finding unless the defendant has been subjected to a psychiatric examination resulting in the conclusions that his mental condition is gravely abnormal; that his criminal conduct has been characterized by a pattern of repetitive or compulsive behavior or by persistent aggressive behavior with heedless indifference to consequences; and that such condition makes him a serious danger to others.

(4) The defendant is a multiple offender whose criminality was so extensive that a sentence of imprisonment for an extended term is warranted.

The Court shall not make such a finding unless:

(a) the defendant is being sentenced for two or more felonies, or is already under sentence of imprisonment for felony, and the sentences of imprisonment involved will run concurrently under Section 7.06; or

(b) the defendant admits in open court the commission of one or more other felonies and asks that they be taken into account when he is sentenced; and

(c) the longest sentences of imprisonment authorized for each of the defendant's crimes, including admitted crimes taken into account, if made to run consecutively would exceed in length the minimum and maximum of the extended term imposed.

STATUS OF SECTION

Presented to the Institute in Tentative Draft No. 2 and considered at the May 1954 meeting.

Reprinted in Tentative Draft No. 4.

Resubmitted to the Institute, with verbal changes in paragraph (c) of Subsection (4), in Proposed Final Draft No. 1 and approved at the May 1961 meeting.

For Commentary, see Tentative Draft No. 2, p. 38.

Section 7.04. Criteria for Sentence of Extended Term of Imprisonment; Misdemeanors and Petty Misdemeanors.

The Court may sentence a person who has been convicted of a misdemeanor or petty misdemeanor to an extended term of imprisonment if it finds one or more of the grounds specified in this Section. The finding of the Court shall be incorporated in the record.

(1) The defendant is a persistent offender whose commitment for an extended term is necessary for protection of the public.

The Court shall not make such a finding unless the defendant has previously been convicted of two crimes, committed at different times when he was over [insert Juvenile Court age] years of age.

(2) The defendant is a professional criminal whose commitment for an extended term is necessary for protection of the public.

The Court shall not make such a finding unless:

(a) the circumstances of the crime show that the defendant has knowingly devoted himself to criminal activity as a major source of livelihood; or

(b) the defendant has substantial income or resources not explained to be derived from a source other than criminal activity.

(3) The defendant is a chronic alcoholic, narcotic addict, prostitute or person of abnormal mental condition who requires rehabilitative treatment for a substantial period of time.

The Court shall not make such a finding unless, with respect to the particular category to which the defendant belongs, the Director of Correction has certified that there is a specialized institution or facility which is satisfactory for the rehabilitative treatment of such persons and which otherwise meets the requirements of Section 6.09, Subsection (2).

(4) The defendant is a multiple offender whose criminality was so extensive that a sentence of imprisonment for an extended term is warranted.

The Court shall not make such a finding unless:

(a) the defendant is being sentenced for a number of misdemeanors or petty misdemeanors or is already under sentence of imprisonment for crime of such grades, or admits in open court the commission of one or more such crimes and asks that they be taken into account when he is sentenced; and

(b) maximum fixed sentences of imprisonment for each of the defendant's crimes, including admitted crimes taken into account, if made to run consecutively, would exceed in length the maximum period of the extended term imposed.

STATUS OF SECTION

Presented to the Institute in Tentative Draft No. 2 for consideration at the May 1954 meeting.

Reprinted in Tentative Draft No. 4.

Resubmitted to the Institute, with verbal changes, in Proposed Final Draft No. 1 and approved at the May 1961 meeting.

The form of the second paragraph of Subsection (3) has been changed to reflect the fact that, under Section 6.11, extended term commitments of misdemeanants and petty misdemeanants are commitments to the Department of Correction and not to a designated institution.

For Commentary, see Tentative Draft No. 2, p. 45.

Section 7.05. Former Conviction in Another Jurisdiction; Definition and Proof of Conviction; Sentence Taking into Account Admitted Crimes Bars Subsequent Conviction for Such Crimes.

(1) For purposes of paragraph (1) of Section 7.03 or 7.04, a conviction of the commission of a crime in another jurisdiction shall constitute a previous conviction. Such conviction shall be deemed to have been of a felony if sentence of death or of imprisonment in excess of one year was authorized under the law of such other jurisdiction, of a misdemeanor if sentence of imprisonment in excess of thirty days but not in excess of a year was authorized and of a petty misdemeanor if sentence of imprisonment for not more than thirty days was authorized.

(2) An adjudication by a court of competent jurisdiction that the defendant committed a crime constitutes a conviction for purposes of Sections 7.03 to 7.05 inclusive, although sentence or the execution thereof was suspended, provided that the time to appeal has expired and that the defendant was not pardoned on the ground of innocence.

(3) Prior conviction may be proved by any evidence, including fingerprint records made in connection with arrest, conviction or imprisonment, that reasonably satisfies the Court that the defendant was convicted.

(4) When the defendant has asked that other crimes admitted in open court be taken into account when he is sentenced and the Court has not rejected such request, the sentence shall bar the prosecution or conviction of the defendant in this State for any such admitted crime.

STATUS OF SECTION

Presented to the Institute in Tentative Draft No. 2 and considered at the May 1954 meeting.

Reprinted in Tentative Draft No. 4.

Resubmitted to the Institute, with verbal changes, in Proposed Final Draft No. 1 and approved at the May 1961 meeting.

For Commentary, see Tentative Draft No. 2, p. 47.

Section 7.06. Multiple Sentences; Concurrent and Consecutive Terms.

(1) <u>Sentences of Imprisonment for More Than One Crime.</u> When multiple sentences of imprisonment are imposed on a defendant for more than one crime, including a crime for which a previous suspended sentence or sentence of probation has been revoked, such multiple sentences shall run concurrently or consecutively as the Court determines at the time of sentence, except that:

> (a) a definite and an indefinite term shall run concurrently and both sentences shall be satisfied by service of the indefinite term; and

> (b) the aggregate of consecutive definite terms shall not exceed one year; and

> (c) the aggregate of consecutive indefinite terms shall not exceed in minimum or maximum length the longest extended term authorized for the highest grade and degree of crime for which any of the sentences was imposed; and

> (d) not more than one sentence for an extended term shall be imposed.

(2) <u>Sentences of Imprisonment Imposed at Different Times.</u> When a defendant who has previously been sentenced to imprisonment is subsequently sentenced to another term for a crime committed prior to the former sentence, other than a crime committed while in custody:

> (a) the multiple sentences imposed shall so far as possible conform to Subsection (1) of this Section; and

> (b) whether the Court determines that the terms shall run concurrently or consecutively, the defendant

shall be credited with time served in imprisonment on the prior sentence in determining the permissible aggregate length of the term or terms remaining to be served; and

(c) when a new sentence is imposed on a prisoner who is on parole, the balance of the parole term on the former sentence shall be deemed to run during the period of the new imprisonment.

(3) <u>Sentence of Imprisonment for Crime Committed While on Parole.</u> When a defendant is sentenced to imprisonment for a crime committed while on parole in this State, such term of imprisonment and any period of reimprisonment that the Board of Parole may require the defendant to serve upon the revocation of his parole shall run concurrently, unless the Court orders them to run consecutively.

(4) <u>Multiple Sentences of Imprisonment in Other Cases.</u> Except as otherwise provided in this Section, multiple terms of imprisonment shall run concurrently or consecutively as the Court determines when the second or subsequent sentence is imposed.

(5) <u>Calculation of Concurrent and Consecutive Terms of Imprisonment.</u>

(a) When indefinite terms run concurrently, the shorter minimum terms merge in and are satisfied by serving the longest minimum term and the shorter maximum terms merge in and are satisfied by discharge of the longest maximum term.

(b) When indefinite terms run consecutively, the minimum terms are added to arrive at an aggregate minimum to be served equal to the sum of all minimum terms and the maximum terms are added to arrive at an aggregate maximum equal to the sum of all maximum terms.

(c) When a definite and an indefinite term run consecutively, the period of the definite term is added to both the minimum and maximum of the indefinite term and both sentences are satisfied by serving the indefinite term.

(6) **Suspension of Sentence or Probation and Imprisonment; Multiple Terms of Suspension and Probation.** When a defendant is sentenced for more than one offense or a defendant already under sentence is sentenced for another offense committed prior to the former sentence:

(a) the Court shall not sentence to probation a defendant who is under sentence of imprisonment [with more than thirty days to run] or impose a sentence of probation and a sentence of imprisonment [, except as authorized by Section 6.02(3)(b)]; and

(b) multiple periods of suspension or probation shall run concurrently from the date of the first such disposition; and

(c) when a sentence of imprisonment is imposed for an indefinite term, the service of such sentence shall satisfy a suspended sentence on another count or a prior suspended sentence or sentence to probation; and

(d) when a sentence of imprisonment is imposed for a definite term, the period of a suspended sentence on another count or a prior suspended sentence or sentence to probation shall run during the period of such imprisonment.

(7) **Offense Committed While Under Suspension of Sentence or Probation.** When a defendant is convicted of an offense committed while under suspension of sentence or

on probation and such suspension or probation is not revoked:

 (a) if the defendant is sentenced to imprisonment for an indefinite term, the service of such sentence shall satisfy the prior suspended sentence or sentence to probation; and

 (b) if the defendant is sentenced to imprisonment for a definite term, the period of the suspension or probation shall not run during the period of such imprisonment; and

 (c) if sentence is suspended or the defendant is sentenced to probation, the period of such suspension or probation shall run concurrently with or consecutively to the remainder of the prior periods, as the Court determines at the time of sentence.

STATUS OF SECTION

Previous version of Section presented to the Institute in Tentative Draft No. 2 and considered at the May 1954 meeting.

Reprinted in Tentative Draft No. 4.

Thereafter the Section was extensively revised. It was expanded to include not only multiple sentences of imprisonment but also multiple sentences involving terms of suspension and probation.

Resubmitted to the Institute in Proposed Final Draft No. 1 and approved at the May 1961 meeting.

For Commentary, see Tentative Draft No. 2, p. 50.

Section 7.07. Procedure on Sentence; Pre-sentence Investigation and Report; Remand for Psychiatric Examination; Transmission of Records to Department of Correction.

(1) The Court shall not impose sentence without first ordering a pre-sentence investigation of the defendant and according due consideration to a written report of such investigation where:

§ 7.07

(a) the defendant has been convicted of a felony; or

(b) the defendant is less than twenty-two years of age and has been convicted of a crime; or

(c) the defendant will be [placed on probation or] sentenced to imprisonment for an extended term.

(2) The Court may order a pre-sentence investigation in any other case.

(3) The pre-sentence investigation shall include an analysis of the circumstances attending the commission of the crime, the defendant's history of delinquency or criminality, physical and mental condition, family situation and background, economic status, education, occupation and personal habits and any other matters that the probation officer deems relevant or the Court directs to be included.

(4) Before imposing sentence, the Court may order the defendant to submit to psychiatric observation and examination for a period of not exceeding sixty days or such longer period as the Court determines to be necessary for the purpose. The defendant may be remanded for this purpose to any available clinic or mental hospital or the Court may appoint a qualified psychiatrist to make the examination. The report of the examination shall be submitted to the Court.

(5) Before imposing sentence, the Court shall advise the defendant or his counsel of the factual contents and the conclusions of any pre-sentence investigation or psychiatric examination and afford fair opportunity, if the defendant so requests, to controvert them. The sources of confidential information need not, however, be disclosed.

(6) The Court shall not impose a sentence of imprisonment for an extended term unless the ground therefor has been established at a hearing after the conviction of the defendant and on written notice to him of the ground proposed. Subject to the limitation of Subsection (5) of this Section, the defendant shall have the right to hear and controvert the evidence against him and to offer evidence upon the issue.

(7) If the defendant is sentenced to imprisonment, a copy of the report of any pre-sentence investigation or psychiatric examination shall be transmitted forthwith to the Department of Correction [or other state department or agency] or, when the defendant is committed to the custody of a specific institution, to such institution.

STATUS OF SECTION

Presented to the Institute in Tentative Draft No. 2 and considered at the May 1954 meeting.

Reprinted in Tentative Draft No. 4.

As originally presented to the Institute the draft included alternate Subsection (1)(a) as follows: "the defendant has been convicted of a felony for the first time." On reconsideration, the paragraph was omitted on the ground that while this limitation may be necessary in some jurisdictions, it has no place in a model code.

As originally presented to the Institute paragraph (1)(b) fixed an age of less than twenty-one years. This was changed to less than twenty-two years, to conform to the definition of young adult offender in Section 6.05.

The brackets in paragraph (1)(c) were added to take account of the possibility that the requirement of an investigation prior to sentence of probation, rather than in the course of supervision, may be impractical in many jurisdictions and may thus have the undesired effect of discouraging probationary disposition.

Resubmitted to the Institute in Proposed Final Draft No. 1 and approved at the May 1961 meeting.

For Commentary, see Tentative Draft No. 2, p. 52.

Section 7.08. Commitment for Observation; Sentence of Imprisonment for Felony Deemed Tentative for Period of One Year; Re-sentence on Petition of Commissioner of Correction.

(1) If, after pre-sentence investigation, the Court desires additional information concerning an offender convicted of a felony or misdemeanor before imposing sentence, it may order that he be committed, for a period not exceeding ninety days, to the custody of the Department of Correction, or, in the case of a young adult offender, to the custody of the Division of Young Adult Correction, for observation and study at an appropriate reception or classification center. The Department and the Board of Parole, or the Young Adult Divisions thereof, shall advise the Court of their findings and recommendations on or before the expiration of such ninety-day period. If the offender is thereafter sentenced to imprisonment, the period of such commitment for observation shall be deducted from the maximum term and from the minimum, if any, of such sentence.

(2) When a person has been sentenced to imprisonment upon conviction of a felony, whether for an ordinary or extended term, the sentence shall be deemed tentative, to the extent provided in this Section, for the period of one year following the date when the offender is received in custody by the Department of Correction [or other state department or agency].

(3) If, as a result of the examination and classification by the Department of Correction [or other state department or agency] of a person under sentence of imprisonment upon conviction of a felony, the Commissioner of Correction [or other department head] is satisfied that the sentence of the Court may have been based upon a misapprehension as to the history, character or physical or mental

condition of the offender, the Commissioner, during the period when the offender's sentence is deemed tentative under Subsection (2) of this Section shall file in the sentencing Court a petition to re-sentence the offender. The petition shall set forth the information as to the offender that is deemed to warrant his re-sentence and may include a recommendation as to the sentence to be imposed.

(4) The Court may dismiss a petition filed under Subsection (3) of this Section without a hearing if it deems the information set forth insufficient to warrant reconsideration of the sentence. If the Court is of the view that the petition warrants such reconsideration, a copy of the petition shall be served on the offender, who shall have the right to be heard on the issue and to be represented by counsel.

(5) When the Court grants a petition filed under Subsection (3) of this Section, it shall re-sentence the offender and may impose any sentence that might have been imposed originally for the felony of which the defendant was convicted. The period of his imprisonment prior to re-sentence and any reduction for good behavior to which he is entitled shall be applied in satisfaction of the final sentence.

(6) For all purposes other than this Section, a sentence of imprisonment has the same finality when it is imposed that it would have if this Section were not in force.

(7) Nothing in this Section shall alter the remedies provided by law for vacating or correcting an illegal sentence.

STATUS OF SECTION

Presented to the Institute in Tentative Draft No. 2 and considered at the May 1954 meeting.

Reprinted in Tentative Draft No. 4.

Subsection (1) was added and verbal changes made.

Resubmitted to the Institute in Proposed Final Draft No. 1 and approved at the May 1961 meeting.

In the first sentence of Subsection (1) the words "convicted of a felony or misdemeanor" have been added.

For Commentary, see Tentative Draft No. 2, p. 56.

Section 7.09. Credit for Time of Detention Prior to Sentence; Credit for Imprisonment Under Earlier Sentence for the Same Crime.

(1) When a defendant who is sentenced to imprisonment has previously been detained in any state or local correctional or other institution following his [conviction of] [arrest for] the crime for which such sentence is imposed, such period of detention following his [conviction] [arrest] shall be deducted from the maximum term, and from the minimum, if any, of such sentence. The officer having custody of the defendant shall furnish a certificate to the Court at the time of sentence, showing the length of such detention of the defendant prior to sentence in any state or local correctional or other institution, and the certificate shall be annexed to the official records of the defendant's commitment.

(2) When a judgment of conviction is vacated and a new sentence is thereafter imposed upon the defendant for the same crime, the period of detention and imprisonment theretofore served shall be deducted from the maximum term, and from the minimum, if any, of the new sentence. The officer having custody of the defendant shall furnish a certificate to the Court at the time of sentence, showing the period of imprisonment served under the original sentence, and the certificate shall be annexed to the official records of the defendant's new commitment.

STATUS OF SECTION

Presented to the Institute in Proposed Final Draft No. 1 and approved at the May 1961 meeting.

A verbal change has been made in the title of the Section.

PART II. DEFINITION OF SPECIFIC CRIMES

OFFENSES AGAINST EXISTENCE OR STABILITY OF THE STATE

[This category of offenses, including treason, sedition, espionage and like crimes, was excluded from the scope of the Model Penal Code. These offenses are peculiarly the concern of the federal government. The Constitution itself defines treason: "Treason against the United States shall consist only in levying War against them, or in adhering to their Enemies, giving them Aid and Comfort. . . ." Article III, Section 3; cf. Pennsylvania v. Nelson, 350 U.S. 497 (supersession of state sedition legislation by federal law). Also, the definition of offenses against the stability of the state is inevitably affected by special political considerations. These factors militated against the use of the Institute's limited resources to attempt to draft "model" provisions in this area. However we provide at this point in the Plan of the Model Penal Code for an Article 200, where definitions of offenses against the existence or stability of the state may be incorporated.]

OFFENSES INVOLVING DANGER TO THE PERSON

ARTICLE 210. CRIMINAL HOMICIDE

Section 210.0. Definitions.

In Articles 210-213, unless a different meaning plainly is required:

(1) "human being" means a person who has been born and is alive;

(2) "bodily injury" means physical pain, illness or any impairment of physical condition;

(3) "serious bodily injury" means bodily injury which creates a substantial risk of death or which causes serious, permanent disfigurement, or protracted loss or impairment of the function of any bodily member or organ;

(4) "deadly weapon" means any firearm, or other weapon, device, instrument, material or substance, whether animate or inanimate, which in the manner it is used or is intended to be used is known to be capable of producing death or serious bodily injury.

STATUS OF SECTION

Presented to the Institute as Section 201.60 of Tentative Draft No. 9, and considered at the May 1959 meeting.

The Section was reprinted as Section 211.4 in Tentative Draft No. 11, page 9. One minor verbal change has been made: the words "permanent or," which appeared just before the words "protracted loss" in clause (3), have been deleted as superfluous.

Section 210.1. Criminal Homicide.

(1) A person is guilty of criminal homicide if he purposely, knowingly, recklessly or negligently causes the death of another human being.

(2) Criminal homicide is murder, manslaughter or negligent homicide.

STATUS OF SECTION

Presented to the Institute in Tentative Draft No. 9, and considered at the May 1959 meeting.

The Section was then numbered 201.1.

For Commentary, see Tentative Draft No. 9, p. 25.

The terms "purposely, knowingly, recklessly or negligently" are defined in Section 2.02. Supra p. 25. The definition of negligence requires proof of "substantial and unjustifiable risk" and "gross deviation" from the standard of reasonable care. Part I of the Code also defines the excuses and justifications, e.g., self-defense, which render a homicide non-criminal.

Section 210.2. Murder.

(1) Except as provided in Section 210.3(1)(b), criminal homicide constitutes murder when:

    (a) it is committed purposely or knowingly; or

    (b) it is committed recklessly under circumstances manifesting extreme indifference to the value of human life. Such recklessness and indifference are presumed if the actor is engaged or is an accomplice in the commission of, or an attempt to commit, or flight after committing or attempting to commit robbery, rape or deviate sexual intercourse by force or threat of force, arson, burglary, kidnapping or felonious escape.

§§ 210.3, 210.4

(2) Murder is a felony of the first degree [but a person convicted of murder may be sentenced to death, as provided in Section 210.6].

STATUS OF SECTION

Presented to the Institute as Section 201.2 of Tentative Draft No. 9, and considered at the May 1959 meeting.

For Commentary, see Tentative Draft No. 9, p. 28.

The only substantive change is the insertion of the reference to deviate sexual intercourse in paragraph (b) of subsection (1).

Section 210.3. Manslaughter.

(1) Criminal homicide constitutes manslaughter when:

(a) it is committed recklessly; or

(b) a homicide which would otherwise be murder is committed under the influence of extreme mental or emotional disturbance for which there is reasonable explanation or excuse. The reasonableness of such explanation or excuse shall be determined from the viewpoint of a person in the actor's situation under the circumstances as he believes them to be.

(2) Manslaughter is a felony of the second degree.

STATUS OF SECTION

Presented to the Institute as Section 201.3 of Tentative Draft No. 9, and considered at the May 1959 meeting.

For Commentary, see Tentative Draft No. 9, p. 40.

Section 210.4. Negligent Homicide.

(1) Criminal homicide constitutes negligent homicide when it is committed negligently.

(2) Negligent homicide is a felony of the third degree.

STATUS OF SECTION

Presented to the Institute as Section 201.4 of Tentative Draft No. 9, and considered at the May 1959 meeting.

For Commentary, see Tentative Draft No. 9, p. 49.

Section 210.5. Causing or Aiding Suicide.

(1) *Causing Suicide as Criminal Homicide.* **A person may be convicted of criminal homicide for causing another to commit suicide only if he purposely causes such suicide by force, duress or deception.**

(2) *Aiding or Soliciting Suicide as an Independent Offense.* **A person who purposely aids or solicits another to commit suicide is guilty of a felony of the second degree if his conduct causes such suicide or an attempted suicide, and otherwise of a misdemeanor.**

STATUS OF SECTION

Presented to the Institute as Section 201.5 of Tentative Draft No. 9, and considered at the May 1959 meeting.

For Commentary, see Tentative Draft No. 9, p. 56.

The section was recommitted to the Reporters for consideration of various proposals and comments. It has been substantially revised.

Subsection (1) formerly read: "A person is deemed to have caused the death of another who commits suicide only if he purposely causes such suicide by force, duress or fraud." Although the comments made it clear that the object and effect of this formulation were to subject such behavior to the penalty for murder or manslaughter, as the case might be, some readers of the original text misunderstood it as defining in subsection (1) an offense for which subsection (2) prescribed the penalties. The revision eliminates the possibility of misconstruction. "Deception" has been substituted for "fraud" because we do not wish to leave open a possible interpretation of "fraud" as requiring motive of personal gain.

Subsection (2) formerly authorized second degree felony penalties "if suicide occurs." This has been changed to require proof of a causal relationship between a solicitation to commit suicide and the subsequent self-destructive behavior of the person solicited. We do not wish to permit severe penalties for soliciting suicide where, for example, the suicide occurs a year after the alleged solicitation, or where a number of people in a crowd watching a death-bent man on a high ledge urge him to jump.

We have also reduced bare solicitation that does not lead to any attempt at suicide to the level of a misdemeanor. Penalties for ineffectual aiding and soliciting suicide may reasonably be mitigated even where we would not mitigate for ineffectual aid or solicitation of an ordinary criminal offense to be committed against a third person. Cf. Section 2.06—*Complicity,* and Section 5.02—*Solicitation.* The instinct of self-preservation will in nearly all cases be sufficient to forestall harmful consequences from solicitation to suicide. Thus such solicitation is intrinsically less dangerous than solicitation of criminal behavior to be directed against others.

Section 210.6. Sentence of Death for Murder; Further Proceedings to Determine Sentence.

(1) Death Sentence Excluded. When a defendant is found guilty of murder, the Court shall impose sentence for a felony of the first degree if it is satisfied that:

(a) none of the aggravating circumstances enumerated in Subsection (3) of this Section was established by the evidence at the trial or will be established if further proceedings are initiated under Subsection (2) of this Section; or

(b) substantial mitigating circumstances, established by the evidence at the trial, call for leniency; or

(c) the defendant, with the consent of the prosecuting attorney and the approval of the Court, pleaded guilty to murder as a felony of the first degree; or

(d) the defendant was under 18 years of age at the time of the commission of the crime; or

(e) the defendant's physical or mental condition calls for leniency; or

(f) although the evidence suffices to sustain the verdict, it does not foreclose all doubt respecting the defendant's guilt.

(2) *Determination by Court or by Court and Jury.* Unless the Court imposes sentence under Subsection (1) of this Section, it shall conduct a separate proceeding to determine whether the defendant should be sentenced for a felony of the first degree or sentenced to death. The proceeding shall be conducted before the Court alone if the defendant was convicted by a Court sitting without a jury or upon his plea of guilty or if the prosecuting attorney and the defendant waive a jury with respect to sentence. In other cases it shall be conducted before the Court sitting with the jury which determined the defendant's guilt or, if the Court for good cause shown discharges that jury, with a new jury empanelled for the purpose.

In the proceeding, evidence may be presented as to any matter that the Court deems relevant to sentence, including but not limited to the nature and circumstances of the crime, the defendant's character, background, history, mental and physical condition and any of the aggravating or mitigating circumstances enumerated in Subsections (3) and (4) of this Section. Any such evidence which the Court deems to have probative force may be received, regardless of its admissibility under the exclusionary rules of evidence, provided that the defendant's counsel is accorded a fair opportunity to rebut any hearsay statements. The prosecuting attorney and the defendant or his counsel shall be permitted to present argument for or against sentence of death.

The determination whether sentence of death shall be imposed shall be in the discretion of the Court, except that when the proceeding is conducted before the Court sitting with a jury, the Court shall not impose sentence of death unless it submits to the jury the issue whether the defendant should be sentenced to death or to imprisonment and the jury returns a verdict that the sentence should be death. If the jury is unable to reach a unanimous verdict, the Court shall dismiss the jury and impose sentence for a felony of the first degree.

The Court, in exercising its discretion as to sentence, and the jury, in determining upon its verdict, shall take into account the aggravating and mitigating circumstances enumerated in Subsections (3) and (4) and any other facts that it deems relevant, but it shall not impose or recommend sentence of death unless it finds one of the aggravating circumstances enumerated in Subsection (3) and further finds that there are no mitigating circumstances sufficiently substantial to call for leniency. When the issue is submitted to the jury, the Court shall so instruct and also shall inform the jury of the nature of the sentence of imprisonment that may be imposed, including its implication with respect to possible release upon parole, if the jury verdict is against sentence of death.

Alternative formulation of Subsection (2):

(2) Determination by Court. Unless the Court imposes sentence under Subsection (1) of this Section, it shall conduct a separate proceeding to determine whether the defendant should be sentenced for a felony of the first degree or sentenced to death. In the proceeding, the Court, in accordance with Section 7.07, shall consider the report of the pre-sentence investigation and, if a psychiatric examination has been ordered, the report of such examination. In addition, evidence may be presented as to any matter that the Court deems relevant to sentence, including but not limited to the nature and circumstances of the crime, the defendant's character, background, history, mental and physical condition and any of the aggravating or mitigating circumstances enumerated in Subsections (3) and (4) of this Section. Any such evidence which the Court deems to

have probative force may be received, regardless of its admissibility under the exclusionary rules of evidence, provided that the defendant's counsel is accorded a fair opportunity to rebut any hearsay statements. The prosecuting attorney and the defendant or his counsel shall be permitted to present argument for or against sentence of death.

The determination whether sentence of death shall be imposed shall be in the discretion of the Court. In exercising such discretion, the Court shall take into account the aggravating and mitigating circumstances enumerated in Subsections (3) and (4) and any other facts that it deems relevant but shall not impose sentence of death unless it finds one of the aggravating circumstances enumerated in Subsection (3) and further finds that there are no mitigating circumstances sufficiently substantial to call for leniency.

(3) Aggravating Circumstances.

(a) The murder was committed by a convict under sentence of imprisonment.

(b) The defendant was previously convicted of another murder or of a felony involving the use or threat of violence to the person.

(c) At the time the murder was committed the defendant also committed another murder.

(d) The defendant knowingly created a great risk of death to many persons.

(e) The murder was committed while the defendant was engaged or was an accomplice in the commission of, or an attempt to commit, or flight after committing or attempting to commit robbery, rape or deviate sexual intercourse by force or threat of force, arson, burglary or kidnapping.

(f) The murder was committed for the purpose of avoiding or preventing a lawful arrest or effecting an escape from lawful custody.

(g) The murder was committed for pecuniary gain.

(h) The murder was especially heinous, atrocious or cruel, manifesting exceptional depravity.

(4) *Mitigating Circumstances.*

(a) The defendant has no significant history of prior criminal activity.

(b) The murder was committed while the defendant was under the influence of extreme mental or emotional disturbance.

(c) The victim was a participant in the defendant's homicidal conduct or consented to the homicidal act.

(d) The murder was committed under circumstances which the defendant believed to provide a moral justification or extenuation for his conduct.

(e) The defendant was an accomplice in a murder committed by another person and his participation in the homicidal act was relatively minor.

(f) The defendant acted under duress or under the domination of another person.

(g) At the time of the murder, the capacity of the defendant to appreciate the criminality [wrongfulness] of his conduct or to conform his conduct to the requirements of law was impaired as a result of mental disease or defect or intoxication.

(h) The youth of the defendant at the time of the crime.

STATUS OF SECTION

Presented to the Institute as Section 201.6 of Tentative Draft No. 9, and considered at the May 1959 meeting.

Revised to reflect the action taken by the Institute, the principal change being the reversal of Subsection (2) and Alternative (2), to express a preference for determination of the issue in contested cases by a method which employs the jury rather than the court alone.

For Commentary, see Tentative Draft No. 9, p. 63.

Subsection (2) has been further revised to reflect the firm opinion of both the Advisory Committee and the Council that even if the supplementary proceeding is conducted before the Court sitting with a jury, the Court should have the power (1) to withhold the issue of capital punishment from the jury and sentence to imprisonment, and (2) to sentence to imprisonment notwithstanding a jury verdict in favor of sentence of death. It was, in short, desired that, unless a jury is dispensed with, a capital sentence rest on the concurrent judgment of the jury and the Court, as is required now in Illinois and Maryland. There was substantial support for this position at the May 1959 meeting, although motions on the subject were all tabled.

Paragraph (e) of Subsection (3) has been revised to include reference to "deviate sexual intercourse" by force, thus making the language parallel to Section 210.2(1)(b).

The word "significant" has been inserted before "history" in Subsection (4)(a) in order to meet the concern expressed by some Institute members lest any trivial and remote conviction bar consideration of an otherwise law-abiding life as a mitigating factor.

The Code does not include provisions governing the execution of capital punishment. Though this topic must be dealt with in a jurisdiction authorizing sentence of death, including the method of execution and the traditional exemptions for pregnant women and persons insane at the time of execution, the primarily correctional preoccupation of the Code led to the omission of this subject.

ARTICLE 211. ASSAULT; RECKLESS ENDANGERING; THREATS

Section 211.0. Definitions.

In this Article, the definitions given in Section 210.0 apply unless a different meaning plainly is required.

Section 211.1. Assault.

(1) Simple Assault. A person is guilty of assault if he:

(a) attempts to cause or purposely, knowingly or recklessly causes bodily injury to another; or

(b) negligently causes bodily injury to another with a deadly weapon; or

(c) attempts by physical menace to put another in fear of imminent serious bodily harm.

Simple assault is a misdemeanor unless committed in a fight or scuffle entered into by mutual consent, in which case it is a petty misdemeanor.

(2) Aggravated Assault. A person is guilty of aggravated assault if he:

(a) attempts to cause serious bodily injury to another, or causes such injury purposely, knowingly or recklessly under circumstances manifesting extreme indifference to the value of human life; or

(b) attempts to cause or purposely or knowingly causes bodily injury to another with a deadly weapon.

Aggravated assault under paragraph (a) is a felony of the second degree; aggravated assault under paragraph (b) is a felony of the third degree.

STATUS OF SECTION

Presented to the Institute as Section 201.10 of Tentative Draft No. 9, and considered at the May 1959 meeting.

For Commentary, see Tentative Draft No. 9, p. 81.

The Section was reprinted in Tentative Draft No. 11, which was before the May 1960 meeting.

The section has been revised in form and substance. Previous drafts called the offense "bodily injury"; we have now gone back to the traditional term "assault," on the ground that retention of the familiar term will enhance acceptability of our proposals. We have also expressly included attempts within the definition of assault. In previous drafts, the section was limited to actual batteries, and we relied on the general attempt provisions of Part I to reach unsuccessful efforts to inflict bodily injury. Again, this is not a change of substance, but a deference to the traditional scope of the "assault" concept.

The substantive change is in the last sentence of the section. Formerly, all aggravated assaults were felonies of the second degree, and there was no category of assault between the second degree felony (10 year maximum) and the misdemeanor (one year maximum) covered by Subsection (1). It is now provided that assaults falling within paragraph (b) of Subsection (2) be classified as felonies of the third degree (five year maximum). These are assaults with a deadly weapon where it does not appear that there was intent to do serious bodily harm or the type of recklessness referred to in paragraph (a). It would be unnecessarily harsh, for example, to subject a person to ten years maximum imprisonment for a mere attempt to inflict minor injury with a knife or club. In particular circumstances the use of such implements would often support an inference of purpose or recklessness leading to a second degree conviction; and use of a firearm to shoot at the victim would almost certainly lead to that conclusion. But a judgment as to the seriousness of the actor's ill-will should not follow automatically from classification of the implement he employs, when the imposition of very heavy sentences is the issue.

Section 211.2. Recklessly Endangering Another Person.

A person commits a misdemeanor if he recklessly engages in conduct which places or may place another person in danger of death or serious bodily injury. Recklessness and danger shall be presumed where a person knowingly points a firearm at or in the direction of another, whether or not the actor believed the firearm to be loaded.

STATUS OF SECTION

A different version of this offense was submitted to the Institute as Section 201.11 of Tentative Draft No. 9, reprinted with verbal changes as Section 211.2 of Tentative Draft No. 11.

For Commentary, see Tentative Draft No. 9, p. 86.

The earlier drafts specified that pointing a firearm at another or exhibiting a deadly weapon "in a rude, angry, or threatening manner" should be a misdemeanor whether or not it was reckless. The present draft requires proof of recklessness, but supplies a presumption of recklessness and danger in the case of pointing firearms. For example, the pointing of an unloaded gun at another in the course of a drama should not be criminal. As for rude or threatening exhibition of deadly weapons, this behavior is adequately dealt with in other sections concerned with threats (Section 211.3 below) and disorderly conduct (Section 250.2, below). See also provisions as to possessing firearms for criminal purpose. Section 5.06. Supra p. 88.

Section 211.3. Terroristic Threats.

A person is guilty of a felony of the third degree if he threatens to commit any crime of violence with purpose to terrorize another or to cause evacuation of a building, place of assembly, or facility of public transportation, or otherwise to cause serious public inconvenience, or in reckless disregard of the risk of causing such terror or inconvenience.

STATUS OF SECTION

This section derives from Section 211.3 of Tentative Draft No. 11, considered at the May 1960 meeting.

For Commentary, see Tentative Draft No. 11, p. 8.

The earlier draft attempted to deal simultaneously with two classes of misbehavior, terroristic threats and coercion. We now believe these would be better handled in separate sections. See proposed Section 212.5 below. Where, as in the present section, the object is to prevent serious alarm for personal safety, such as may arise from letters or anonymous telephone calls threatening death, kidnapping or bombing, the class of threats can be narrowly defined, and the gravity of the offense can be related both to the seriousness of the threat and the disturbing character of the psychological result intended or risked by the actor. Moreover, in the case of terroristic threats there is no occasion to exempt from criminal liability on the ground of the actor's possibly benign ultimate purpose, as is appropriate in connection with the offense of coercion.

ARTICLE 212. KIDNAPPING AND RELATED OFFENSES; COERCION.

Section 212.0. Definitions.

In this Article, the definitions given in Section 210.0 apply unless a different meaning plainly is required.

Section 212.1. Kidnapping.

A person is guilty of kidnapping if he unlawfully removes another from his place of residence or business, or a substantial distance from the vicinity where he is found, or if he unlawfully confines another for a substantial period in a place of isolation, with any of the following purposes:

    (a) to hold for ransom or reward, or as a shield or hostage; or

    (b) to facilitate commission of any felony or flight thereafter; or

    (c) to inflict bodily injury on or to terrorize the victim or another; or

    (d) to interfere with the performance of any governmental or political function.

Kidnapping is a felony of the first degree unless the actor voluntarily releases the victim alive and in a safe place prior to trial, in which case it is a felony of the second degree. A removal or confinement is unlawful within the meaning of this Section if it is accomplished by force, threat or deception, or, in the case of a person who is under the age of 14 or incompetent, if it is accomplished without the consent of a parent, guardian or other person responsible for general supervision of his welfare.

§§ 212.3, 212.4

STATUS OF SECTION

Presented to the Institute in Tentative Draft No. 11, and considered at the May 1960 meeting.

For Commentary, see Tentative Draft No. 11, p. 11.

The text has been revised only to make clear that release "alive and in a safe place" must be by voluntary act of the kidnapper in order to reduce the offense to the level of second degree felony. Rescue of the victim by the police will not avail the kidnapper.

Section 212.2. Felonious Restraint.

A person commits a felony of the third degree if he knowingly:

(a) restrains another unlawfully in circumstances exposing him to risk of serious bodily injury; or

(b) holds another in a condition of involuntary servitude.

STATUS OF SECTION

Presented to the Institute in Tentative Draft No. 11, and considered at the May 1960 meeting.

For Commentary, see Tentative Draft No. 11, p. 21.

Minor verbal changes have been made. The requirement of knowledge has been made explicit.

Section 212.3. False Imprisonment.

A person commits a misdemeanor if he knowingly restrains another unlawfully so as to interfere substantially with his liberty.

STATUS OF SECTION

Presented to the Institute in Tentative Draft No. 11, and considered at the May 1960 meeting.

For Commentary, see Tentative Draft No. 11, p. 22.

Minor verbal changes have been made, paralleling those in Section 212.2.

Section 212.4 Interference with Custody.

(1) *Custody of Children.* A person commits an offense if he knowingly or recklessly takes or entices any child under the age of 18 from the custody of its parent, guardian or other lawful custodian, when he has no privilege to do so. It is an affirmative defense that:

> (a) the actor believed that his action was necessary to preserve the child from danger to its welfare; or

> (b) the child, being at the time not less than 14 years old, was taken away at its own instigation without enticement and without purpose to commit a criminal offense with or against the child.

Proof that the child was below the critical age gives rise to a presumption that the actor knew the child's age or acted in reckless disregard thereof. The offense is a misdemeanor unless the actor, not being a parent or person in equivalent relation to the child, acted with knowledge that his conduct would cause serious alarm for the child's safety, or in reckless disregard of a likelihood of causing such alarm, in which case the offense is a felony of the third degree.

(2) *Custody of Committed Persons.* A person is guilty of a misdemeanor if he knowingly or recklessly takes or entices any committed person away from lawful custody when he is not privileged to do so. "Committed person" means, in addition to anyone committed under judicial warrant, any orphan, neglected or delinquent child, mentally defective or insane person, or other dependent or incompetent person entrusted to another's custody by or through a recognized social agency or otherwise by authority of law.

STATUS OF SECTION

Presented to the Institute in Tentative Draft No. 11, and considered at the May 1960 meeting.

For Commentary, see Tentative Draft No. 11, p. 23.

Only minor verbal changes have been made.

Section 212.5. Criminal Coercion.

(1) <u>Offense Defined.</u> **A person is guilty of criminal coercion if, with purpose unlawfully to restrict another's freedom of action to his detriment, he threatens to:**

 (a) commit any criminal offense; or

 (b) accuse anyone of a criminal offense; or

 (c) expose any secret tending to subject any person to hatred, contempt or ridicule, or to impair his credit or business repute; or

 (d) take or withhold action as an official, or cause an official to take or withhold action.

It is an affirmative defense to prosecution based on paragraphs (b), (c) or (d) that the actor believed the accusation or secret to be true or the proposed official action justified and that his purpose was limited to compelling the other to behave in a way reasonably related to the circumstances which were the subject of the accusation, exposure or proposed official action, as by desisting from further misbehavior, making good a wrong done, refraining from taking any action or responsibility for which the actor believes the other disqualified.

(2) <u>Grading.</u> Criminal coercion is a misdemeanor unless the threat is to commit a felony or the actor's purpose is felonious, in which cases the offense is a felony of the third degree.

STATUS OF SECTION

This Section derives from Section 211.3 of Tentative Draft No. 11, considered at the May 1960 meeting.

For Commentary, see Tentative Draft No. 11, p. 8.

For reasons stated above in connection with Section 211.3, we have separated the problem of coercion from that of terroristic threats. In the present section, embracing broader categories of threats, the prosecution will have to show that the coercion was not for benign purposes. For example, threats designed to deter the "victim" from continuing to take narcotics or gamble away his fortune would not be criminal under the present section.

The proposed affirmative defenses associated with the newly added categories of threats exclude from criminality some categories of threats which should obviously be privileged.

Subsection (2) is designed to prevent inconsistency between the present Section and the grading provided elsewhere for certain offenses partaking of the nature of coercion. For example, extortion of petty sums is only a misdemeanor under Section 223.1(2)(b); it should therefore not be possible to prosecute it as a felony under the present Section.

ARTICLE 213. SEXUAL OFFENSES

Section 213.0. Definitions.

In this Article, the definitions given in Section 210.0 apply unless a different meaning plainly is required.

Section 213.1. Rape and Related Offenses.

(1) Rape. A male who has sexual intercourse with a female not his wife is guilty of rape if:

    (a) he compels her to submit by force or by threat of imminent death, serious bodily injury, extreme pain or kidnapping, to be inflicted on anyone; or

    (b) he has substantially impaired her power to appraise or control her conduct by administering or employing without her knowledge drugs, intoxicants or other means for the purpose of preventing resistance; or

    (c) the female is unconscious; or

    (d) the female is less than 10 years old.

Rape is a felony of the second degree unless (i) in the course thereof the actor inflicts serious bodily injury upon anyone, or (ii) the victim was not a voluntary social companion of the actor upon the occasion of the crime and had not previously permitted him sexual liberties, in which cases the offense is a felony of the first degree. Sexual intercourse includes intercourse per os or per anum, with some penetration however slight; emission is not required.

(2) Gross Sexual Imposition. A male who has sexual intercourse with a female not his wife commits a felony of the third degree if:

(a) he compels her to submit by any threat that would prevent resistance by a woman of ordinary resolution; or

(b) he knows that she suffers from a mental disease or defect which renders her incapable of appraising the nature of her conduct; or

(c) he knows that she is unaware that a sexual act is being committed upon her or that she submits because she falsely supposes that he is her husband.

STATUS OF SECTION

Presented to the Institute as Section 207.4 of Tentative Draft No. 4, and considered at the May 1955 meeting.

For Commentary, see Tentative Draft No. 4, p. 241.

A number of changes have been made. The substantial ones are noted in the following paragraphs:

Subsection (1)(a) formerly required that the threats be directed against the woman or a member of her family, except that a "threat to commit any felony of the first degree" would suffice even if that felony was to be committed against a person not related to the woman. We believe that the general objective of reaching all "compelling" threats is better accomplished in the revised draft. For example, threat of serious injury to a girl's escort will be covered, although the infliction of serious injury might not be a felony of the first degree. Threat of kidnapping is now specified among the types of threat that suffice for rape conviction, whereas formerly we relied on the formulation with regard to first degree felonies to embrace kidnapping threats. Since, when we came to draft our kidnapping provisions, we did not make all kidnapping felonies of the first degree, it became necessary to provide expressly for kidnapping.

Subsection (1)(c) formerly referred to the case of a victim who was "physically powerless to resist." This has been dropped because, taken literally, it would have condemned as rape any intercourse with a person so disabled, even with her consent. Where intercourse is forced on such a woman against her will, paragraph (a) sufficiently covers the case.

Subsection (2)(a) is a provision favored by the Institute at the May 1955 meeting, which had before it also an alternative referring to threats "reasonably calculated to prevent resistance."

Subsection (2)(b) is a much-narrowed version of a provision which evoked considerable resistance at the 1955 meeting, and which the Reporters agreed to reconsider. The earlier version would have made it a felony for a man to have intercourse with a woman if he knew that she submitted because of "substantially complete incapacity to appraise or control" her own conduct because of mental illness, intoxication, etc. There was a somewhat complicated clause designed to exclude situations where intercourse occurred following joint indulgence in drugs or liquor. The revised draft limits criminality to situations of known mental disease or defect so serious as to render the woman "incapable of appraising the nature of her own conduct." Conditions affecting only the woman's capacity to "control" herself sexually will not involve criminal liability. Also, by specifying that the woman must lack capacity to appraise "the nature" of her conduct, we make it clear that we are not talking about appraisals involving value judgments or consideration of remote consequences of the immediate acts. The typical case that remains within the revised clause would be the case of intercourse with a woman known to the defendant to be manifestly and seriously deranged.

Provisions relating to consensual relations with adolescents and minor wards formerly appearing in Subsections (2)(d) and (3) of Section 207.4, Tentative Draft No. 4, will be found below in new Section 213.3—*Corruption of Minors and Seduction.* Other provisions of former Section 207.4 will be found below in new Section 213.6—*Provisions Generally Applicable to Article 213.*

Section 213.2. Deviate Sexual Intercourse by Force or Imposition.

(1) By Force or Its Equivalent. **A person who engages in deviate sexual intercourse with another person, or who causes another to engage in deviate sexual intercourse, commits a felony of the second degree if:**

(a) **he compels the other person to participate by force or by threat of imminent death, serious bodily injury, extreme pain or kidnapping, to be inflicted on anyone; or**

(b) **he has substantially impaired the other person's power to appraise or control his conduct, by ad-**

ministering or employing without the knowledge of the other person drugs, intoxicants or other means for the purpose of preventing resistance; or

   (c) the other person is unconscious; or

   (d) the other person is less than 10 years old.

Deviate sexual intercourse means sexual intercourse per os or per anum between human beings who are not husband and wife, and any form of sexual intercourse with an animal.

(2) **By Other Imposition.** A person who engages in deviate sexual intercourse with another person, or who causes another to engage in deviate sexual intercourse, commits a felony of the third degree if:

   (a) he compels the other person to participate by any threat that would prevent resistance by a person of ordinary resolution; or

   (b) he knows that the other person suffers from a mental disease or defect which renders him incapable of appraising the nature of his conduct; or

   (c) he knows that the other person submits because he is unaware that a sexual act is being committed upon him.

STATUS OF SECTION

Presented to the Institute as Section 207.5 of Tentative Draft No. 4, and considered at the May 1955 meeting.

For Commentary, see Tentative Draft No. 4, p. 276.

Substantial changes in Subsections (1)(a), (2)(b), and (3) parallel changes in the corresponding subsections of Section 213.1, discussed above.

Subsection (4) of the earlier draft has been dropped. It dealt with deviate sexual relations between consenting adults, and with public solicitation of such relations. The Institute voted against including private homosexuality not involving force, imposition or corruption of the young as an offense in the Model Penal Code. Public solicitation, whether of homosexual or heterosexual relations, is dealt with in connection with the offense of prostitution in Sections 251.2 and 251.3 below.

The definition of deviate sexual intercourse in Subsection (1) of the present draft replaces Subsection (5) of the 1955 draft. The previous definition involved an unworkable cross-reference to our rape section (which, it will be recalled, treats some perverse forms of sexual aggression as rape).

Provisions relating to consensual relations with adolescents and minor wards, formerly appearing in Subsections (2)(d) and (3) of Section 207.5, T.D. No. 4, will be found below in new Section 213.3—*Corruption of Minors and Seduction.* Other provisions of former Section 207.5 will be found below in new Section 213.6—*Provisions Generally Applicable to Article 213.*

Section 213.3. Corruption of Minors and Seduction.

(1) <u>Offense Defined.</u> A male who has sexual intercourse with a female not his wife, or any person who engages in deviate sexual intercourse or causes another to engage in deviate sexual intercourse, is guilty of an offense if:

(a) the other person is less than [16] years old and the actor is at least [4] years older than the other person; or

(b) the other person is less than 21 years old and the actor is his guardian or otherwise responsible for general supervision of his welfare; or

(c) the other person is in custody of law or detained in a hospital or other institution and the actor has supervisory or disciplinary authority over him; or

(d) the other person is a female who is induced to participate by a promise of marriage which the actor does not mean to perform.

Art. 213 147 § 213.4

(2) Grading. An offense under paragraph (a) of Subsection (1) is a felony of the third degree. Otherwise an offense under this section is a misdemeanor.

STATUS OF SECTION

This new Section incorporates similar provisions appearing in Subsections (2) and (3) of Sections 207.4 and 207.5 of Tentative Draft No. 4, which was considered at the May 1955 meeting.

For Commentary, see Tentative Draft No. 4, pp. 250-259, 263, 280.

It seemed desirable as a matter of form to consolidate parallel provisions formerly repeated in two sections, one dealing with ordinary heterosexual relations, the other with deviate sexual intercourse. Another advantage of the present form is that it segregates these consensual transactions from the cases of force and imposition dealt with in Sections 213.1 and 213.2.

A substantive change associated with the consolidation is that we suggest a single "age of consent" in paragraph (a) of Subsection (1), viz. 16. In former Section 207.5(2)(d), the age of consent for deviate sexual relations was placed at 18. Since the legislative choice of a particular "age of consent" in the 15-18 year range has a certain degree of arbitrariness in any event, it seems sufficient to suggest a single age, indicating the qualified nature of the recommendation by placing the figure in brackets. The Comment will, as before, review the grounds upon which a legislature might choose to make the critical age somewhat higher in the case of homosexual relations.

Subsection (1)(b) has been revised so that only guardians and others responsible for supervising the young, e.g., probation officers, camp supervisors, may be penalized. The previous draft reached anyone responsible for "care, treatment, protection, or education," a formula which, upon reconsideration, seemed too broad in its possible impact on doctor-patient and teacher-student relationships.

Subsection (1)(c) has been limited to personnel having "supervisory or disciplinary authority" over the victim. Formerly any person "associated" with the institution would have been covered. This would have extended the offense to situations not involving presumptive abuse of custodial authority.

Section 213.4. Sexual Assault.

A person who subjects another not his spouse to any sexual contact is guilty of sexual assault, a misdemeanor, if:

(1) he knows that the contact is offensive to the other person; or

(2) he knows that the other person suffers from a mental disease or defect which renders him or her incapable of appraising the nature of his or her conduct; or

(3) he knows that the other person is unaware that a sexual act is being committed; or

(4) the other person is less than 10 years old; or

(5) he has substantially impaired the other person's power to appraise or control his or her conduct, by administering or employing without the other's knowledge drugs, intoxicants or other means for the purpose of preventing resistance; or

(6) the other person is less than [16] years old and the actor is at least [four] years older than the other person; or

(7) the other person is less than 21 years old and the actor is his guardian or otherwise responsible for general supervision of his welfare; or

(8) the other person is in custody of law or detained in a hospital or other institution and the actor has supervisory or disciplinary authority over him.

Sexual contact is any touching of the sexual or other intimate parts of the person of another for the purpose of arousing or gratifying sexual desire of either party.

STATUS OF SECTION

Presented to the Institute as Section 207.6 of Tentative Draft No. 4, and considered at the May 1955 meeting.

For Commentary, see Tentative Draft No. 4, p. 292.

The Section has been substantially revised.

Section 207.6(1) (a) made sexual contact criminal if there was "no consent." This seems too strict a standard of criminality, considering the frequency with which tentative sexual advances are made without explicit assurance of consent.

Under Section 207.6(2) the offense was a felony if the victim suffered serious physical injury or if the offensive contact was with specified erogenous areas. Questions of criminal liability for bodily injury should, in our present view, be considered under the sections specifically addressed to that subject, viz. Sections 211.1 and 211.2. Further consideration led also to the dropping of the felony classification for sexual touching of particular parts of the body. It is hard to believe that there is a significant criminological distinction between sexually aggressive males who press their attentions to the point of touching genitalia and others who stop or are interrupted just short of that.

Other changes have been made to conform with parallel provisions in Sections 213.1 and 213.2. See also Section 213.6 below for *"Provisions Generally Applicable to Article 213."*

Section 213.5. Indecent Exposure.

A person commits a misdemeanor if, for the purpose of arousing or gratifying sexual desire of himself or of any person other than his spouse, he exposes his genitals under circumstances in which he knows his conduct is likely to cause affront or alarm.

STATUS OF SECTION

Presented to the Institute in Tentative Draft No. 13, and considered at the May 1961 meeting.

For Commentary, see Tentative Draft No. 13, p. 82.

Only minor verbal changes have been made.

Section 213.6. Provisions Generally Applicable to Article 213.

(1) Mistake as to Age. Whenever in this Article the criminality of conduct depends on a child's being below the age of 10, it is no defense that the actor did not know

§ 213.6   150   Model Penal Code

the child's age, or reasonably believed the child to be older than 10. When criminality depends on the child's being below a critical age other than 10, it is a defense for the actor to prove that he reasonably believed the child to be above the critical age.

(2) Spouse Relationships. Whenever in this Article the definition of an offense excludes conduct with a spouse, the exclusion shall be deemed to extend to persons living as man and wife, regardless of the legal status of their relationship. The exclusion shall be inoperative as respects spouses living apart under a decree of judicial separation. Where the definition of an offense excludes conduct with a spouse or conduct by a woman, this shall not preclude conviction of a spouse or woman as accomplice in a sexual act which he or she causes another person, not within the exclusion, to perform.

(4) Sexually Promiscuous Complainants. It is a defense to prosecution under Section 213.3. and paragraphs (6), (7) and (8) of Section 213.4 for the actor to prove by a preponderance of the evidence that the alleged victim had, prior to the time of the offense charged, engaged promiscuously in sexual relations with others.

(5) Prompt Complaint. No prosecution may be instituted or maintained under this Article unless the alleged offense was brought to the notice of public authority within [3] months of its occurrence or, where the alleged victim was less than [16] years old or otherwise incompetent to make complaint, within [3] months after a parent, guardian or other competent person specially interested in the victim learns of the offense.

(6) Testimony of Complainants. No person shall be convicted of any felony under this Article upon the uncor-

roborated testimony of the alleged victim. Corroboration may be circumstantial. In any prosecution before a jury for an offense under this Article, the jury shall be instructed to evaluate the testimony of a victim or complaining witness with special care in view of the emotional involvement of the witness and the difficulty of determining the truth with respect to alleged sexual activities carried out in private.

STATUS OF SECTION

This is a new section into which have been incorporated subsections formerly parts of various sections of this Article.

For Commentary, see Tentative Draft No. 4, p. 244 ("Female Not the Wife"); p. 253 ("Mistake as to Age of Female"); pp. 254, 259 ("Previous Unchastity"); p. 264 ("Prompt Complaint"); p. 263 ("Corroboration").

The only significant change is in Subsection (6) where the corrobation requirement has been limited to felony prosecutions, and a sentence has been added to require special caution as to complainant testimony, whether in felony or misdemeanor cases. Corroboration requirements are presently common in seduction statutes, occasionally encountered in rape statutes, not usual in legislation dealing with sodomy or indecent exposure. A uniform policy on all sex offenses has a prima facie validity; but Wigmore's attack on *any* such requirement gives one pause in extending it to new areas. In addition, it has been argued that a rigid requirement of corroboration would virtually preclude prosecutions in typical cases of minor sexual assault in dark theaters and crowded subways.

There seems less reason to hesitate about bringing sodomy and indecent exposure within the policy of "prompt complaint" in Subsection (5). The Advisors and Council approved a shortening of the period to three months, from the six months proposed in Tentative Draft No. 4.

OFFENSES AGAINST PROPERTY

ARTICLE 220. ARSON, CRIMINAL MISCHIEF, AND OTHER PROPERTY DESTRUCTION

Section 220.1. Arson and Related Offenses.

(1) *Arson.* A person is guilty of arson, a felony of the second degree, if he starts a fire or causes an explosion with the purpose of:

    (a) destroying a building or occupied structure of another; or

    (b) destroying or damaging any property, whether his own or another's, to collect insurance for such loss. It shall be an affirmative defense to prosecution under this paragraph that the actor's conduct did not recklessly endanger any building or occupied structure of another or place any other person in danger of death or bodily injury.

(2) *Reckless Burning or Exploding.* A person commits a felony of the third degree if he purposely starts a fire or causes an explosion, whether on his own property or another's, and thereby recklessly:

    (a) places another person in danger of death or bodily injury; or

    (b) places a building or occupied structure of another in danger of damage or destruction.

(3) *Failure to Control or Report Dangerous Fire.* A person who knows that a fire is endangering life or a substantial amount of property of another and fails to take reasonable measures to put out or control the fire, when he

can do so without substantial risk to himself, or to give a prompt fire alarm, commits a misdemeanor if:

(a) he knows that he is under an official, contractual, or other legal duty to prevent or combat the fire; or

(b) the fire was started, albeit lawfully, by him or with his assent, or on property in his custody or control.

(4) *Definitions.* "Occupied structure" includes a ship, trailer, sleeping car, airplane, or other vehicle, structure or place adapted for overnight accommodation of persons or for carrying on business therein, whether or not a person is actually present. Property is that of another, for the purposes of this section, if anyone other than the actor has a possessory or proprietary interest therein. If a building or structure is divided into separately occupied units, any unit not occupied by the actor is an occupied structure of another.

STATUS OF SECTION

Presented to the Institute in Tentative Draft No. 11, and considered at the May 1960 meeting.

For Commentary, see Tentative Draft No. 11, p. 34.

Minor changes have been made to conform to votes and suggestions of the Institute, notably deletion of a proposed paragraph (c) in Subsection (3), which would have required a person to report or control a dangerous fire if he was in a peculiarly favorable position to do so without risk or inconvenience.

Section 220.2. Causing or Risking Catastrophe.

(1) *Causing Catastrophe.* A person who causes a catastrophe by explosion, fire, flood, avalanche, collapse of building, release of poison gas, radioactive material or other harmful or destructive force or substance, or by any other means of causing potentially widespread injury or damage, commits a felony of the second degree if he does so purposely

or knowingly, or a felony of the third degree if he does so recklessly.

(2) <u>Risking Catastrophe.</u> A person is guilty of a misdemeanor if he recklessly creates a risk of catastrophe in the employment of fire, explosives or other dangerous means listed in Subsection (1).

(3) <u>Failure to Prevent Catastrophe.</u> A person who knowingly or recklessly fails to take reasonable measures to prevent or mitigate a catastrophe commits a misdemeanor if:

    (a) he knows that he is under an official, contractual or other legal duty to take such measures; or

    (b) he did or assented to the act causing or threatening the catastrophe.

STATUS OF SECTION

Presented to the Institute in Tentative Draft No. 11 and considered at the May 1960 meeting.

For Commentary, see Tentative Draft No. 11, p. 52.

Changed only to delete from Subsection (3), pursuant to direction of the Institute, a paragraph (c) which required a person to prevent or mitigate a catastrophe if he was in a peculiarly favorable position to do so without risk or inconvenience. Minor verbal changes have also been made.

Section 220.3. Criminal Mischief.

(1) <u>Offense Defined.</u> A person is guilty of criminal mischief if he:

    (a) damages tangible property of another purposely, recklessly, or by negligence in the employment of fire, explosives, or other dangerous means listed in Section 220.2(1); or

(b) purposely or recklessly tampers with tangible property of another so as to endanger person or property; or

(c) purposely or recklessly causes another to suffer pecuniary loss by deception or threat.

(2) <u>Grading</u>. Criminal mischief is a felony of the third degree if the actor purposely causes pecuniary loss in excess of $5,000, or a substantial interruption or impairment of public communication, transportation, supply of water, gas or power, or other public service. It is a misdemeanor if the actor purposely causes pecuniary loss in excess of $100, or a petty misdemeanor if he purposely or recklessly causes pecuniary loss in excess of $25. Otherwise criminal mischief is a violation.

STATUS OF SECTION

Presented to the Institute originally as Sections 206.50 and 205.51 of Tentative Draft No. 2, and considered at the May 1954 meeting. Revised to present form in Tentative Draft No. 11, which was considered by the Institute at the May 1960 meeting.

For Commentary, see Tentative Draft No. 2, pp. 126, 129.

ARTICLE 221. BURGLARY AND OTHER CRIMINAL INTRUSION

Section 221.0. Definitions.

In this Article, unless a different meaning plainly is required:

(1) "occupied structure" means any structure, vehicle or place adapted for overnight accommodation of persons, or for carrying on business therein, whether or not a person is actually present.

(2) "night" means the period between thirty minutes past sunset and thirty minutes before sunrise.

STATUS OF SECTION

The definition of occupied structure derives from Subsection (1) of Section 221.1—*Burglary* in Tentative Draft No. 11, considered at the May 1960 meeting.

For Commentary, see Tentative Draft No. 11, p. 58.

The definition of "night" has been added in view of the introduction in Sections 221.1(2) and 221.2(1) of grading based on commission of certain offenses at night. The considerations which are significant in this connection are that darkness facilitates commission of the offense, increases the alarm of the victims, and hampers identification of suspects. Such darkness does not occur at sunset, but at some time during the ensuing hour. Our selection of an interval of 30 minutes has support in some current legislation, including safety regulations under the motor vehicle codes and the Federal Aviation Act.

Section 221.1. Burglary.

(1) <u>Burglary Defined</u>. A person is guilty of burglary if he enters a building or occupied structure, or separately secured or occupied portion thereof, with purpose to commit a crime therein, unless the premises are at the time open to

the public or the actor is licensed or privileged to enter. It is an affirmative defense to prosecution for burglary that the building or structure was abandoned.

(2) <u>Grading</u>. Burglary is a felony of the second degree if it is perpetrated in the dwelling of another at night, or if, in the course of committing the offense, the actor:

    (a) purposely, knowingly or recklessly inflicts or attempts to inflict bodily injury on anyone; or

    (b) is armed with explosives or a deadly weapon.

Otherwise, burglary is a felony of the third degree. An act shall be deemed "in the course of committing" an offense if it occurs in an attempt to commit the offense or in flight after the attempt or commission.

(3) <u>Multiple Convictions</u>. A person may not be convicted both for burglary and for the offense which it was his purpose to commit after the burglarious entry or for an attempt to commit that offense, unless the additional offense constitutes a felony of the first or second degree.

STATUS OF SECTION

Presented to the Institute in Tentative Draft No. 11, and considered at the May 1960 meeting.

For Commentary, see Tentative Draft No. 11, p. 54.

Several minor revisions have been made in the light of discussion at the meeting. The language in the first sentence referring to "premises . . . open to the public" has been added so as to make it clear that entry into premises accessible to the public cannot be prosecuted as burglary even if the proprietor sought to restrict the implied license, for example, by posting notice at the door of a department store that loiterers and shoplifters are forbidden to enter.

The word "therein" has been inserted in Subsection (1) to make it clear that the mere purpose to commit criminal trespass by intrusion into the premises does not satisfy the criminal purpose requirement for burglary.

Subsection (3) has been put in terms of multiple convictions rather than multiple sentences. The multiple sentence aspects of the problem are dealt with in Section 7.06. Supra p. 114.

Section 221.2. Criminal Trespass.

(1) <u>Buildings and Occupied Structures</u>. A person commits an offense if, knowing that he is not licensed or privileged to do so, he enters or surreptitiously remains in any building or occupied structure, or separately secured or occupied portion thereof. An offense under this Subsection is a misdemeanor if it is committed in a dwelling at night. Otherwise it is a petty misdemeanor.

(2) <u>Defiant Trespasser</u>. A person commits an offense if, knowing that he is not licensed or privileged to do so, he enters or remains in any place as to which notice against trespass is given by:

    (a) actual communication to the actor; or

    (b) posting in a manner prescribed by law or reasonably likely to come to the attention of intruders; or

    (c) fencing or other enclosure manifestly designed to exclude intruders.

An offense under this Subsection constitutes a petty misdemeanor if the offender defies an order to leave personally communicated to him by the owner of the premises or other authorized person. Otherwise it is a violation.

(3) <u>Defenses</u>. It is an affirmative defense to prosecution under this Section that:

(a) a building or occupied structure involved in an offense under Subsection (1) was abandoned; or

(b) the premises were at the time open to members of the public and the actor complied with all lawful conditions imposed on access to or remaining in the premises; or

(c) the actor reasonably believed that the owner of the premises, or other person empowered to license access thereto, would have licensed him to enter or remain.

STATUS OF SECTION

A draft on criminal trespass was first submitted at the May 1954 meeting of the Institute as Sections 206.53 and 206.54 of Tentative Draft No. 2.

For Commentary, see Tentative Draft No. 2, p. 132.

A revision was submitted as Section 221.2 of Tentative Draft No. 11 in 1960, the changes being designed to integrate criminal trespass provisions with the then newly drafted section on burglary.

The Section is now further revised to reflect discussion at the 1960 meeting of the Institute and to take account of the fact that in May 1961, the Institute approved a reduction of the penalty for petty misdemeanors from a maximum of 90 days to a maximum of 30 days. See Section 6.08. Supra p. 100.

The present draft classifies criminal trespass as a petty misdemeanor where it is in a building or occupied structure (Subsection 1) or in defiance of a personal order to leave (Subsection 2). The previous draft classified criminal trespass as a petty misdemeanor where the actor "broke into" the premises or knew that his presence would "cause apprehension." With the reduction of the maximum for petty misdemeanors, it becomes possible to abandon the rather refined legislative distinctions by which we sought to exclude minor trespasses from the possibility of 90 day jail sentences. This also solves the verbal problem inherent in our calling "criminal trespass" a "violation," which we elsewhere declare to be non-criminal.

We have provided that criminal trespass in a dwelling at night is a misdemeanor. This change grew out of the discussion of burglary at the May 1960 meeting. Some members expressed concern that these especially terrifying intrusions would not be adequately penalized in view of the required proof in burglary of purpose to commit crime. Furthermore, the decision that burglary "in the dwelling of another at night" should be included among the class of aggravated burglaries —see Section 221.1(2)—suggests a parallel distinction in the classification of criminal trespass.

The affirmative defense provided in Subsection (3) in respect to premises open to the public parallels the conception of licensed entry which we have introduced in the burglary section. The primary objective is to exclude criminal prosecution for mere presence of a person in a place where the public generally is invited. Persons who become undesirable by virtue of disorderly conduct may of course be prosecuted for that offense. The Section is not intended to preclude resort by the occupant to civil remedies for trespass, including his privilege, whatever it may be, of barring entry or ejecting. In controversies such as have arisen in the "sit-in" cases, the effect of the present proposal would be merely to make it explicitly an issue whether the conditions imposed on access to premises open to the public were "lawful." They might be unlawful by virtue of federal law relating to facilities of interstate transportation, statutory or common law requirements of non-discrimination in places to which the public resorts, or for other reason.

ARTICLE 222. ROBBERY

Section 222.1. Robbery.

(1) <u>Robbery Defined</u>. A person is guilty of robbery if, in the course of committing a theft, he:

    (a) inflicts serious bodily injury upon another; or

    (b) threatens another with or purposely puts him in fear of immediate serious bodily injury; or

    (c) commits or threatens immediately to commit any felony of the first or second degree.

An act shall be deemed "in the course of committing a theft" if it occurs in an attempt to commit theft or in flight after the attempt or commission.

(2) <u>Grading</u>. Robbery is a felony of the second degree, except that it is a felony of the first degree if in the course of committing the theft the actor attempts to kill anyone, or purposely inflicts or attempts to inflict serious bodily injury.

STATUS OF SECTION

Presented to the Institute in Tentative Draft No. 11, and considered at the May 1960 meeting.

For Commentary, see Tentative Draft No. 11, p. 68.

Subsection (1)(a) formerly read "recklessly inflicts", relying on provisions in the General Part of the Code that a requirement of recklessness is satisfied by proof of purpose or knowledge. But Section 2.02, supra p. 25, also makes it unnecessary to specify "recklessly," since it provides that absent specification, the culpability requirement is purpose, knowledge or recklessness.

ARTICLE 223. THEFT AND RELATED OFFENSES

Section 223.0. Definitions.

In this Article, unless a different meaning plainly is required:

(1) "deprive" means: (a) to withhold property of another permanently or for so extended a period as to appropriate a major portion of its economic value, or with intent to restore only upon payment of reward or other compensation; or (b) to dispose of the property so as to make it unlikely that the owner will recover it.

(2) "financial institution" means a bank, insurance company, credit union, building and loan association, investment trust or other organization held out to the public as a place of deposit of funds or medium of savings or collective investment.

(3) "government" means the United States, any State, county, municipality, or other political unit, or any department, agency or subdivision of any of the foregoing, or any corporation or other association carrying out the functions of government.

(4) "movable property" means property the location of which can be changed, including things growing on, affixed to, or found in land, and documents although the rights represented thereby have no physical location. "Immovable property" is all other property.

(5) "obtain" means: (a) in relation to property, to bring about a transfer or purported transfer of a legal interest in the property, whether to the obtainer or another; or (b) in relation to labor or service, to secure performance thereof.

(6) "property" means anything of value, including real estate, tangible and intangible personal property, contract rights, choses-in-action and other interests in or claims to wealth, admission or transportation tickets, captured or domestic animals, food and drink, electric or other power.

(7) "property of another" includes property in which any person other than the actor has an interest which the actor is not privileged to infringe, regardless of the fact that the actor also has an interest in the property and regardless of the fact that the other person might be precluded from civil recovery because the property was used in an unlawful transaction or was subject to forfeiture as contraband. Property in possession of the actor shall not be deemed property of another who has only a security interest therein, even if legal title is in the creditor pursuant to a conditional sales contract or other security agreement.

STATUS OF SECTION

Definitions applicable to property offenses were presented to the Institute as Section 206.64 of Tentative Draft No. 2, reprinted as Section 206.63 of Tentative Draft No. 4. These drafts were before the May meetings of the Institute in 1954 and 1955.

The definition of "deprive" in Subsection (1) is new. The utility of the definition is that it provides a single concept embracing both permanent and prolonged withholding of property from the rightful owner. Cf. § 15-3 of the Ill. Rev. Crim. Code of 1961. For want of such a concept, it was necessary in earlier drafts to provide separate sections dealing with permanent deprivations and "prolonged or seriously prejudicial deprivations." See Tentative Draft No. 1, Section 206.1(2); Tentative Draft No. 2, Sections 206.1(1) and 206.6(1). Compare Section 223.2 of the present draft.

For Commentary on the problem of non-permanent deprivation, see Tentative Draft No. 1, p. 69, and Tentative Draft No. 2, p. 88.

"Financial institution" has been substituted for "credit institution," following the lead of the revisers of the Illinois Code, who incorporated the definition from our Tentative Draft.

§ 223.1

The definition of "property of another" was presented to the Institute in Section 206.1(4) of Tentative Draft No. 1, and considered at the May 1953 meeting. Equivalent provisions cast as substantive rules of law were presented to the Institute in Tentative Draft No. 2, Sections 206.11 and 206.12, considered at the May 1954 meeting.

For Commentary, see Tentative Draft No. 1, p. 78, and Tentative Draft No. 2, pp. 100, 102.

Minor verbal changes have been made.

Section 223.1. Consolidation of Theft Offenses; Grading; Provisions Applicable to Theft Generally.

(1) Consolidation of Theft Offenses. Conduct denominated theft in this Article constitutes a single offense embracing the separate offenses heretofore known as larceny, embezzlement, false pretense, extortion, blackmail, fraudulent conversion, receiving stolen property, and the like. An accusation of theft may be supported by evidence that it was committed in any manner that would be theft under this Article, notwithstanding the specification of a different manner in the indictment or information, subject only to the power of the Court to ensure fair trial by granting a continuance or other appropriate relief where the conduct of the defense would be prejudiced by lack of fair notice or by surprise.

(2) Grading of Theft Offenses.

(a) Theft constitutes a felony of the third degree if the amount involved exceeds $500, or if the property stolen is a firearm, automobile, or other motor-propelled vehicle, or in the case of theft by receiving stolen property, if the receiver is in the business of buying or selling stolen property.

(b) Theft not within the preceding paragraph constitutes a misdemeanor, except that if the property was not taken from the person or by threat, or in breach of a fiduciary obligation, and the actor proves by a preponderance of the evidence that the amount involved was less than $50, the offense constitutes a petty misdemeanor.

(c) The amount involved in a theft shall be deemed to be the highest value, by any reasonable standard, of the property or services which the actor stole or attempted to steal. Amounts involved in thefts committed pursuant to one scheme or course of conduct, whether from the same person or several persons, may be aggregated in determining the grade of the offense.

(3) Claim of Right. It is an affirmative defense to prosecution for theft that the actor:

(a) was unaware that the property or service was that of another; or

(b) acted under an honest claim of right to the property or service involved or that he had a right to acquire or dispose of it as he did; or

(c) took property exposed for sale, intending to purchase and pay for it promptly, or reasonably believing that the owner, if present, would have consented.

(4) Theft from Spouse. It is no defense that theft was from the actor's spouse, except that misappropriation of household and personal effects, or other property normally accessible to both spouses, is theft only if it occurs after the parties have ceased living together.

STATUS OF SECTION

Subsection (1) on Consolidation of Theft Offenses derives from Section 206.60 of Tentative Draft No. 2, considered by the Institute at the May 1954 meeting. That Section was reprinted in Tentative Draft No. 4, for the May 1955 meeting.

§ 223.1

For Commentary on the problem of consolidation, see Tentative Draft No. 1, p. 101.

Subsection (2) on Grading of Theft Offenses derives from Section 206.15 of Tentative Draft No. 2, considered by the Institute at the May 1954 meeting. That Section was reprinted in Tentative Draft No. 4, for the May 1955 meeting.

For Commentary, see Tentative Draft No. 2, p. 108.

The grading provisions have been revised in form and in certain substantial respects, but the essential scheme is that heretofore approved by the Institute. The important changes are as follows: theft from the person or by threat is made a misdemeanor by paragraph (b) of Subsection (2) even if the amount involved be less than $50. This is a middle position between the old draft, under which such thefts, like other petty thefts, were petty misdemeanors, and suggestions by some members of the Institute that all theft by threat or from the person should be punishable as felony. We have withdrawn from the position taken in the earlier draft that the offense should be a felony where breach of trust is involved, however petty the amount. Thus, by raising the grading of petty theft from the person or by threat, and by reducing the grading of petty theft in breach of trust, we arrive at a uniform policy for petty theft with any of these aggravating circumstances.

Subsection (3) on Claim of Right derives from Section 206.10 of Tentative Draft No. 2, considered by the Institute at the May 1954 meeting. That section was reprinted in Tentative Draft No. 4, for the May 1955 meeting.

For Commentary, see Tentative Draft No. 2, p. 98, and Tentative Draft No. 1, p. 56. Paragraph (b) is somewhat broadened to admit the defense where the actor, although not in a position to claim that the property belongs to him, honestly believes that he is entitled to acquire it and that his privilege extended to the use of force or other unlawful method. An example might be where an employee threatens his employer in some way covered by Section 223.4, but only for the purpose of compelling the employer to pay wages which the employee believes to be due. If the employee acted with the prescribed belief in his right to acquire "as he did," he would not be guilty of theft although he might be punishable under other sections of the Code for assault or threat. See discussion in Tentative Draft No. 1, p. 57. The claim of right language of the present draft has the additional advantage of applicability not only to property but also to services, which may be the subject of theft under Section 223.7. Following suggestions at the May 1954 meeting, the subsection incorporates in paragraph (c) the defense of reasonable belief that the owner, if present, would have consented to a taking of property exposed for sale.

Subsection (4) on Theft from Spouse derives from Section 206.13, a much broader and more complicated provision that dealt with defenses and mitigations in relation to thefts involving members of a common household. By vote of the Institute the former section was recommitted to the Reporters for consideration of an alternative such as is embodied in the present draft.

Two other sections that appeared in earlier drafts are dropped from the present draft because equivalent provisions have been included in the General Part of the Code. They were Section 206.61 of Tentative Draft No. 2, defining "consent" in relation to property offenses, and Section 206.62, authorizing a court to dismiss prosecution for property offenses "involving inconsequential amounts within a customary license or toleration. . . ." These sections appeared in Tentative Draft No. 2 and were reprinted in Tentative Draft No. 4.

For Commentary, see Tentative Draft No. 2, pp. 135, 136.

Section 223.2. Theft by Unlawful Taking or Disposition.

(1) <u>Movable Property.</u> A person is guilty of theft if he takes, or exercises unlawful control over, movable property of another with purpose to deprive him thereof.

(2) <u>Immovable Property.</u> A person is guilty of theft if he unlawfully transfers immovable property of another or any interest therein with purpose to benefit himself or another not entitled thereto.

STATUS OF SECTION

Presented to the Institute as Section 206.1 of Tentative Draft No. 2, and considered at the May 1954 meeting.

Reprinted in Tentative Draft No. 4.

For Commentary, see Tentative Draft No. 2, p. 59; see also Tentative Draft No. 1, p. 61.

"Purpose to deprive" in Subsection (1) covers prolonged as well as permanent deprivations. See comment on definition of "deprive" in note on status of Section 223.0. The scope of this Subsection is therefore broadened so as to make unnecessary former Section 206.6(1) which separately defined an offense of theft by prolonged deprivation. Except for this, there are only verbal changes in this Section.

§ 223.3

Section 223.3. Theft by Deception.

A person is guilty of theft if he obtains property of another by deception. A person deceives if he purposely:

(a) creates or reinforces a false impression, including false impressions as to law, value, intention or other state of mind; but deception as to a person's intention to perform a promise shall not be inferred from the fact alone that he did not subsequently perform the promise; or

(b) prevents another from acquiring information which would affect his judgment of a transaction; or

(c) fails to correct a false impression which the deceiver previously created or reinforced, or which the deceiver knows to be influencing another to whom he stands in a fiduciary or confidential relationship; or

(d) fails to disclose a known lien, adverse claim or other legal impediment to the enjoyment of property which he transfers or encumbers in consideration for the property obtained, whether such impediment is or is not valid, or is or is not a matter of official record.

The term "deceive" does not, however, include falsity as to matters having no pecuniary significance, or puffing by statements unlikely to deceive ordinary persons in the group addressed.

STATUS OF SECTION

Presented to the Institute as Section 206.2 of Tentative Draft No. 2, and considered at the May 1954 meeting.

Reprinted in Tentative Draft No. 4.

For Commentary, see Tentative Draft No. 2, p. 65.

The Section has been simplified, especially by substituting the brief reference to "puffing" in the final sentence, in place of a cumbersome elaboration of the same idea in Subsection (3) of the former draft.

Section 223.4. Theft by Extortion.

A person is guilty of theft if he obtains property of another by threatening to:

    (a) inflict bodily injury on anyone or commit any other criminal offense; or

    (b) accuse anyone of a criminal offense; or

    (c) expose any secret tending to subject any person to hatred, contempt or ridicule, or to impair his credit or business repute; or

    (d) take or withhold action as an official, or cause an official to take or withhold action; or

    (e) bring about or continue a strike, boycott or other collective unofficial action, if the property is not demanded or received for the benefit of the group in whose interest the actor purports to act; or

    (f) testify or provide information or withhold testimony or information with respect to another's legal claim or defense; or

    (g) inflict any other harm which would not benefit the actor.

It is an affirmative defense to prosecution based on paragraphs (b), (c) or (d) that the property obtained by threat of accusation, exposure, lawsuit or other invocation of official action was honestly claimed as restitution or indemnification for harm done in the circumstances to which such accusation, exposure, lawsuit or other official action relates, or as compensation for property or lawful services.

STATUS OF SECTION

Presented to the Institute as Section 206.3 of Tentative Draft No. 2, and considered at the May 1954 meeting.

§§ 223.5, 223.6

Reprinted in Tentative Draft No. 4.

For Commentary, see Tentative Draft No. 2, p. 74.

The Reporters were directed to reconsider the effect of paragraph (b) [paragraph (d) of the former draft] on the situation where a person asserting a civil claim to compensation for personal injury threatens to file a criminal complaint. The affirmative defense provided in the last sentence of the Subsection assures proper disposition of such cases, i.e., it is made criminal to threaten prosecution if and only if the actor thereby obtains or attempts to obtain more than he believes is due him. The same policy is expressed in Section 242.5—*Compounding.*

Section 223.5. Theft of Property Lost, Mislaid, or Delivered by Mistake.

A person who comes into control of property of another that he knows to have been lost, mislaid, or delivered under a mistake as to the nature or amount of the property or the identity of the recipient is guilty of theft if, with purpose to deprive the owner thereof, he fails to take reasonable measures to restore the property to a person entitled to have it.

STATUS OF SECTION

This is a condensed version of Section 206.5 of Tentative Draft No. 2, considered by the Institute at the May 1954 meeting. It is deemed unnecessary to attempt to spell out, as Section 206.5 did, what are "reasonable measures," e.g. delivery to law officers or to the operator of a vehicle where the property was found.

For Commentary, see Tentative Draft No. 2, p. 83.

Section 223.6. Receiving Stolen Property.

(1) Receiving. A person is guilty of theft if he receives, retains, or disposes of movable property of another knowing that it has been stolen, or believing that it has probably been stolen, unless the property is received, retained, or disposed with purpose to restore it to the owner.

Art. 223 171 § 223.6

"Receiving" means acquiring possession, control or title, or lending on the security of the property.

(2) <u>Presumption of Knowledge.</u> The requisite knowledge or belief is presumed in the case of a dealer who:

(a) is found in possession or control of property stolen from two or more persons on separate occasions; or

(b) has received stolen property in another transaction within the year preceding the transaction charged; or

(c) being a dealer in property of the sort received, acquires it for a consideration which he knows is far below its reasonable value.

"Dealer" means a person in the business of buying or selling goods.

STATUS OF SECTION

Presented to the Institute as Section 206.8 of Tentative Draft No. 2, and considered at the May 1954 meeting.

For Commentary, see Tentative Draft No. 2, p. 93.

The Section has been revised and simplified. The present draft abandons a distinction formerly made between dealers and others with respect to the mental state required for conviction. This distinction was criticised in the course of the debates at the May 1954 meeting. We have also dropped provisions calling for notification to the police by dealers acquiring from children under 16, or in other suspicious circumstances, in the view that such requirements, if imposed at all, should be part of regulatory statutes outside the penal code.

Revised Subsection (2) does not include a provision of the old draft raising a presumption of the dealer's knowledge if he has previously been convicted of theft. The rational basis for such a presumption was thought to be so tenuous as to raise constitutional questions.

Section 223.7. Theft of Services.

(1) A person is guilty of theft if he obtains services which he knows are available only for compensation, by deception or threat, or by false token or other means to avoid payment for the service. "Services" includes labor, professional service, telephone or other public service, accommodation in hotels, restaurants or elsewhere, admission to exhibitions, use of vehicles or other movable property. Where compensation for service is ordinarily paid immediately upon the rendering of such service, as in the case of hotels and restaurants, refusal to pay or absconding without payment or offer to pay gives rise to a presumption that the service was obtained by deception as to intention to pay.

(2) A person commits theft if, having control over the disposition of services of others, to which he is not entitled, he diverts such services to his own benefit or to the benefit of another not entitled thereto.

STATUS OF SECTION

Equivalent provisions appeared as Section 206.7 and Subsections (3) and (4) of Section 206.6 in Tentative Draft No. 2, considered by the Institute at the May 1954 meeting. These provisions have been consolidated without significant change of substance.

For Commentary, see Tentative Draft No. 2, pp. 89, 91; Tentative Draft No. 1, p. 98.

Section 223.8. Theft by Failure to Make Required Disposition of Funds Received.

A person who obtains property upon agreement, or subject to a known legal obligation, to make specified payment or other disposition, whether from such property or its proceeds or from his own property in equivalent amount, is guilty of theft if he deals with the property obtained as his own and fails to make the required payment or disposition. The foregoing applies notwithstanding that it may be impossible to identify particular property as belonging to the victim at the time of the actor's failure to make the required payment or disposition. An officer or employee of the government or of a financial institution is presumed: (i) to know any legal obligation relevant to his criminal liability under this Section, and (ii) to have dealt with the property as his own if he fails to pay or account upon lawful demand, or if an audit reveals a shortage or falsification of accounts.

STATUS OF SECTION

Presented to the Institute as Section 206.4 of Tentative Draft No. 2, and considered at the May 1953 meeting.

Reprinted in Tentative Draft No. 4.

For Commentary, see Tentative Draft No. 2, p. 80.

The original draft was recommitted to the Reporters for consideration of various suggestions to circumscribe its scope, and the present draft represents a substantial revision along these lines. Presumptions against private fiduciaries have been eliminated, and the presumption based on failure to pay or account arises only on lawful demand.

Section 223.9. Unauthorized Use of Automobiles and Other Vehicles.

A person commits a misdemeanor if he operates another's automobile, airplane, motorcycle, motorboat, or other motor-propelled vehicle without consent of the owner. It is an affirmative defense to prosecution under this Section that the actor reasonably believed that the owner would have consented to the operation had he known of it.

STATUS OF SECTION

Presented to the Institute as Section 206.6(2) in Tentative Draft No. 2.

Reprinted in Tentative Draft No. 4.

For Commentary, see Tentative Draft No. 2, p. 89.

The Section has been substantially revised. It formerly penalized the "taking" of any vehicle or draft or riding animal "without consent." Operation of motor vehicles is obviously the practical problem to be dealt with, because of the danger to the vehicle and to other persons from unauthorized operation. So far as draught and riding animals are concerned, we now believe that the definition of "deprive" in Section 223.0(1) makes our theft provisions adequate to reach all serious misappropriations of animals.

The last sentence of the revised Section introduces the defense of reasonable belief that the owner would have consented. This appears necessary to exempt from criminal liability a good deal of informal borrowing of automobiles by members of the same household or friends of the owner. Cf. Section 223.1(3)(c).

ARTICLE 224. FORGERY AND FRAUDULENT PRACTICES

Section 224.0 Definitions.

In this Article, the definitions given in Section 223.0 apply unless a different meaning plainly is required.

Section 224.1. Forgery.

(1) Definition. A person is guilty of forgery if, with purpose to defraud or injure anyone, or with knowledge that he is facilitating a fraud or injury to be perpetrated by anyone, the actor:

    (a) alters any writing of another without his authority; or

    (b) makes, completes, executes, authenticates, issues or transfers any writing so that it purports to be the act of another who did not authorize that act, or to have been executed at a time or place or in a numbered sequence other than was in fact the case, or to be a copy of an original when no such original existed; or

    (c) utters any writing which he knows to be forged in a manner specified in paragraphs (a) or (b).

"Writing" includes printing or any other method of recording information, money, coins, tokens, stamps, seals, credit cards, badges, trade-marks, and other symbols of value, right, privilege, or identification.

(2) Grading. Forgery is a felony of the second degree if the writing is or purports to be part of an issue of money, securities, postage or revenue stamps, or other instruments issued by the government, or part of an issue of stock, bonds or other instruments representing interests in or claims

§ 224.0   Model Penal Code

against any property or enterprise. Forgery is a felony of the third degree if the writing is or purports to be a will, deed, contract, release, commercial instrument, or other document evidencing, creating, transferring, altering, terminating, or otherwise affecting legal relations. Otherwise forgery is a misdemeanor.

STATUS OF SECTION

Presented to the Institute as Section 223.1 of Tentative Draft No. 11, and considered at the May 1960 meeting.

For Commentary, see Tentative Draft No. 11, p. 78.

Subsection (1) of the former draft defined forgery with less particularity than the present draft: "A writing or other object is forged if and only if it is so made or altered as to convey a false impression as to authorship, authority, date, or other aspect of its authenticity." The word "authenticity" was relied on both as a catch-all to reach all forms of essential falsification and as a criterion by which to distinguish forgery from ordinary false pretense by misrepresentation of facts outside the document. The draft was criticised as inadequate for the latter purpose. For example, it was said that the test of authenticity did not clearly exclude from forgery such cases as the keeping of duplicate misleading books of account, or the fraudulent "padding" of a payroll by an employee of a corporation.

The present draft meets this criticism. The greater specificity, however, makes the provisions inappropriate to deal with "forgery" of "objects" other than writings. Accordingly it has become necessary to provide separately for fraudulent simulation of antique or rare objects. See Section 224.2, below.

There has been inserted in subsection (1) an additional basis for culpability, namely, "with knowledge that he is facilitating a fraud or injury to be perpetrated by anyone." This is to make it clear that a forger commits an offense even though he does not defraud the person to whom he sells or passes the forged writings, as where the transferee takes with knowledge of the forgery for the purpose of passing the writings as authentic.

The grading provisions in Subsection (2) have been revised principally by deleting provisions making it a third degree felony to forge records and accounts kept by or for the government. This matter is dealt with in Section 241.8 which covers all forms of tampering with public records. Section 241.8 classifies such tampering as a misdemeanor, except where the tampering is with purpose to defraud or injure, in which case it is a felony.

Section 224.2. Simulating Objects of Antiquity, Rarity, Etc.

A person commits a misdemeanor if, with purpose to defraud anyone or with knowledge that he is facilitating a fraud to be perpetrated by anyone, he makes, alters or utters any object so that it appears to have value because of antiquity, rarity, source, or authorship which it does not possess.

STATUS OF SECTION

This is a new section, the subject-matter of which was formerly comprehended in Section 224.1—*Forgery*. The occasion for separate treatment of forgery of "objects" is stated above in the explanation of revised Section 224.1.

Section 224.3. Fraudulent Destruction, Removal or Concealment of Recordable Instruments.

A person commits a felony of the third degree if, with purpose to deceive or injure anyone, he destroys, removes or conceals any will, deed, mortgage, security instrument or other writing for which the law provides public recording.

STATUS OF SECTION

Presented to the Institute as Section 223.2 of Tentative Draft No. 11, and considered at the May 1960 meeting.

For Commentary, see Tentative Draft No. 11, p. 97.

Section 224.4. Tampering with Records.

A person commits a misdemeanor if, knowing that he has no privilege to do so, he falsifies, destroys, removes or conceals any writing or record, with purpose to deceive or injure anyone or to conceal any wrongdoing.

STATUS OF SECTION

Presented to the Institute as Section 223.3 of Tentative Draft No. 11 and considered at the May 1960 meeting.

For Commentary, see Tentative Draft No. 11, p. 98.

Section 224.5. Bad Checks.

A person who issues or passes a check or similar sight order for the payment of money, knowing that it will not be honored by the drawee, commits a misdemeanor. For the purposes of this Section as well as in any prosecution for theft committed by means of a bad check, an issuer is presumed to know that the check or order (other than a post-dated check or order) would not be paid, if:

(a) the issuer had no account with the drawee at the time the check or order was issued; or

(b) payment was refused by the drawee for lack of funds, upon presentation within 30 days after issue, and the issuer failed to make good within 10 days after receiving notice of that refusal.

STATUS OF SECTION

Presented to the Institute as Section 206.22 of Tentative Draft No. 2, and considered at the May 1954 meeting.

For Commentary, see Tentative Draft No. 2, p. 117.

The offense has been reclassified from petty misdemeanor to misdemeanor in view of dissatisfaction expressed in the 1954 debates with regard to classification of the offense as a petty misdemeanor. The Institute's subsequent decision to reduce the maximum imprisonment for petty misdemeanors from 90 to 30 days reinforces the position of those who take the graver view of the offense of passing small bad checks. It should be recalled that if the check is over $500, the passer could be prosecuted for felonious theft by deception, under Sections 223.1(2) and 223.3.

Section 224.6. Credit Cards.

A person commits an offense if he uses a credit card for the purpose of obtaining property or services with knowledge that:

(a) the card is stolen or forged; or

(b) the card has been revoked or cancelled; or

(c) for any other reason his use of the card is unauthorized.

It is an affirmative defense to prosecution under paragraph (c) if the actor proves by a preponderance of the evidence that he had the purpose and ability to meet all obligations to the issuer arising out of his use of the card. "Credit card" means a writing purporting to evidence an undertaking to pay for property or services delivered or rendered to or upon the order of a designated person or bearer. An offense under this Section is a felony of the third degree if the value of the property or services secured or sought to be secured by means of the credit card exceeds $500; otherwise it is a misdemeanor.

STATUS OF SECTION

This is a new section to fill a gap in the law relating to false pretense and fraudulent practices. Sections 223.3 and 223.7 cover theft of property or services by deception. It is doubtful whether they reach the credit card situation because the user of a stolen or cancelled credit card does not obtain goods by any deception practiced upon or victimizing the seller. The seller will collect from the issuer of the credit card, because credit card issuers assume the risk of misuse of cards in order to encourage sellers to honor the cards readily. Thus it is the non-deceived issuer who is the victim of the practice.

The proposed grading parallels the grading by amount in the theft sections of the Code except that, as in the case of bad checks, we do not provide for anything less than a misdemeanor even when the amounts are quite small. The rationale, in the case of both credit cards and bad checks, is that these methods of defrauding lend themselves to repeated violation by transients so as to undermine reliance on useful credit mechanisms.

Section 224.7. Deceptive Business Practices.

A person commits a misdemeanor if in the course of business he:

(a) uses or possesses for use a false weight or measure, or any other device for falsely determining or recording any quality or quantity; or

(b) sells, offers or exposes for sale, or delivers less than the represented quantity of any commodity or service; or

(c) takes or attempts to take more than the represented quantity of any commodity or service when as buyer he furnishes the weight or measure; or

(d) sells, offers or exposes for sale adulterated or mislabeled commodities. "Adulterated" means varying from the standard of composition or quality prescribed by or pursuant to any statute providing criminal penalties for such variance, or set by established commercial usage. "Mislabeled" means varying from the standard of truth or disclosure in labeling prescribed by or pursuant to any statute providing criminal penalties for such variance, or set by established commercial usage; or

(e) makes a false or misleading statement in any advertisement addressed to the public or to a substantial segment thereof for the purpose of promoting the purchase or sale of property or services; or

(f) makes a false or misleading written statement for the purpose of obtaining property or credit; or

(g) makes a false or misleading written statement for the purpose of promoting the sale of securities, or omits information required by law to be disclosed in written documents relating to securities.

It is an affirmative defense to prosecution under this Section if the defendant proves by a preponderance of the evidence that his conduct was not knowingly or recklessly deceptive.

STATUS OF SECTION

Presented to the Institute as Section 206.24 of Tentative Draft No. 2, and considered at the May 1954 meeting.

For Commentary, see Tentative Draft No. 2, p. 121.

A substantial change in paragraph (d) is the introduction of the standard of "established commercial usage" in addition to standards prescribed by statute or regulation.

Minor verbal changes have also been made.

Section 224.8. Commercial Bribery and Breach of Duty to Act Disinterestedly.

(1) A person commits a misdemeanor if he solicits, accepts or agrees to accept any benefit as consideration for knowingly violating or agreeing to violate a duty of fidelity to which he is subject as:

    (a) agent or employee of another;

    (b) trustee, guardian, or other fiduciary;

    (c) lawyer, physician, accountant, appraiser, or other professional adviser or informant;

    (d) officer, director, partner, manager or other participant in the direction of the affairs of an incorporated or unincorporated association; or

    (e) arbitrator or other purportedly disinterested adjudicator or referee.

(2) A person who holds himself out to the public as being engaged in the business of making disinterested selection, appraisal, or criticism of commodities or services commits a misdemeanor if he solicits, accepts or agrees to accept any benefit to influence his selection, appraisal or criticism.

(3) A person commits a misdemeanor if he confers, or offers or agrees to confer, any benefit the acceptance of which would be criminal under this Section.

STATUS OF SECTION

Presented to the Institute as Section 223.10 of Tentative Draft No. 11, and considered at the May 1961 meeting.

For Commentary, see Tentative Draft No. 11, p. 113.

The phrase "being engaged in the business of" has been added in Subsection (2) in order to confine the Subsection to professional critics, commercial rating agencies, and the like, excluding individual endorsements of products by prominent athletes, actors, and the like. These endorsements are probably vulnerable to attack as "unfair methods of competition," but like "puffing" of wares are unlikely to deceive most members of the audience as respects the disinterestedness of the endorsement.

Section 224.9. Rigging Publicly Exhibited Contest.

(1) A person commits a misdemeanor if, with purpose to prevent a publicly exhibited contest from being conducted in accordance with the rules and usages purporting to govern it, he:

>**(a) confers or offers or agrees to confer any benefit upon, or threatens any injury to a participant, official or other person associated with the contest or exhibition; or**

>**(b) tampers with any person, animal or thing.**

(2) Soliciting or Accepting Benefit for Rigging. A person commits a misdemeanor if he knowingly solicits, accepts or agrees to accept any benefit the giving of which would be criminal under Subsection (1).

(3) Participation in Rigged Contest. A person commits a misdemeanor if he knowingly engages in, sponsors, produces, judges, or otherwise participates in a publicly exhibited contest knowing that the contest is not being conducted in compliance with the rules and usages purporting to govern it, by reason of conduct which would be criminal under this Section.

STATUS OF SECTION

Presented to the Institute as Section 223.9 of Tentative Draft No. 11 and considered at the May 1960 meeting.

For Commentary, see Tentative Draft No. 11, p. 107.

The Section has been revised mainly in form. Subsection (1)(a) formerly referred explicity to bribing a participant so that he would "not use his best efforts"; but this seems to be adequately covered by the general prohibition against attempts to subvert the "rules and usages" proporting to govern the exhibition. The knowledge element of the offense has been made explicit in Subsections (2) and (3).

Section 224.10. Defrauding Secured Creditors.

A person commits a misdemeanor if he destroys, removes, conceals, encumbers, transfers or otherwise deals with property subject to a security interest with purpose to hinder enforcement of that interest.

STATUS OF SECTION

Presented to the Institute as Section 223.7 of Tentative Draft No. 11 and considered at the May 1960 meeting.

For Commentary, see Tentative Draft No. 11, p. 98.

Section 224.11. Fraud in Insolvency.

A person commits a misdemeanor if, knowing that proceedings have been or are about to be instituted for the appointment of a receiver or other person entitled to administer property for the benefit of creditors, or that any other composition or liquidation for the benefit of creditors has been or is about to made, he:

> **(a) destroys, removes, conceals, encumbers, transfers, or otherwise deals with any property with purpose to defeat or obstruct the claim of any creditor, or otherwise to obstruct the operation of any law relating to administration of property for the benefit of creditors; or**

(b) knowingly falsifies any writing or record relating to the property; or

(c) knowingly misrepresents or refuses to disclose to a receiver or other person entitled to administer property for the benefit of creditors, the existence, amount or location of the property, or any other information which the actor could be legally required to furnish in relation to such administration.

STATUS OF SECTION

Presented to the Institute as Section 223.8 of Tentative Draft No. 11 and considered at the May 1960 meeting.

For Commentary, see Tentative Draft No. 11, p. 100.

Section 224.12. Receiving Deposits in a Failing Financial Institution.

An officer, manager or other person directing or participating in the direction of a financial institution commits a misdemeanor if he receives or permits the receipt of a deposit, premium payment or other investment in the institution knowing that:

(1) due to financial difficulties the institution is about to suspend operations or go into receivership or reorganization; and

(2) the person making the deposit or other payment is unaware of the precarious situation of the institution.

STATUS OF SECTION

Presented to the Institute as Section 206.23 of Tentative Draft No. 2 and considered at the May 1954 meeting.

For Commentary, see Tentative Draft No. 2, p. 119.

The Section was reprinted in Tentative Draft No. 4.

Clause (1) has been revised to tighten the knowledge requirement. Defendant must now be shown to have known, in effect, that the institution was closing, whereas formerly knowledge of insolvency or "failing condition" sufficed. The definition of "financial institution" appears in Section 223.0 and is made applicable here by Section 224.0.

Section 224.13. Misapplication of Entrusted Property and Property of Government or Financial Institution.

A person commits an offense if he applies or disposes of property that has been entrusted to him as a fiduciary, or property of the government or of a financial institution, in a manner which he knows is unlawful and involves substantial risk of loss or detriment to the owner of the property or to a person for whose benefit the property was entrusted. The offense is a misdemeanor if the amount involved exceeds $50; otherwise it is a petty misdemeanor. "Fiduciary" includes trustee, guardian, executor, administrator, receiver and any person carrying on fiduciary functions on behalf of a corporation or other organization which is a fiduciary.

STATUS OF SECTION

Presented to the Institute as Section 206.40 of Tentative Draft No. 2, and considered at the May 1954 meeting.

The Section was reprinted in Tentative Draft No. 4.

For Commentary, see Tentative Draft No. 2, p. 124.

The Section has been substantially revised. Provisions of the earlier draft setting up presumptions and unusual allocations of burden of proof were questioned at the meeting, and have been eliminated. The scope of the Section has also been narrowed by taking out commercial bailees and by requiring in all cases proof that defendant knew his action involved substantial risk of loss or detriment.

Section 224.14. Securing Execution of Documents by Deception.

A person commits a misdemeanor if by deception he causes another to execute any instrument affecting or likely to affect the pecuniary interest of any person.

STATUS OF SECTION

Presented to the Institute as Section 206.20 of Tentative Draft No. 2, and considered at the May 1954 meeting.

For Commentary, see Tentative Draft No. 2, p. 113.

The Section has been revised in form and substance. Previous drafts dealt with "threat" as well as deception. That became unnecessary with the adoption of our general section on criminal coercion (212.5).

The documents to which the Section relates are now characterized as those "affecting or likely to affect the pecuniary interest of any person," where formerly we said "deed, contract, trust, will, license, lease or other document disposing of property or incurring a pecuniary obligation, contingent or otherwise." The new, more comprehensive language clearly reaches such cases as execution of releases or extensions of time for payment of obligations. A proposal to extend the Section to non-pecuniary instruments such as agreements on custody of children or written statements given to law enforcement officers was considered and rejected.

The second sentence of former Section 206.20 has been deleted as unnecessary. It sought to exclude overlapping of this Section with certain other Sections of the Code. The problem of overlapping is solved by our general provision in Sections 1.07 and 7.06 against cumulative convictions and sentences based on the same conduct.

Tentative Draft No. 2 contained a Section 206.21 making it a misdemeanor to use intimidation or deception "to secure employment." This section has been dropped. So far as intimidation is concerned, we propose to rely on Section 212.5—*Criminal Coercion*. As for deception in securing employment, there is sufficient doubt as to the propriety and utility of making this an offense (see Commentary in Tentative Draft No. 2, p. 114) that it was classified as a mere "violation" in the previous draft. Divorced from the problem of coerced employment relations, it hardly merits inclusion in the Code.

In the course of considering Section 206.21, the question was raised whether misdemeanor penalties were adequate for "labor racketeering." See notation following Section 206.21 when it was reprinted in Tentative Draft No. 4. Threats of violence in the context of labor disputes (and, more generally, in the context of group struggles over political, religious or racial issues) present a social danger quite distinct from and more serious than threats to personal security of individuals. This problem is met by the grading provisions of Section 212.5—*Criminal Coercion*, where either the gravity of the threat or the nature of the demand may raise the offense to the felony classification.

OFFENSES AGAINST THE FAMILY

ARTICLE 230. OFFENSES AGAINST THE FAMILY

Section 230.1. Bigamy and Polygamy.

(1) <u>Bigamy.</u> A married person is guilty of bigamy, a misdemeanor, if he contracts or purports to contract another marriage, unless at the time of the subsequent marriage:

 (a) the actor believes that the prior spouse is dead; or

 (b) the actor and the prior spouse have been living apart for five consecutive years throughout which the prior spouse was not known by the actor to be alive; or

 (c) a Court has entered a judgment purporting to terminate or annul any prior disqualifying marriage, and the actor does not know that judgment to be invalid; or

 (d) the actor reasonably believes that he is legally eligible to remarry.

(2) <u>Polygamy.</u> A person is guilty of polygamy, a felony of the third degree, if he marries or cohabits with more than one spouse at a time in purported exercise of the right of plural marriage. The offense is a continuing one until all cohabitation and claim of marriage with more than one spouse terminates. This section does not apply to parties to a polygamous marriage, lawful in the country of which they are residents or nationals, while they are in transit through or temporarily visiting this State.

(3) <u>Other Party to Bigamous or Polygamous Marriage.</u> A person is guilty of bigamy or polygamy, as the case may

§ 230.2

be, if he contracts or purports to contract marriage with another knowing that the other is thereby committing bigamy or polygamy.

STATUS OF SECTION

Presented to the Institute as Section 207.2 of Tentative Draft No. 4, and considered at the May 1955 meeting.

For Commentary, see Tentative Draft No. 4, p. 220.

Paragraph (c) in Subsection (1) has been added to lighten the burden of exculpation for a defendant who remarries following an out-of-state divorce. The thought is that a person with any sophistication in law may be uncertain as to the validity of a foreign divorce. It seems harsh to subject him to a criminal bigamy prosecution, especially since the questionable divorce may be that of his second spouse from another person.

The previous draft contained a subsection penalizing "bigamous cohabitation," i.e., living together in this State following a bigamous marriage in another State. The purpose was to prevent evasion of the bigamy law by the simple device of having the bigamous marriage performed in a jurisdiction where the parties do not live. The Advisors and the Council doubted that this was a problem of substantial dimensions or that penal sanctions would be useful in dealing with it. In addition, drafting and enforcing a penal provision would be difficult in view of complexities deriving from conflict-of-laws and statutes of limitations.

Subsection (3) has been revised. Formerly it provided a misdemeanor penalty for the other party to a bigamous or polygamous marriage. It now makes the other party guilty of bigamy or polygamy, as the case may be, depending on the nature of the arrangement he knows that he is getting into. Polygamy is a felony under Subsection (2).

Section 230.2. Incest.

A person is guilty of incest, a felony of the third degree, if he knowingly marries or cohabits or has sexual intercourse with an ancestor or descendant, a brother or sister of the whole or half blood [or an uncle, aunt, nephew or niece of the whole blood]. "Cohabit" means to live together under the representation or appearance of being married. The

relationships referred to herein include blood relationships without regard to legitimacy, and relationship of parent and child by adoption.

STATUS OF SECTION

Presented to the Institute as Section 207.3 of Tentative Draft No. 4, and considered at the May 1955 meeting.

For Commentary, see Tentative Draft No. 4, p. 231.

Minor changes suggested at the Institute meeting have been made. The uncle-aunt-nephew-niece cases have been bracketed in the text to indicate some doubt whether they belong in the category of "felonious incest," in view of the severity of the penalty and condemnation, and acceptance of uncle-niece marriage for some religious groups, e.g., in Rhode Island law. Our Comments recognize that the marriage regulations of a state may circumscribe marriage more strictly than the incest law, but that is a different question from the proper scope to be accorded to the felony of incest. Relations between uncles and under-age nieces would be "statutory rape" under Section 213.3(1).

Section 230.3. Abortion.

(1) <u>Unjustified Abortion.</u> A person who purposely and unjustifiably terminates the pregnancy of another otherwise than by a live birth commits a felony of the third degree or, where the pregnancy has continued beyond the twenty-sixth week, a felony of the second degree.

(2) <u>Justifiable Abortion.</u> A licensed physician is justified in terminating a pregnancy if he believes there is substantial risk that continuance of the pregnancy would gravely impair the physical or mental health of the mother or that the child would be born with grave physical or mental defect, or that the pregnancy resulted from rape, incest, or other felonious intercourse. All illicit intercourse with a girl below the age of 16 shall be deemed felonious for

purposes of this subsection. Justifiable abortions shall be performed only in a licensed hospital except in case of emergency when hospital facilities are unavailable. [Additional exceptions from the requirement of hospitalization may be incorporated here to take account of situations in sparsely settled areas where hospitals are not generally accessible.]

(3) *Physicians' Certificates; Presumption from Non-Compliance.* No abortion shall be performed unless two physicians, one of whom may be the person performing the abortion, shall have certified in writing the circumstances which they believe to justify the abortion. Such certificate shall be submitted before the abortion to the hospital where it is to be performed and, in the case of abortion following felonious intercourse, to the prosecuting attorney or the police. Failure to comply with any of the requirements of this Subsection gives rise to a presumption that the abortion was unjustified.

(4) *Self-Abortion.* A woman whose pregnancy has continued beyond the twenty-sixth week commits a felony of the third degree if she purposely terminates her own pregnancy otherwise than by a live birth, or if she uses instruments, drugs or violence upon herself for that purpose. Except as justified under Subsection (2), a person who induces or knowingly aids a woman to use instruments, drugs or violence upon herself for the purpose of terminating her pregnancy otherwise than by a live birth commits a felony of the third degree whether or not the pregnancy has continued beyond the twenty-sixth week.

(5) *Pretended Abortion.* A person commits a felony of the third degree if, representing that it is his purpose to perform an abortion, he does an act adapted to cause abortion in a pregnant woman although the woman is in fact not

pregnant, or the actor does not believe she is. **A person charged with unjustified abortion under Subsection (1) or an attempt to commit that offense may be convicted thereof upon proof of conduct prohibited by this Subsection.**

(6) <u>Distribution of Abortifacients.</u> **A person who sells, offers to sell, possesses with intent to sell, advertises, or displays for sale anything specially designed to terminate a pregnancy, or held out by the actor as useful for that purpose, commits a misdemeanor, unless:**

> (a) the sale, offer or display is to a physician or druggist or to an intermediary in a chain of distribution to physicians or druggists; or

> (b) the sale is made upon prescription or order of a physician; or

> (c) the possession is with intent to sell as authorized in paragraphs (a) and (b); or

> (d) the advertising is addressed to persons named in paragraph (a) and confined to trade or professional channels not likely to reach the general public.

(7) <u>Section Inapplicable to Prevention of Pregnancy.</u> **Nothing in this Section shall be deemed applicable to the prescription, administration or distribution of drugs or other substances for avoiding pregnancy, whether by preventing implantation of a fertilized ovum or by any other method that operates before, at or immediately after fertilization.**

STATUS OF SECTION

Presented to the Institute as Section 207.11 of Tentative Draft No. 9, and considered at the May 1959 meeting.

For Commentary, see Tentative Draft No. 9, p. 146.

Changes, for the most part formal, reflect decisions and suggestions at the meeting. In particular the meeting voted in favor of including "statutory rape" among the occasions for justified abortion. This is accomplished by the reference in Subsection (2) to "other felonious intercourse," which takes in all the third degree felony cases in Subsection (2) of Section 213.1, including cases of intimidation and impersonation. The sentence in Subsection (2) relating to illicit intercourse with girls under 16 is necessary because the Institute has excluded from felonious intercourse cases of sexual relations between children who do not differ in age by more than four years. See 213.3(a).

The 1955 draft required performance in a hospital and the filing of physicians' certificates if the abortion was to be justified. There was strong support for making hospitalization a condition of legality, and strong opposition to making a physician guilty of a felony where he performed a therapeutic abortion in a hospital but neglected to comply precisely with the filing requirements. The solution offered in the present draft is to separate these two classes of requirement. Hospitalization, where practicable, remains a condition of justification under Subsection (2). Noncompliance with filing requirements gives rise solely to a presumption that abortion was unjustified under Subsection (3).

Section 230.4. Endangering Welfare of Children.

A parent, guardian, or other person supervising the welfare of a child under 18 commits a misdemeanor if he knowingly endangers the child's welfare by violating a duty of care, protection or support.

STATUS OF SECTION

Presented to the Institute as § 207.13 of Tentative Draft No. 9, and considered at the May 1959 meeting.

For Commentary, see Tentative Draft No. 9, p. 183.

The Section then referred to "physical or moral" welfare. It was suggested that "mental" be added. The Reporter accepted the suggestion, but concluded that there was no reason to qualify the word "welfare" with any of the adjectives. They have been deleted.

Section 230.5. Persistent Non-Support.

A person commits a misdemeanor if he persistently fails to provide support which he can provide and which he knows he is legally obliged to provide to a spouse, child or other dependent.

STATUS OF SECTION

Presented to the Institute as § 207.14 of Tentative Draft No. 9, and considered at the May 1955 meeting.

For Commentary, see Tentative Draft No. 9, p. 188.

OFFENSES AGAINST PUBLIC ADMINISTRATION

ARTICLE 240. BRIBERY AND CORRUPT INFLUENCE

Section 240.0. Definitions.

In Articles 240-243, unless a different meaning plainly is required:

(1) "benefit" means gain or advantage, or anything regarded by the beneficiary as gain or advantage, including benefit to any other person or entity in whose welfare he is interested, but not an advantage promised generally to a group or class of voters as a consequence of public measures which a candidate engages to support or oppose;

(2) "government" includes any branch, subdivision or agency of the government of the State or any locality within it;

(3) "harm" means loss, disadvantage or injury, or anything so regarded by the person affected, including loss, disadvantage or injury to any other person or entity in whose welfare he is interested;

(4) "official proceeding" means a proceeding heard or which may be heard before any legislative, judicial, administrative or other governmental agency or official authorized to take evidence under oath, including any referee, hearing examiner, commissioner, notary or other person taking testimony or deposition in connection with any such proceeding;

(5) "party official" means a person who holds an elective or appointive post in a political party in the

United States by virtue of which he directs or conducts, or participates in directing or conducting party affairs at any level of responsibility;

(6) "pecuniary benefit" is benefit in the form of money, property, commercial interests or anything else the primary significance of which is economic gain;

(7) "public servant" means any officer or employee of government, including legislators and judges, and any person participating as juror, advisor, consultant or otherwise, in performing a governmental function; but the term does not include witnesses;

(8) "administrative proceeding" means any proceeding the outcome of which is required to be based on a record or documentation prescribed by law, or in which law or regulation is particularized in application to individuals.

STATUS OF SECTION

Presented to the Institute as Section 208.50 of Tentative Draft No. 8, and considered at the May 1958 meeting.

In addition to minor verbal changes, the definitions of "pecuniary benefit" and "administrative proceeding" have been added for purposes discussed below in connection with Sections 240.1 and 240.2.

Section 240.1. Bribery in Official and Political Matters.

A person is guilty of bribery, a felony of the third degree, if he offers, confers or agrees to confer upon another, or solicits, accepts or agrees to accept from another:

(1) any pecuniary benefit as consideration for the recipient's decision, opinion, recommendation, vote or other exercise of discretion as a public servant, party official or voter; or

(2) any benefit as consideration for the recipient's decision, vote, recommendation or other exercise of official discretion in a judicial or administrative proceeding; or

(3) any benefit as consideration for a violation of a known duty as public servant or party official.

It is no defense to prosecution under this section that a person whom the actor sought to influence was not qualified to act in the desired way whether because he had not yet assumed office, or lacked jurisdiction, or for any other reason.

STATUS OF SECTION

Presented to the Institute as Section 208.10 of Tentative Draft No. 8, and considered at the May 1958 meeting.

For Commentary, see Tentative Draft No. 8, p. 102.

The Section has been substantially revised. The previous draft employed the word "corruptly" to characterize the forbidden influence. Although that word is often used in extant legislation and judicial opinions, it is ambiguous in application to two important categories of cases: (i) where the alleged briber seeks to justify his conduct on the ground that he sought only to counter opposing "corrupt" offers, or to influence an official to make the decision which he should in any event make; and (ii) where the alleged bribe is an offer of appointment or promotion in the public service, or of political support, in exchange for like commitments by the offeree.

Accordingly, with the approval of the Advisors and the Council, the Section has been revised so that it no longer employs the word "corruptly." Instead, paragraph (1) now prohibits unqualifiedly the giving or receiving of any *pecuniary* benefit to influence official or political discretion. Offers of non-pecuniary benefits, e.g. political support, honorific appointments, are penalized, under paragraph (2), only in connection with attempts to influence judicial and administrative proceedings. "Administrative proceeding" is defined in Section 240.0 so as to include quasi-judicial proceedings and, also, some proceedings directed toward formulation of regulations, if the law contemplates that the outcome shall be based on evidence and findings. The definition will also cover some actions that might be called "executive" or "administrative," where the official action applies a general rule to an individual, e.g. in granting or revoking a license, awarding veteran's disability compensation or social security pay.

Section 240.1 departs from the earlier draft also in requiring that the benefit be "in consideration" of the official action or agreement therefor. This is the more conventional formula in bribery legislation, and prevents application of the bribery sanction to situations where gifts are given in the mere hope of influence, without any agreement by the donee. We deal with gifts to officials elsewhere. See Section 240.6.

Section 240.2. Threats and Other Improper Influence in Official and Political Matters.

(1) <u>Offenses Defined</u>. A person commits an offense if he:

(a) threatens unlawful harm to any person with purpose to influence his decision, opinion, recommendation, vote or other exercise of discretion as a public servant, party official or voter; or

(b) threatens harm to any public servant with purpose to influence his decision, opinion, recommendation, vote or other exercise of discretion in a judicial or administrative proceeding; or

(c) threatens harm to any public servant or party official with purpose to influence him to violate his duty; or

(d) privately addresses to any public servant who has or will have an official discretion in a judicial or administrative proceeding any representation, entreaty, argument or other communication designed to influence the outcome on the basis of considerations other than those authorized by law.

It is no defense to prosecution under this Section that a person whom the actor sought to influence was not qualified to act in the desired way, whether because he had not yet assumed office, or lacked jurisdiction, or for any other reason.

§ 240.3

(2) **Grading.** An offense under this Section is a misdemeanor unless the actor threatened to commit a crime or made a threat with purpose to influence a judicial or administrative proceeding, in which cases the offense is a felony of the third degree.

STATUS OF SECTION

Presented to the Institute as Sections 208.11 and 208.14 of Tentative Draft No. 8, and considered at the May 1958 meeting. For Commentary, see Tentative Draft No. 8, pp. 107, 111.

Section 208.11 dealt with threats made to influence "corruptly." For the reasons given above in discussing Section 240.1, we have revised the present section to avoid reliance on the ambiguous word "corruptly."

The title and scope of revised Section 240.2 have been somewhat broadened to include the non-threat influences of paragraph (d). This paragraph derives from Section 208.14 of Tentative Draft No. 8, which also employed the term "corruptly." Section 208.14 is dropped as a separate section in the present submission.

Section 240.3. Compensation for Past Official Behavior.

A person commits a misdemeanor if he solicits, accepts or agrees to accept any pecuniary benefit as compensation for having, as public servant, given a decision, opinion, recommendation or vote favorable to another, or for having otherwise exercised a discretion in his favor, or for having violated his duty. A person commits a misdemeanor if he offers, confers or agrees to confer compensation acceptance of which is prohibited by this Section.

STATUS OF SECTION

Presented to the Institute as Section 208.12 of Tentative Draft No. 8, and considered at the May 1958 meeting.

For Commentary, see Tentative Draft No. 8, p. 109.

"Pecuniary benefit" has been substituted in place of "anything of pecuniary value" in the previous draft, thus employing the same term here as in Section 240.1.

Section 240.4. Retaliation for Past Official Action.

A person commits a misdemeanor if he harms another by any unlawful act in retaliation for anything lawfully done by the latter in the capacity of public servant.

STATUS OF SECTION

Presented to the Institute as Section 208.13 of Tentative Draft No. 8, and considered at the May 1958 meeting.

For Commentary, see Tentative Draft No. 8, p. 110.

Section 240.5. Gifts to Public Servants by Persons Subject to Their Jurisdiction.

(1) <u>Regulatory and Law Enforcement Officials</u>. No public servant in any department or agency exercising regulatory functions, or conducting inspections or investigations, or carrying on civil or criminal litigation on behalf of the government, or having custody of prisoners, shall solicit, accept or agree to accept any pecuniary benefit from a person known to be subject to such regulation, inspection, investigation or custody, or against whom such litigation is known to be pending or contemplated.

(2) <u>Officials Concerned with Government Contracts and Pecuniary Transactions</u>. No public servant having any discretionary function to perform in connection with contracts, purchases, payments, claims or other pecuniary transactions of the government shall solicit, accept or agree to accept any pecuniary benefit from any person known to be interested in or likely to become interested in any such contract, purchase, payment, claim or transaction.

(3) <u>Judicial and Administrative Officials</u>. No public servant having judicial or administrative authority and no

public servant employed by or in a court or other tribunal having such authority, or participating in the enforcement of its decisions, shall solicit, accept or agree to accept any pecuniary benefit from a person known to be interested in or likely to become interested in any matter before such public servant or a tribunal with which he is associated.

(4) Legislative Officials. No legislator or public servant employed by the legislature or by any committee or agency thereof shall solicit, accept or agree to accept any pecuniary benefit from any person known to be interested in a bill, transaction or proceeding, pending or contemplated, before the legislature or any committee or agency thereof.

(5) Exceptions. This Section shall not apply to:

(a) fees prescribed by law to be received by a public servant, or any other benefit for which the recipient gives legitimate consideration or to which he is otherwise legally entitled; or

(b) gifts or other benefits conferred on account of kinship or other personal, professional or business relationship independent of the official status of the receiver; or

(c) trivial benefits incidental to personal, professional or business contacts and involving no substantial risk of undermining official impartiality.

(6) Offering Benefits Prohibited. No person shall knowingly confer, or offer or agree to confer, any benefit prohibited by the foregoing Subsections.

(7) Grade of Offense. An offense under this Section is a misdemeanor.

STATUS OF SECTION

Presented to the Institute as Section 208.15 of Tentative Draft No. 8, and considered at the May 1958 meeting.

For Commentary, see Tentative Draft No. 8, p. 114.

Minor verbal changes have been made.

Section 240.6. Compensating Public Servant for Assisting Private Interests in Relation to Matters Before Him.

(1) **Receiving Compensation.** A public servant commits a misdemeanor if he solicits, accepts or agrees to accept compensation for advice or other assistance in preparing or promoting a bill, contract, claim, or other transaction or proposal as to which he knows that he has or is likely to have an official discretion to exercise.

(2) **Paying Compensation.** A person commits a misdemeanor if he pays or offers or agrees to pay compensation to a public servant with knowledge that acceptance by the public servant is unlawful.

STATUS OF SECTION

Presented to the Institute as Section 208.16 of Tentative Draft No. 8, and considered at the May 1958 meeting.

For Commentary, see Tentative Draft No. 8, p. 115.

The Section has been revised in form and somewhat narrowed in scope. The previous draft applied to compensation for any "services in relation to any matter" as to which the official had a discretion. In the course of the debates, members of the Institute pointed out that this made the section applicable to all supplementary private compensation to officials exercising discretion, whether or not the payment was designed or likely to secure favorable action on particular proposals of the payor. The old language would also have encompassed compensation for non-promotional services; for example, an undertaker in a small town, who also served as coroner, might have been forbidden to accept compensation for funeral services. Accordingly the present draft has been restricted to advice and assistance in promoting legislation, claims against the government, and the like.

Subsection (2) has been changed to require proof of knowledge of illegality in prosecuting a layman for compensating a public servant for services. The public servant who is at the same time engaged in the private practice of law or other profession may be expected to know the applicable ethical and legal rules. The same cannot be expected of the private client, who may not even be aware that the lawyer, whom he has regularly retained, now occupies a relevant governmental post.

Section 240.7. Selling Political Endorsement; Special Influence.

(1) Selling Political Endorsement. A person commits a misdemeanor if he solicits, receives, agrees to receive, or agrees that any political party or other person shall receive, any pecuniary benefit as consideration for approval or disapproval of an appointment or advancement in public service, or for approval or disapproval of any person or transaction for any benefit conferred by an official or agency of government. "Approval" includes recommendation, failure to disapprove, or any other manifestation of favor or acquiescence. "Disapproval" includes failure to approve, or any other manifestation of disfavor or nonacquiescence.

(2) Other Trading in Special Influence. A person commits a misdemeanor if he solicits, receives or agrees to receive any pecuniary benefit as consideration for exerting special influence upon a public servant or procuring another to do so. "Special influence" means power to influence through kinship, friendship or other relationship, apart from the merits of the transaction.

(3) Paying for Endorsement or Special Influence. A person commits a misdemeanor if he offers, confers or agrees to confer any pecuniary benefit receipt of which is prohibited by this Section.

STATUS OF SECTION

Presented to the Institute as Section 208.7 of Tentative Draft No. 8, and considered at the May 1958 meeting.

For Commentary, see Tentative Draft No. 8, p. 116.

Minor verbal changes have been made. The words "or agrees that any political party or other person shall receive" have been inserted in Subsection (1) to make the Section clearly applicable to situations like United States v. Shirey, 359 U.S. 255, 79 S. Ct. 746 (1959). There the Supreme Court held, by a vote of five to four, that 18 U.S.C. §214 does reach cases where the money is to be received by a political party rather than by the politician on his own account.

§§ 241.0, 241.1

ARTICLE 241. PERJURY AND OTHER FALSIFICATION IN OFFICIAL MATTERS

Section 241.0. Definitions.

In this Article, unless a different meaning plainly is required:

    (1) the definitions given in Section 240.0 apply; and

    (2) "statement" means any representation, but includes a representation of opinion, belief or other state of mind only if the representation clearly relates to state of mind apart from or in addition to any facts which are the subject of the representation.

STATUS OF SECTION

Section 208.20(1) of Tentative Draft No. 6, considered at the May 1957 meeting, is the source of the definitions of "official proceeding" and "statement," terms employed in the following sections. "Official proceeding" is now defined in Section 240.0, which is here incorporated by reference.

For Commentary, see Tentative Draft No. 6, pp. 101, 115.

Section 241.1. Perjury.

    (1) <u>Offense Defined.</u> A person is guilty of perjury, a felony of the third degree, if in any official proceeding he makes a false statement under oath or equivalent affirmation, or swears or affirms the truth of a statement previously made, when the statement is material and he does not believe it to be true.

    (2) <u>Materiality.</u> Falsification is material, regardless of the admissibility of the statement under rules of evidence, if it could have affected the course or outcome of the proceeding. It is no defense that the declarant mistakenly

believed the falsification to be immaterial. **Whether a falsification is material in a given factual situation is a question of law.**

(3) Irregularities No Defense. It is not a defense to prosecution under this Section that the oath or affirmation was administered or taken in an irregular manner or that the declarant was not competent to make the statement. A document purporting to be made upon oath or affirmation at any time when the actor presents it as being so verified shall be deemed to have been duly sworn or affirmed.

(4) Retraction. No person shall be guilty of an offense under this Section if he retracted the falsification in the course of the proceeding in which it was made before it became manifest that the falsification was or would be exposed and before the falsification substantially affected the proceeding.

(5) Inconsistent Statements. Where the defendant made inconsistent statements under oath or equivalent affirmation, both having been made within the period of the statute of limitations, the prosecution may proceed by setting forth the inconsistent statements in a single count alleging in the alternative that one or the other was false and not believed by the defendant. In such case it shall not be necessary for the prosecution to prove which statement was false but only that one or the other was false and not believed by the defendant to be true.

(6) Corroboration. No person shall be convicted of an offense under this Section where proof of falsity rests solely upon contradiction by testimony of a single person other than the defendant.

STATUS OF SECTION

Presented to the Institute as Section 208.20 of Tentative Draft No. 6, and considered at the May 1957 meeting.

For Commentary, see Tentative Draft No. 6, p. 100.

Minor verbal changes have been made to incorporate suggestions advanced at the meeting. Definitions previously included in Subsection (1) have been transposed to Sections 240.0 and 241.0 since they are applicable at a number of points in this Article.

Section 241.2. False Swearing.

(1) <u>False Swearing in Official Matters</u>. A person who makes a false statement under oath or equivalent affirmation, or swears or affirms the truth of such a statement previously made, when he does not believe the statement to be true, is guilty of a misdemeanor if:

    (a) the falsification occurs in an official proceeding; or

    (b) the falsification is intended to mislead a public servant in performing his official function.

(2) <u>Other False Swearing</u>. A person who makes a false statement under oath or equivalent affirmation, or swears or affirms the truth of such a statement previously made, when he does not believe the statement to be true, is guilty of a petty misdemeanor, if the statement is one which is required by law to be sworn or affirmed before a notary or other person authorized to administer oaths.

(3) <u>Perjury Provisions Applicable</u>. Subsections (3) to (6) of Section 241.1 apply to the present Section.

STATUS OF SECTION

Presented to the Institute as Section 208.21 of Tentative Draft No. 6, and considered at the May 1957 meeting.

For Commentary, see Tentative Draft No. 6, p. 140.

The only substantial change is the revision of Subsection (2) so as to eliminate criminal liability for falsification in private affidavits. The possibilities of abuse referred to in the Comments on the earlier draft persuaded the Advisory Committee to confine this Section to affidavits "required by law."

Section 241.3. Unsworn Falsification to Authorities.

(1) <u>In General.</u> A person commits a misdemeanor if, with purpose to mislead a public servant in performing his official function, he:

(a) makes any written false statement which he does not believe to be true; or

(b) purposely creates a false impression in a written application for any pecuniary or other benefit, by omitting information necessary to prevent statements therein from being misleading; or

(c) submits or invites reliance on any writing which he knows to be forged, altered or otherwise lacking in authenticity; or

(d) submits or invites reliance on any sample, specimen, map, boundary-mark, or other object which he knows to be false.

(2) <u>Statements "Under Penalty."</u> A person commits a petty misdemeanor if he makes a written false statement which he does not believe to be true, on or pursuant to a form bearing notice, authorized by law, to the effect that false statements made therein are punishable.

(3) <u>Perjury Provisions Applicable.</u> Subsections (3) to (6) of Section 241.1 apply to the present section.

STATUS OF SECTION

Presented to the Institute as Section 208.22 of Tentative Draft No. 6, and considered at the May 1957 meeting.

For Commentary, see Tentative Draft No. 6, p. 141.

Minor verbal changes have been made.

Section 241.4. False Alarms to Agencies of Public Safety.

A person who knowingly causes a false alarm of fire or other emergency to be transmitted to or within any organization, official or volunteer, for dealing with emergencies involving danger to life or property commits a misdemeanor.

STATUS OF SECTION

Presented to the Institute as Section 208.23 of Tentative Draft No. 6, and considered at the May 1957 meeting.

For Commentary, see Tentative Draft No. 6, p. 143.

Section 241.5. False Reports to Law Enforcement Authorities.

(1) <u>Falsely Incriminating Another</u>. A person who knowingly gives false information to any law enforcement officer with purpose to implicate another commits a misdemeanor.

(2) <u>Fictitious Reports</u>. A person commits a petty misdemeanor if he:

    (a) reports to law enforcement authorities an offense or other incident within their concern knowing that it did not occur; or

    (b) pretends to furnish such authorities with information relating to an offense or incident when he knows he has no information relating to such offense or incident.

STATUS OF SECTION

Presented to the Institute as Section 208.24 of Tentative Draft No. 6, and considered at the May 1957 meeting.

For Commentary, see Tentative Draft No. 6, p. 144.

Subsection (2) has been revised to eliminate a requirement of proof that the actor "cause[d] a law enforcement officer to act in reliance on [the] false information." The ever-awkward issue of causation ought not to be introduced needlessly into prosecution for minor offenses. The Institute's decision in May 1961 to reduce the penalty for petty misdemeanors to a maximum of 30 days makes it easier and more desirable to eliminate the issue of causation. False information of the sort covered by this Section would almost always lead to some police action in reliance thereon anyway. Accordingly, since we are dealing with behavior that is highly likely to have antisocial consequences, and with actors who are consciously falsifying, the minor penalty may be prescribed without inquiry into actual result of the misbehavior.

Section 241.6. Tampering With Witnesses and Informants; Retaliation Against Them.

(1) <u>Tampering</u>. A person commits an offense if, believing that an official proceeding or investigation is pending or about to be instituted, he attempts to induce or otherwise cause a witness or informant to:

(a) testify or inform falsely; or

(b) withhold any testimony, information, document or thing; or

(c) elude legal process summoning him to testify or supply evidence; or

(d) absent himself from any proceeding or investigation to which he has been legally summoned.

The offense is a felony of the third degree if the actor employs force, deception, threat or offer of pecuniary benefit. Otherwise it is a misdemeanor.

(2) <u>Retaliation Against Witness or Informant</u>. A person commits a misdemeanor if he harms another by any unlawful act in retaliation for anything lawfully done in the capacity of witness or informant.

§ 241.7

(3) **Witness or Informant Taking Bribe.** A person commits a felony of the third degree if he solicits, accepts or agrees to accept any benefit in consideration of his doing any of the things specified in clauses (a) to (d) of Subsection (1).

STATUS OF SECTION

Presented to the Institute as Section 208.25 of Tentative Draft No. 8, and considered at the May 1958 meeting.

For Commentary, see Tentative Draft No. 8, p. 121.

Minor verbal changes have been made.

Section 241.7. Tampering With or Fabricating Physical Evidence.

A person commits a misdemeanor if, believing that an official proceeding or investigation is pending or about to be instituted, he:

(a) alters, destroys, conceals or removes any record, document or thing with purpose to impair its verity or availability in such proceeding or investigation; or

(b) makes, presents or uses any record, document or thing knowing it to be false and with purpose to mislead a public servant who is or may be engaged in such proceeding or investigation.

STATUS OF SECTION

Presented to the Institute as Section 208.26 of Tentative Draft No. 8, and considered at the May 1958 meeting.

For Commentary, see Tentative Draft No. 8, p. 121.

Minor verbal changes have been made.

Section 241.8. Tampering With Public Records or Information.

(1) <u>Offense Defined</u>. A person commits an offense if he:

(a) knowingly makes a false entry in, or false alteration of, any record, document or thing belonging to, or received or kept by, the government for information or record, or required by law to be kept by others for information of the government; or

(b) makes, presents or uses any record, document or thing knowing it to be false, and with purpose that it be taken as a genuine part of information or records referred to in paragraph (a); or

(c) purposely and unlawfully destroys, conceals, removes or otherwise impairs the verity or availability of any such record, document or thing.

(2) <u>Grading</u>. An offense under this Section is a misdemeanor unless the actor's purpose is to defraud or injure anyone, in which case the offense is a felony of the third degree.

STATUS OF SECTION

Presented to the Institute as Section 208.27 of Tentative Draft No. 8, and considered at the May 1958 meeting.

For Commentary, see Tentative Draft No. 8, p. 122.

The provision for conviction of felony where there is purpose to injure or defraud is new, and is explained in the final paragraph of the Status Note on revised Section 224.1 above.

Section 241.9. Impersonating a Public Servant.

A person commits a misdemeanor if he falsely pretends to hold a position in the public service with purpose to induce another to submit to such pretended official authority or otherwise to act in reliance upon that pretense to his prejudice.

STATUS OF SECTION

Presented to the Institute as Section 208.28 of Tentative Draft No. 8, and considered at the May 1958 meeting.

For Commentary, see Tentative Draft No. 8, p. 123.

The previous draft covered substantially the same ground as the present section, but graded the offense into two categories: a petty misdemeanor where there was any purpose to induce reliance on the pretense, and a misdemeanor where the accused did "any act" in the pretended capacity of law enforcement officer. The Reporter reconsidered this classification in view of the Institute's action in May 1961 reducing the penalty for petty misdemeanors.

Further study led to the conclusion that there was no need for two classes of offense here, that impersonation with intent to induce "reliance" should not be criminal unless the "victim" was to be prejudiced in some way, and that "submission" by the victim to pretended authority expresses the desired criterion more clearly than the previous draft.

ARTICLE 242. OBSTRUCTING GOVERNMENTAL OPERATIONS; ESCAPES

Section 242.0. Definitions.

In this Article, unless another meaning plainly is required, the definitions given in Section 240.0 apply.

STATUS OF SECTION

As a separate statement with respect to Article 242, this Section is new. But cf. Section 208.50 of Tentative Draft No. 8.

Section 242.1. Obstructing Administration of Law or Other Governmental Function.

A person commits a misdemeanor if he purposely obstructs, impairs or perverts the administration of law or other governmental function by force, violence, physical interference or obstacle, breach of official duty, or any other unlawful act, except that this Section does not apply to flight by a person charged with crime, refusal to submit to arrest, failure to perform a legal duty other than an official duty, or any other means of avoiding compliance with law without affirmative interference with governmental functions.

STATUS OF SECTION

Presented to the Institute as Section 208.30 of Tentative Draft No. 8, and considered at the May 1958 meeting.

For Commentary, see Tentative Draft No. 8, p. 125.

Section 242.2. Resisting Arrest or Other Law Enforcement.

A person commits a misdemeanor if, for the purpose of preventing a public servant from effecting a lawful arrest

§ 242.3

or discharging any other duty, the person creates a substantial risk of bodily harm to the public servant or anyone else, or employs means justifying or requiring substantial force to overcome the resistance.

STATUS OF SECTION

Presented to the Institute as Section 208.31 of Tentative Draft No. 8, and considered at the May 1958 meeting.

For Commentary, see Tentative Draft No. 8, p. 129.

Minor verbal changes have been made.

Section 242.3. Hindering Apprehension or Prosecution.

A person commits an offense if, with purpose to hinder the apprehension, prosecution, conviction or punishment of another for crime, he:

(a) harbors or conceals the other; or

(b) provides or aids in providing a weapon, transportation, disguise or other means of avoiding apprehension or effecting escape; or

(c) conceals or destroys evidence of the crime, or tampers with a witness, informant, document or other source of information, regardless of its admissibility in evidence; or

(d) warns the other of impending discovery or apprehension, except that this paragraph does not apply to a warning given in connection with an effort to bring another into compliance with law; or

(e) volunteers false information to a law enforcement officer.

The offense is a felony of the third degree if the conduct which the actor knows has been charged or is liable to be charged against the person aided would constitute a felony of the first or second degree. Otherwise it is a misdemeanor.

STATUS OF SECTION

Presented to the Institution as Subsection (1) of Section 208.32 of Tentative Draft No. 9, and considered at the May 1959 meeting.

For Commentary, see Tentative Draft No. 9, p. 195.

Paragraph (d) has been amended by adding the exception to take care of cases like fellow-motorists warning speeders to slow down for a speed trap, or a lawyer advising a client to discontinue illegal activities.

Paragraph (e) formerly read: "attempts to mislead law enforcement officers by volunteering information which he knows to be false." The purpose clause at the beginning of the section seems adequate to define the guilty state of mind.

Section 242.4. Aiding Consummation of Crime.

A person commits an offense if he purposely aids another to accomplish an unlawful object of a crime, as by safeguarding the proceeds thereof or converting the proceeds into negotiable funds. The offense is a felony of the third degree if the principal offense was a felony of the first or second degree. Otherwise it is a misdemeanor.

STATUS OF SECTION

Presented to the Institute as Subsection (2) of Section 208.32 in Tentative Draft No. 9, and considered at the May 1959 meeting.

For Commentary, see Tentative Draft No. 9, p. 202.

The Section has been reworded to make it clear that the actor's purpose is to facilitate the consummation of the criminal plan.

Section 242.5. Compounding.

A person commits a misdemeanor if he accepts or agrees to accept any pecuniary benefit in consideration of refraining from reporting to law enforcement authorities the commission or suspected commission of any offense or information relating to an offense. It is an affirmative defense to prosecution under this Section that the pecuniary benefit did not exceed an amount which the actor believed to be due as restitution or indemnification for harm caused by the offense.

STATUS OF SECTION

Presented to the Institute as Section 208.32A of Tentative Draft No. 9, and considered at the May 1959 meeting.

For Commentary, see Tentative Draft No. 9, p. 203.

The Section has been limited to "pecuniary" benefits, and the issue of restitution or indemnification has been made an affirmative defense.

Section 242.6. Escape.

(1) Escape. A person commits an offense if he unlawfully removes himself from official detention or fails to return to official detention following temporary leave granted for a specific purpose or limited period. "Official detention" means arrest, detention in any facility for custody of persons under charge or conviction of crime or alleged or found to be delinquent, detention for extradition or deportation, or any other detention for law enforcement purposes; but "official detention" does not include supervision of probation or parole, or constraint incidental to release on bail.

(2) Permitting or Facilitating Escape. A public servant concerned in detention commits an offense if he knowingly or recklessly permits an escape. Any person who knowingly causes or facilitates an escape commits an offense.

(3) Effect of Legal Irregularity in Detention. Irregularity in bringing about or maintaining detention, or lack

of jurisdiction of the committing or detaining authority, shall not be a defense to prosecution under this Section if the escape is from a prison or other custodial facility or from detention pursuant to commitment by official proceedings. In the case of other detentions, irregularity or lack of jurisdiction shall be a defense only if:

(a) the escape involved no substantial risk of harm to the person or property of anyone other than the detainee; or

(b) the detaining authority did not act in good faith under color of law.

(4) Grading of Offenses. An offense under this Section is a felony of the third degree where:

(a) the detainee was under arrest for or detained on a charge of felony or following conviction of crime; or

(b) the actor employs force, threat, deadly weapon or other dangerous instrumentality to effect the escape; or

(c) a public servant concerned in detention of persons convicted of crime purposely facilitates or permits an escape from a detention facility.

Otherwise an offense under this section is a misdemeanor.

STATUS OF SECTION

Presented to the Institute as Section 208.33 of Tentative Draft No. 8, and considered at the May 1958 meeting.

For Commentary, see Tentative Draft No. 8, p. 132.

Paragraph (a) of Subsection (4) has been reworded to make clear the original intent to treat as a felony any escape from arrest for felony. In addition, the phrase "following conviction of crime" alters the substance of the prior draft, which here referred to escapes following conviction of "felony." The effect of this change is to make it felonious to escape from a jail or other place of confinement under a misdemeanor sentence, even though no dangerous means within the contemplation of paragraph (b) is employed.

One of the Reporters presently favors the following substitute for paragraph (a): "the detainee was held following conviction of any crime or on a judicial commitment to answer a charge of any crime." This would mean that a person who escapes from the custody of an arresting officer would be guilty of a misdemeanor only, even though the arrest was for a felony. Conflicting considerations are of course involved. On the one hand, we should like to have severe sanctions against escape of guilty felons from arrest. On the other hand, many are arrested who are innocent or will never be found guilty. It seems harsh to make a felon out of an innocent person who flees from arrest. Moreover, prosecution for escape necessarily occurs only on recapture. If the accused is convicted of the principal offense plus the misdemeanor of escape, the Court and Parole Board will have adequate opportunity to take the escape into consideration in assessing punishment. Escape from arrest would be felonious in any event, under paragraph (b), if force or other dangerous means is employed. The privilege of the policeman to use necessary force to prevent even "non-dangerous" escape would not be impaired.

Section 242.7. Implements for Escape; Other Contraband.

(1) <u>Escape Implements</u>. **A person commits a misdemeanor if he unlawfully introduces within a detention facility, or unlawfully provides an inmate with, any weapon, tool or other thing which may be useful for escape. An inmate commits a misdemeanor if he unlawfully procures, makes, or otherwise provides himself with, or has in his possession, any such implement of escape. "Unlawfully" means surreptitiously or contrary to law, regulation or order of the detaining authority.**

(2) <u>Other Contraband</u>. **A person commits a petty misdemeanor if he provides an inmate with anything which the actor knows it is unlawful for the inmate to possess.**

STATUS OF SECTION

Presented to the Institute as Section 208.34 of Tentative Draft No. 8, and considered at the May 1958 meeting.

For Commentary, see Tentative Draft No. 8, p. 137.

Subsection (1) above restates the substance of Section 208.34 with improvements in form. Subsection (2) has been added to provide a petty sanction against the introduction of gambling paraphernalia, cigarettes, liquor and other things forbidden to inmates. This Subsection will be a useful adjunct to Subsection (1) where there is any doubt that the object "may be useful for escape."

Section 242.8. Bail Jumping; Default in Required Appearance.

A person set at liberty by court order, with or without bail, upon condition that he will subsequently appear at a specified time and place, commits a misdemeanor if, without lawful excuse, he fails to appear at that time and place. The offense constitutes a felony of the third degree where the required appearance was to answer to a charge of felony, or for disposition of any such charge, and the actor took flight or went into hiding to avoid apprehension, trial or punishment. This Section does not apply to obligations to appear incident to release under suspended sentence or on probation or parole.

STATUS OF SECTION

Presented to the Institute as Section 208.35 of Tentative Draft No. 8, and considered at the May 1958 meeting.

For Commentary, see Tentative Draft No. 8, p. 138.

ARTICLE 243. ABUSE OF OFFICE

Section 243.0. Definitions.

In this Article, unless a different meaning plainly is required, the definitions given in Section 240.0 apply.

Section 243.1. Official Oppression.

A person acting or purporting to act in an official capacity or taking advantage of such actual or purported capacity commits a misdemeanor if, knowing that his conduct is illegal, he:

    (a) subjects another to arrest, detention, search, seizure, mistreatment, dispossession, assessment, lien or other infringement of personal or property rights; or

    (b) denies or impedes another in the exercise or enjoyment of any right, privilege, power or immunity.

STATUS OF SECTION

Presented to the Institute as Section 208.40 of Tentative Draft No. 9, and considered at the May 1959 meeting.

For Commentary, see Tentative Draft No. 9, p. 212.

Minor verbal changes have been made.

Section 243.2. Speculating or Wagering on Official Action or Information.

A public servant commits a misdemeanor if, in contemplation of official action by himself or by a governmental unit with which he is associated, or in reliance on information to which he has access in his official capacity and which has not been made public, he:

(1) acquires a pecuniary interest in any property, transaction or enterprise which may be affected by such information or official action; or

(2) speculates or wagers on the basis of such information or official action; or

(3) aids another to do any of the foregoing.

STATUS OF SECTION

Presented to the Institute as Section 208.18 of Tentative Draft No. 8, and considered at the May 1958 meeting.

For Commentary, see Tentative Draft No. 8, p. 118.

The Section has been revised by consolidating into Subsection (2) three Subsections which ran as follows in the tentative draft:

(2) he sells short any commodity or security, or makes any other business commitment which will be affected by the contemplated official action or by public release of the information; or

(3) he speculates in any other way in the matter, transaction or enterprise which is the subject of such information or official action; or

(4) he wagers upon such action or information . . .

OFFENSES AGAINST PUBLIC ORDER AND DECENCY

ARTICLE 250. RIOT, DISORDERLY CONDUCT, AND RELATED OFFENSES

Section 250.1. Riot; Failure to Disperse.

(1) Riot. A person is guilty of riot, a felony of the third degree, if he participates with [two] or more others in a course of disorderly conduct:

    (a) with purpose to commit or facilitate the commission of a felony or misdemeanor;

    (b) with purpose to prevent or coerce official action; or

    (c) when the actor or any other participant to the knowledge of the actor uses or plans to use a firearm or other deadly weapon.

(2) Failure of Disorderly Persons to Disperse Upon Official Order. Where [three] or more persons are participating in a course of disorderly conduct likely to cause substantial harm or serious inconvenience, annoyance or alarm, a peace officer or other public servant engaged in executing or enforcing the law may order the participants and others in the immediate vicinity to disperse. A person who refuses or knowingly fails to obey such an order commits a misdemeanor.

STATUS OF SECTION

Presented to the Institute as Subsections (2) and (3) of Section 250.1 of Tentative Draft No. 13, and considered at the May 1961 meeting.

Art. 250 § 250.2

For Commentary, see Tentative Draft No. 13, p. 18.

It seemed appropriate to begin Article 250 with a separate section dealing with this category of aggravated disorderly conduct.

Subsection (2) concerning dispersal orders formerly was cast in terms of an order to "desist or disperse." It now seems preferable to omit the reference to desistance for the following reasons. The actual participants in the disorderly conduct are subject to penalty apart from any order, so the Subsection mainly affects "others in the immediate vicinity." It is meaningless to order them to "desist or disperse" since by hypothesis they are not engaged in the disorderly conduct.

Section 250.2. Disorderly Conduct.

(1) <u>Offense Defined</u>. **A person is guilty of disorderly conduct if, with purpose to cause public inconvenience, annoyance or alarm, or recklessly creating a risk thereof, he:**

    (a) engages in fighting or threatening, or in violent or tumultuous behavior; or

    (b) makes unreasonable noise or offensively coarse utterance, gesture or display, or addresses abusive language to any person present; or

    (c) creates a hazardous or physically offensive condition by any act which serves no legitimate purpose of the actor.

"Public" means affecting or likely to affect persons in a place to which the public or a substantial group has access; among the places included are highways, transport facilities, schools, prisons, apartment houses, places of business or amusement, or any neighborhood.

(2) <u>Grading</u>. **An offense under this section is a petty misdemeanor if the actor's purpose is to cause substantial harm or serious inconvenience, or if he persists in disorderly**

conduct after reasonable warning or request to desist. Otherwise disorderly conduct is a violation.

STATUS OF SECTION

Presented to the Institute in Sections 250.1 and 250.8 of Tentative Draft No. 13, and considered at the May 1961 meeting.

For Commentary, see Tentative Draft No. 13, pp. 4, 52.

Verbal changes have been made, including the adoption of "offensively coarse" in clause (b) of Subsection (1) to characterize the category of utterances which embarrass or shock by needless vulgarity of expression. "Coarse" alone is insufficient since in many groups and settings coarse language is not offensive to the hearers.

Section 250.3. False Public Alarms.

A person is guilty of a misdemeanor if he initiates or circulates a report or warning of an impending bombing or other crime or catastrophe, knowing that the report or warning is false or baseless and that it is likely to cause evacuation of a building, place of assembly, or facility of public transport, or to cause public inconvenience or alarm.

STATUS OF SECTION

Presented to the Institute as Section 250.8 of Tentative Draft No. 13, and considered at the May 1961 meeting.

Minor revisions have been made.

For Commentary, see Tentative Draft No. 13, p. 52.

Note that Section 211.3—*Terroristic Threats* provides felony penalties for the person who himself threatens to commit the crime, which threat is likely to cause public inconvenience.

Section 250.4. Harassment.

A person commits a petty misdemeanor if, with purpose to harass another, he:

    (a) makes a telephone call without purpose of legitimate communication; or

(b) insults, taunts or challenges another in a manner likely to provoke violent or disorderly response; or

(c) makes repeated communications anonymously or at extremely inconvenient hours, or in offensively coarse language; or

(d) engages in any other course of harmful conduct serving no legitimate purpose of the actor.

STATUS OF SECTION

Presented to the Institute as Section 250.9 of Tentative Draft No. 13, and considered at the May 1961 meeting.

For Commentary, see Tentative Draft No. 13, p. 52.

The Section has been revised to take account of criticism of the earlier draft because it proscribed only "repeated" telephone conversations, thus failing to reach the culprit caught making a single abusive call, or one who calls several people indiscriminately but none repeatedly.

That portion of the previous draft which dealt with threat or menace of unlawful bodily harm has been deleted in view of the scope of Section 211.3, covering threats generally.

Section 250.5. Public Drunkenness; Drug Incapacitation.

A person is guilty of an offense if he appears in any public place manifestly under the influence of alcohol, narcotics or other drug, not therapeutically administered, to the degree that he may endanger himself or other persons or property, or annoy persons in his vicinity. An offense under this Section constitutes a petty misdemeanor if the actor has been convicted hereunder twice before within a period of one year. Otherwise the offense constitutes a violation.

STATUS OF SECTION

Presented to the Institute as Section 250.11 of Tentative Draft No. 13, and considered at the May 1961 meeting.

For Commentary, see Tentative Draft No. 13, p. 56.

The Section has been revised by adding the phrase referring to therapeutic administration, and by dropping a clause which classified public drunkenness as a petty misdemeanor where "the actor does anything that would violate this article if done purposely." The object of the latter clause, which was obscure, was to authorize the misdemeanor sanction for obstreperous drunks who might not be aware that their actions were creating general annoyance or alarm. But, under revised Section 250.2—*Disorderly Conduct,* recklessness suffices for conviction, and persistence in disorderly conduct after reasonable warning makes the offense a petty misdemeanor. Intoxication normally suffices to establish recklessness. See Section 2.08(2) supra p. 38. Thus adequate penalties for the "drunk and disorderly" are available under Section 250.2.

Section 250.6. Loitering or Prowling.

A person commits a violation if he loiters or prowls in a place, at a time, or in a manner not usual for law-abiding individuals under circumstances that warrant alarm for the safety of persons or property in the vicinity. Among the circumstances which may be considered in determining whether such alarm is warranted is the fact that the actor takes flight upon appearance of a peace officer, refuses to identify himself, or manifestly endeavors to conceal himself or any object. Unless flight by the actor or other circumstance makes it impracticable, a peace officer shall prior to any arrest for an offense under this section afford the actor an opportunity to dispel any alarm which would otherwise be warranted, by requesting him to identify himself and explain his presence and conduct. No person shall be convicted of an offense under this Section if the peace officer did not comply with the preceding sentence, or if it appears at trial that the explanation given by the actor was true and, if believed by the peace officer at the time, would have dispelled the alarm.

STATUS OF SECTION

Presented to the Institute as Section 250.12 of Tentative Draft No. 13, and considered at the May 1961 meeting.

For Commentary, see Tentative Draft No. 13, p. 60.

The principal developments in the Section since Tentative Draft No. 13 are as follows. We have changed the basis of the offense from justifiable "suspicion" that the actor was engaged or about to engage in crime, to justifiable "alarm" for the safety of persons or property. This seems desirable to save the section from attack and possible invalidation as a subterfuge by which the police would be empowered to arrest and search without probable cause.

A second change is the requirement that the peace officer give the actor an opportunity to "dispel any alarm which would otherwise be warranted." Under prior drafts, failure to respond to police requests for identification and explanation were circumstances which might be taken into account in determining whether suspicion or alarm was warranted; but if there was enough without that to justify alarm, the policeman was entitled to arrest (and therefore incidentally search) even though a moment's delay for inquiry would have elicited an explanation which would have satisfied him.

The final clause of the Section takes account of the fact that an incredible but true explanation may be given to the policeman. An arrest may be justified; but when it is subsequently made to appear that, despite the alarming circumstances and the incredible explanation, defendant was in fact engaged in lawful business or other activity, he ought not to be convicted. Indeed, the record of his arrest ought to be expunged.

Section 250.7. Obstructing Highways and Other Public Passages.

(1) A person, who, having no legal privilege to do so, purposely or recklessly obstructs any highway or other public passage, whether alone or with others, commits a violation, or, in case he persists after warning by a law officer, a petty misdemeanor. "Obstructs" means renders impassable without unreasonable inconvenience or hazard. No person shall be deemed guilty of recklessly obstructing in violation of this Subsection solely because of a gathering of persons to hear him speak or otherwise communicate, or solely because of being a member of such a gathering.

(2) A person in a gathering commits a violation if he refuses to obey a reasonable official request or order to move:

    (a) to prevent obstruction of a highway or other public passage; or

    (b) to maintain public safety by dispersing those gathered in dangerous proximity to a fire or other hazard.

An order to move, addressed to a person whose speech or other lawful behavior attracts an obstructing audience, shall not be deemed reasonable if the obstruction can be readily remedied by police control of the size or location of the gathering.

STATUS OF SECTION

Presented to the Institute as Section 250.2 of Tentative Draft No. 13, and considered at the May 1961 meeting.

For Commentary, see Tentative Draft No. 13, p. 37.

The last word in Subsection (2)(b) has been changed from "emergency" to "hazard," accepting a suggestion made at the meeting.

Section 250.8. Disrupting Meetings and Processions.

A person commits a misdemeanor if, with purpose to prevent or disrupt a lawful meeting, procession or gathering, he does any act tending to obstruct or interfere with it physically, or makes any utterance, gesture or display designed to outrage the sensibilities of the group.

STATUS OF SECTION

Presented to the Institute as Section 250.3 of Tentative Draft No. 13, and considered at the May 1961 meeting.

For Commentary, see Tentative Draft No. 13, p. 38.

The classification of this offense has been raised from petty misdemeanor to misdemeanor. With the reduction of the maximum penalty for petty misdemeanors from 90 to 30 days, the petty misdemeanor sanction seemed disproportionately low for some of the more serious offenses embraced by this section, e.g. disruption of a meeting of a legislature or international conference.

Section 250.9. Desecration of Venerated Objects.

A person commits a misdemeanor if he purposely desecrates any public monument or structure, or place of worship or burial, or if he purposely desecrates the national flag or any other object of veneration by the public or a substantial segment thereof in any public place. "Desecrate" means defacing, damaging, polluting or otherwise physically mistreating in a way that the actor knows will outrage the sensibilities of persons likely to observe or discover his action.

STATUS OF SECTION

Presented to the Institute as Section 250.4 of Tentative Draft No. 13, and considered at the May 1961 meeting.

For Commentary, see Tentative Draft No. 13, p. 39.

In the last sentence, the words "outrage the sensibilities of" replace "seriously offend" in the previous draft.

Section 250.10. Abuse of Corpse.

Except as authorized by law, a person who treats a corpse in a way that he knows would outrage ordinary family sensibilities commits a misdemeanor.

STATUS OF SECTION

Presented to the Institute as Section 250.5 of Tentative Draft No. 13, and considered at the May 1961 meeting.

For Commentary, see Tentative Draft No. 13, p. 40.

The word "outrage" replaces "seriously offend" in the previous draft.

Section 250.11. Cruelty to Animals.

A person commits a petty misdemeanor if he purposely or recklessly:

    (1) subjects any animal to cruel mistreatment; or

    (2) subjects any animal in his custody to cruel neglect; or

    (3) kills or injures any animal belonging to another without legal privilege or consent of the owner.

Subsections (1) and (2) shall not be deemed applicable to accepted veterinary practices and activities carried on for scientific research.

STATUS OF SECTION

Presented to the Institute as Section 250.6 of Tentative Draft No. 13, and considered at the May 1961 meeting.

For Commentary, see Tentative Draft No. 13, p. 40.

Section 250.12. Violation of Privacy.

(1) <u>Unlawful Eavesdropping or Surveillance.</u> A person commits a misdemeanor if, except as authorized by law, he:

    (a) trespasses on property with purpose to subject anyone to eavesdropping or other surveillance in a private place; or

    (b) installs in any private place, without the consent of the person or persons entitled to privacy there, any device for observing, photographing, recording, amplifying or broadcasting sounds or events in such place, or uses any such unauthorized installation; or

    (c) installs or uses outside a private place any device for hearing, recording, amplifying or broadcasting sounds originating in such place which would not ordinarily be audible or comprehensible outside, without the consent of the person or persons entitled to privacy there.

"Private place" means a place where one may reasonably expect to be safe from casual or hostile intrusion or surveillance, but does not include a place to which the public or a substantial group thereof has access.

(2) **Other Breach of Privacy of Messages.** A person commits a misdemeanor if, except as authorized by law, he:

(a) intercepts without the consent of the sender or receiver a message by telephone, telegraph, letter or other means of communicating privately; but this paragraph does not extend to (i) overhearing of messages through a regularly installed instrument on a telephone party line or on an extension, or (ii) interception by the telephone company or subscriber incident to enforcement of regulations limiting use of the facilities or to other normal operation and use; or

(b) divulges without the consent of the sender or receiver the existence or contents of any such message if the actor knows that the message was illegally intercepted, or if he learned of the message in the course of employment with an agency engaged in transmitting it.

STATUS OF SECTION

Presented to the Institute as Section 250.10 of Tentative Draft No. 13, and considered at the May 1961 meeting.

For Commentary, see Tentative Draft No. 13, p. 54.

The Section has been substantially revised.

Private place was formerly defined as "any home, office, vehicle, or quarters whose occupant may reasonably expect to be safe, etc." It was objected that many structures other than homes and offices are equally entitled to protection against prying intrusion. The reformulation, therefore, encompasses all places where a person would reasonably expect privacy, except that a highway or open land, or a store or other place where people congregate, does not become a "private place" for purposes of this Section merely because an individual believes himself to be alone there.

§ 250.12

The exceptions articulated in Subsection (2)(a) are new. Idle eavesdropping is annoying but not usually harmful, and the risk is well known to users of telephone party lines and extensions. Particularly obnoxious abuse of privilege can usually be remedied by administrative action of the telephone company. At most, a legislature might wish to proscribe minor misbehavior of this sort as a petty violation, by provision in the code regulating communications rather than in the penal code.

As to interception by the subscriber, dealt with in Subsection (2)(a)(ii), we are taking the position that subscribers may monitor calls on their lines for the purpose, for example, of determining whether forbidden personal or toll calls are being made. A wiretap by the subscriber would not, however, be lawful if done for such a purpose as securing evidence against a spouse or employee. Thus the Section rejects the result reached in *People v. Appelbaum,* 227 App. Div. 43, 97 N.Y. 2d 807, aff'd per cur. 301 N.Y. 738, 95 N. E. 2d 410 (1950). There the Court, construing a statute prohibiting "unlawful" tapping, as applied to a man who had his own phone tapped "to vindicate his paramount rights in respect of marital status," declared:

> The protection of a right of privacy may be subordinated where the circumstances disclose the existence of a paramount right and the use of a telephone line is with the permission of and subordinate to the possessor of that paramount right. Such a paramount right is possessed by the subscriber to a telephone line. When such a subscriber consents to the use of his line, by his employee or by a member of his household, or by his wife, there is a condition implied that the telephone will not be used to the detriment of the subscriber's business, household or marital status. Or the use may be expressly made the subject of such a condition or conditions. In such situations the subscriber may determine if his line is being used to his detriment by those whom he permits to use it. To this end he may have his own line tapped or otherwise checked so that his business may not be damaged, his household relations impaired or his marital status disrupted. When a subscriber exercises this paramount right, the one using the line subject to the implied conditions stated, is using it with the presumed understanding that his otherwise inviolate right of privacy to that extent may be invaded. Such a view preserves the paramount right of the subscriber to determine whether or not a basis exists for discipline in his business, in his household, or for action to protect his marital status.

In 1951 New York enacted §738 of the Penal Law penalizing the use of instruments to overhear and record telephone conversations by anyone other than the "sender or receiver" of the communication.

ARTICLE 251. PUBLIC INDECENCY

Section 251.1. Open Lewdness.

A person commits a petty misdemeanor if he does any lewd act which he knows is likely to be observed by others who would be affronted or alarmed.

STATUS OF SECTION

Presented to the Institute in Tentative Draft No. 13, and considered at the May 1961 meeting.

For Commentary, see Tentative Draft No. 13, p. 82.

Section 251.2. Prostitution and Related Offenses.

(1) Prostitution. A person is guilty of prostitution, a pettty misdemeanor, if he or she:

(a) is an inmate of a house of prostitution or otherwise engages in sexual activity as a business; or

(b) loiters in or within view of any public place for the purpose of being hired to engage in sexual activity.

"Sexual activity" includes homosexual and other deviate sexual relations. A "house of prostitution" is any place where prostitution or promotion of prostitution is regularly carried on by one person under the control, management or supervision of another. An "inmate" is a person who engages in prostitution in or through the agency of a house of prostitution. "Public place" means any place to which the public or any substantial group thereof has access.

(2) Promoting Prostitution. A person who knowingly promotes prostitution of another commits a misdemeanor or felony as provided in Subsection (3). The following acts

shall, without limitation of the foregoing, constitute promoting prostitution:

    (a) owning, controlling, managing, supervising or otherwise keeping, alone or in association with others, a house of prostitution or a prostitution business; or

    (b) procuring an inmate for a house of prostitution or a place in a house of prostitution for one who would be an inmate; or

    (c) encouraging, inducing, or otherwise purposely causing another to become or remain a prostitute; or

    (d) soliciting a person to patronize a prostitute; or

    (e) procuring a prostitute for a patron; or

    (f) transporting a person into or within this state with purpose to promote that person's engaging in prostitution, or procuring or paying for transportation with that purpose; or

    (g) leasing or otherwise permitting a place controlled by the actor, alone or in association with others, to be regularly used for prostitution or the promotion of prostitution, or failure to make reasonable effort to abate such use by ejecting the tenant, notifying law enforcement authorities, or other legally available means; or

    (h) soliciting, receiving, or agreeing to receive any benefit for doing or agreeing to do anything forbidden by this Subsection.

(3) **Grading of Offenses Under Subsection (2).** An offense under Subsection (2) constitutes a felony of the third degree if:

    (a) the offense falls within paragraph (a), (b) or (c) of Subsection (2); or

Art. 251 § 251.2

(b) the actor compels another to engage in or promote prostitution; or

(c) the actor promotes prostitution of a child under 16, whether or not he is aware of the child's age; or

(d) the actor promotes prostitution of his wife, child, ward or any person for whose care, protection or support he is responsible.

Otherwise the offense is a misdemeanor.

(4) <u>Presumption from Living off Prostitutes</u>. A person, other than the prostitute or the prostitute's minor child or other legal dependent incapable of self-support, who is supported in whole or substantial part by the proceeds of prostitution is presumed to be knowingly promoting prostitution in violation of Subsection (2).

(5) <u>Patronizing Prostitutes</u>. A person commits a violation if he hires a prostitute to engage in sexual activity with him, or if he enters or remains in a house of prostitution for the purpose of engaging in sexual activity.

(6) <u>Evidence</u>. On the issue whether a place is a house of prostitution the following shall be admissible evidence: its general repute; the repute of the persons who reside in or frequent the place; the frequency, timing and duration of visits by non-residents. Testimony of a person against his spouse shall be admissible to prove offenses under this Section.

STATUS OF SECTION

Presented to the Institute as Section 207.12 of Tentative Draft No. 9, and considered at the May 1959 meeting.

For Commentary, see Tentative Draft No. 9, p. 169.

The Section was recommitted for further consideration of the position taken in the British Street Offences Act, 1959, 7 & 8 Eliz. 2,

c. 57, strongly favored by Mr. Bethuel Webster and others, that prostitution should not be penalized except as carried on by solicitation in public places. Judge Breitel and others who opposed this position emphasized the importance of repressing the "private" house of prostitution and the "call girl," as profitable elements in organized crime.

Subsection (1) has been revised to meet in part the views of those who are skeptical of the propriety or utility of using the criminal law to repress individual immorality. It no longer purports to reach every engagement in sexual activity for hire. Thus, the possibility of applying the Section to the private mistress whose lover contributes to her support is now excluded. But we adhere, in paragraph (a), to the position of the previous draft that professional prostitution is criminal even if carried on in private. Paragraph (b) adopts the idea that prostitution is also to be repressed when it manifests itself in public solicitation, which may be an annoyance to passersby and an outrage to the moral sensibilities of a large part of the public.

There has been dropped from Subsection (1) language in the previous draft penalizing entry into the state or locality with purpose to engage in prostitution. The attempt provisions of the General Part of this Code adequately cover such inchoate criminal activity.

We have eliminated from Subsection (5) a presumption that a person in a house of prostitution was there for the purpose of patronizing a prostitute. Some members of the Institute objected to it as unnecessary, and it might be harmful if invoked defensively by someone who was present in the house of prostitution in the capacity of operator of the criminal enterprise.

Section 251.3. Loitering to Solicit Deviate Sexual Relations.

A person is guilty of a petty misdemeanor if he loiters in or near any public place for the purpose of soliciting or being solicited to engage in deviate sexual relations.

STATUS OF SECTION

This Section is derived from Subsection (4) of Section 207.5, Tentative Draft No. 4, considered at the May 1955 meeting.

For Commentary, see Tentative Draft No. 4, p. 281.

The earlier version covered deviate sexual intercourse in private, as well as public solicitation. The Institute voted in favor of the

Reporters' recommendation that the Model Penal Code should not extend to private acts not involving force, imposition or corrupting of the young. See Tentative Draft No. 4, p. 276.

The earlier draft dealt with solicitation "in any public place." It did not require "loitering," but excluded solicitation of one with whom the actor had "no previous acquaintance." The object was to preclude application of the statute to purely private conversations between persons having an established intimacy, even if the conversations occur in a public place. The present draft is more clearly directed to indiscriminate seeking or making one's self available for deviate sexual relations.

The principal issue raised in discussion of the present draft was whether to require proof that the solicitation was "for hire," as in the Section on prostitution. Section 251.2(1)(b). The present Section would be superfluous if hire must be shown here, since Section 251.1 penalizes prostitution without regard to whether the sexual relation is normal or deviate.

Those who favored the present Section notwithstanding the apparent inconsistency with the policy of Section 251.2(1)(b) did so upon the ground that the main objective is to suppress the open flouting of prevailing moral standards as a sort of nuisance in public thoroughfares and parks. In the case of females, suppression of professionals is likely to accomplish that objective. In the case of males, there is a greater likelihood that non-professional homosexuals will congregate and behave in a manner grossly offensive to other users of public facilities.

Section 251.4. Obscenity.

(1) **Obscene Defined.** Material is obscene if, considered as a whole, its predominant appeal is to prurient interest, that is, a shameful or morbid interest, in nudity, sex or excretion, and if in addition it goes substantially beyond customary limits of candor in describing or representing such matters. Predominant appeal shall be judged with reference to ordinary adults unless it appears from the character of the material or the circumstances of its dissemination to be designed for children or other specially susceptible audience. Undeveloped photographs, molds, printing plates, and the like, shall be deemed obscene notwithstanding that

processing or other acts may be required to make the obscenity patent or to disseminate it.

(2) Offenses. Subject to the affirmative defense provided in Subsection (3), a person commits a misdemeanor if he knowingly or recklessly:

(a) sells, delivers or provides, or offers or agrees to sell, deliver or provide, any obscene writing, picture, record or other representation or embodiment of the obscene; or

(b) presents or directs an obscene play, dance or performance, or participates in that portion thereof which makes it obscene; or

(c) publishes, exhibits or otherwise makes available any obscene material; or

(d) possesses any obscene material for purposes of sale or other commercial dissemination; or

(e) sells, advertises or otherwise commercially disseminates material, whether or not obscene, by representing or suggesting that it is obscene.

A person who disseminates or possesses obscene material in the course of his business is presumed to do so knowingly or recklessly.

(3) Justifiable and Non-Commercial Private Dissemination. It is an affirmative defense to prosecution under this Section that dissemination was restricted to:

(a) institutions or persons having scientific, educational, governmental or other similar justification for possessing obscene material; or

(b) non-commercial dissemination to personal associates of the actor.

(4) Evidence; Adjudication of Obscenity. In any prosecution under this Section evidence shall be admissible to show:

    (a) the character of the audience for which the material was designed or to which it was directed;

    (b) what the predominant appeal of the material would be for ordinary adults or any special audience to which it was directed, and what effect, if any, it would probably have on conduct of such people;

    (c) artistic, literary, scientific, educational or other merits of the material;

    (d) the degree of public acceptance of the material in the United States;

    (e) appeal to prurient interest, or absence thereof, in advertising or other promotion of the material; and

    (f) the good repute of the author, creator, publisher or other person from whom the material originated.

Expert testimony and testimony of the author, creator, publisher or other person from whom the material originated, relating to factors entering into the determination of the issue of obscenity, shall be admissible. The Court shall dismiss a prosecution for obscenity if it is satisfied that the material is not obscene.

STATUS OF SECTION

Presented to the Institute as Section 207.10 of Tentative Draft No. 6, and considered at the May 1957 meeting.

For Commentary, see Tentative Draft No. 6, p. 5.

A number of changes in form, and some of substance, have been introduced.

The present text does not include an alternative formulation of the offense which appeared in Tentative Draft No. 6, but was voted

§ 251.4   240   Model Penal Code

down by the Institute. Under that alternative the offense would have been defined as "pandering to an interest in obscenity." This proposal and discussion of it will be included in Commentary.

The crucial definition of the term "obscene" has now been placed in the first Subsection. Minor verbal changes have been made. The word "public" has been inserted in the phrase "beyond customary limits of candor in public representation." This only makes explicit what was intended before.

In the present version all offenses have been grouped in Subsection (2). Formerly paragraph (d) appeared as a separate Subsection (5), and paragraph (e) as a separate Subsection (6). Paragraph (d) is limited to "possession," whereas formerly there was reference also to "create, buy, procure" as well as "possess." The extra terms seem superfluous: creating, buying and procuring will normally result in possession, and, where they do not, the actor can frequently be prosecuted on the basis of actual or attempted dissemination. Paragraph (e) prohibits "representing or suggesting" rather than "representing or holding out," as before, with no change in intended meaning.

The explicit requirement of knowledge or recklessness, in Subsection (2), together with the presumption stated at the end of the Subsection, state in a clearer way the intent of the former draft. See Subsection (7) of Section 207.10 of Tentative Draft No. 6, and the culpability requirements made applicable generally to offenses under this Code by Section 2.02. It should be noted that, as between the two alternatives posed in Subsection (7) of the earlier draft, the Institute voted in favor of the rebuttable presumption and against placing the burden of proof upon the defendant to establish that he did not act knowingly or recklessly.

Subsection (3) corresponds to Subsection (4) of former Section 207.10; but paragraphs (a) and (b) of the former draft have been consolidated as paragraph (b) of the present proposal. In the process of consolidation, we have given up some substantive distinctions about which doubts were expressed in earlier discussion. Thus, former Section 207.10(4) prohibited non-gainful dissemination to personal associates: (i) under 16, and (ii) between 16 and 21 if the disseminator more than four years older than the recipient. It was objected against these provisions that they left nominally within reach of the law acts of parents in relation to their children and that commercial exploitation was the real evil to be policed. Tentative Draft No. 4 placed the burden of proof on the person asserting a defense under this Section. This departure from normal proof requirements in criminal prosecutions has now been abandoned.

Subsection (4) incorporates parts of former Subsections (2) and (3). Paragraph (f) has been revised to eliminate "purpose" of the author as a subject of inquiry, and to restrict the "repute" issue to "good repute". The former change was directed by the Institute. The latter change was suggested by an inquiry of Judge Goodrich whether evidence of the general bad repute of an author or publisher might be made part of the state's case in prosecuting a bookseller. The present draft precludes that possibility. Of course evidence of good repute may be rebutted.

The last sentence of Subsection (4), relating to an independent determination by the Court on the issue of obscenity, derives from former Subsection (3) which was tentatively disapproved by a close vote of the Institute. The present version is much simplified and omits provisions, to which most objections were voiced, for judges to consult behavioral scientists and for written submissions by these consultants. What we preserve in the present draft is the independent judgment of the court on the question of obscenity without impairing defendant's right to a jury trial. This is desirable in order to promote statewide uniformity of standards in this critical area. The action of the Supreme Court of the United States in a series of obscenity cases after the Roth decision indicates the large extent to which the question of obscenity is one of law in any case, because of the application of the First Amendment.

ADDITIONAL ARTICLES.

[At this point, a State enacting a new Penal Code may insert additional Articles dealing with special topics such as narcotics, alcoholic beverages, gambling and offenses against tax and trade laws. The Model Penal Code project did not extend to these, partly because a higher priority on limited time and resources was accorded to branches of the penal law which have not received close legislative scrutiny. Also, in legislation dealing with narcotics, liquor, tax evasion, and the like, penal provisions have been so intermingled with regulatory and procedural provisions that the task of segregating one group from the other presents special difficulty for model legislation.]

PART III. TREATMENT AND CORRECTION

ARTICLE 301. SUSPENSION OF SENTENCE; PROBATION

Section 301.1. Conditions of Suspension or Probation.

(1) When the Court suspends the imposition of sentence on a person who has been convicted of a crime or sentences him to be placed on probation, it shall attach such reasonable conditions, authorized by this Section, as it deems necessary to insure that he will lead a law-abiding life or likely to assist him to do so.

(2) The Court, as a condition of its order, may require the defendant:

(a) to meet his family responsibilities;

(b) to devote himself to a specific employment or occupation;

(c) to undergo available medical or psychiatric treatment and to enter and remain in a specified institution, when required for that purpose;

(d) to pursue a prescribed secular course of study or vocational training;

(e) to attend or reside in a facility established for the instruction, recreation or residence of persons on probation;

(f) to refrain from frequenting unlawful or disreputable places or consorting with disreputable persons;

(g) to have in his possession no firearm or other dangerous weapon unless granted written permission;

(h) to make restitution of the fruits of his crime or to make reparation, in an amount he can afford to pay, for the loss or damage caused thereby;

(i) to remain within the jurisdiction of the Court and to notify the Court or the probation officer of any change in his address or his employment;

(j) to report as directed to the Court or the probation officer and to permit the officer to visit his home;

(k) to post a bond, with or without surety, conditioned on the performance of any of the foregoing obligations;

(l) to satisfy any other conditions reasonably related to the rehabilitation of the defendant and not unduly restrictive of his liberty or incompatible with his freedom of conscience.

[(3) When the Court sentences a person who has been convicted of a felony or misdemeanor to be placed on probation, it may require him to serve a term of imprisonment not exceeding thirty days as an additional condition of its order. The term of imprisonment imposed hereunder shall be treated as part of the term of probation, and in the event of a sentence of imprisonment upon the revocation of probation, the term of imprisonment served hereunder shall not be credited toward service of such subsequent sentence.]

(4) The defendant shall be given a copy of this Article and written notice of any requirements imposed pursuant to this Section, stated with sufficient specificity to enable him to guide himself accordingly.

§ 301.2

STATUS OF SECTION

Presented to the Institute in Tentative Draft No. 2 and considered at the May 1954 meeting.

Reprinted in Tentative Draft No. 4.

Subsection (2)(g) was revised to conform conditions of probation with conditions of parole in Section 305.13.

Subsection (3) was added as an optional provision. See note respecting Section 6.02(3)(b), *supra* p. 92.

Resubmitted to the Institute in Proposed Final Draft No. 1 and approved at the May 1961 meeting.

For Commentary, see Tentative Draft No. 2, p. 141.

Section 301.2. Period of Suspension or Probation; Modification of Conditions; Discharge of Defendant.

(1) When the Court has suspended sentence or has sentenced a defendant to be placed on probation, the period of the suspension or probation shall be five years upon conviction of a felony or two years upon conviction of a misdemeanor or a petty misdemeanor, unless the defendant is sooner discharged by order of the Court. The Court, on application of a probation officer or of the defendant, or on its own motion, may discharge the defendant at any time. On conviction of a violation, a suspended sentence constitutes an unconditional discharge.

(2) During the period of the suspension or probation, the Court, on application of a probation officer or of the defendant, or on its own motion, may modify the requirements imposed on the defendant or add further requirements authorized by Section 301.1. The Court shall eliminate any requirement that imposes an unreasonable burden on the defendant.

(3) Upon the termination of the period of suspension or probation or the earlier discharge of the defendant, the defendant shall be relieved of any obligations imposed by the order of the Court and shall have satisfied his sentence for the crime.

STATUS OF SECTION

Presented to the Institute in Tentative Draft No. 4 and considered at the May 1954 meeting.

Reprinted in Tentative Draft No. 4.

Resubmitted to the Institute in Proposed Final Draft No. 1 and approved at the May 1961 meeting.

The last sentence of Subsection (1) has been added to remove an ambiguity as to the effect of suspending sentence on conviction of a violation.

For Commentary, see Tentative Draft No. 2, p. 146.

Section 301.3. Summons or Arrest of Defendant Under Suspended Sentence or on Probation; Commitment Without Bail; Revocation and Resentence.

(1) At any time before the discharge of the defendant or the termination of the period of suspension or probation:

(a) the Court may summon the defendant to appear before it or may issue a warrant for his arrest;

(b) a probation or peace officer, having probable cause to believe that the defendant has failed to comply with a requirement imposed as a condition of the order or that he has committed another crime, may arrest him without a warrant;

(c) the Court, if there is probable cause to believe that the defendant has committed another crime or if he has been held to answer therefor, may commit him without bail, pending a determination of the charge by the Court having jurisdiction thereof;

(d) the Court, if satisfied that the defendant has inexcusably failed to comply with a substantial requirement imposed as a condition of the order or if he has been convicted of another crime, may revoke the suspension or probation and sentence or re-sentence the defendant, as provided in this Section.

(2) When the Court revokes a suspension or probation, it may impose on the defendant any sentence that might have been imposed originally for the crime of which he was convicted, except that the defendant shall not be sentenced to imprisonment unless:

 (a) he has been convicted of another crime; or

 (b) his conduct indicates that his continued liberty involves undue risk that he will commit another crime; or

 (c) such disposition is essential to vindicate the authority of the Court.

STATUS OF SECTION

Presented to the Institute in Tentative Draft No. 2 and considered at the May 1954 meeting.

Reprinted in Tentative Draft No. 4.

Verbal changes were made in paragraphs (2)(b) and (c) with the approval of the Council at its March 1957 meeting.

Resubmitted to the Institute in Proposed Final Draft No. 1 and approved at the May 1961 meeting.

For Commentary, see Tentative Draft No. 2, p. 149.

Section 301.4. Notice and Hearing on Revocation or Modification of Conditions of Suspension or Probation.

The Court shall not revoke a suspension or probation or increase the requirements imposed thereby on the defendant except after a hearing upon written notice to the defendant of the grounds on which such action is proposed. The defendant shall have the right to hear and controvert the evidence against him, to offer evidence in his defense and to be represented by counsel.

STATUS OF SECTION

Presented to the Institute in Tentative Draft No. 2 and considered at the May 1954 meeting.

Reprinted in Tentative Draft No. 4.

Resubmitted to the Institute in Proposed Final Draft No. 1 and approved at the May 1961 meeting.

For Commentary, see Tentative Draft No. 2, p. 152.

[Section 301.5. Order Removing Disqualification or Disability Based on Conviction.

(1) When the Court has suspended sentence or has sentenced the defendant to be placed on probation and the defendant has fully complied with the requirements imposed as a condition of such order and has satisfied the sentence, the Court may order that so long as the defendant is not convicted of another crime, the judgment shall not constitute a conviction for the purpose of any disqualification or disability imposed by law upon conviction of a crime.

(2) Proof of a conviction as relevant evidence upon the trial or determination of any issue or for the purpose of impeaching the defendant as a witness is not a disqualification or disability within the meaning of this Section.]

STATUS OF SECTION

Presented to the Institute in Tentative Draft No. 2 and considered at the May 1954 meeting.

Reprinted in Tentative Draft No. 4.

Resubmitted to the Institute in Proposed Final Draft No. 1 and approved at the May 1961 meeting.

This Section should be eliminated if Section 306.6, dealing with removal of disabilities generally, is adopted.

For Commentary, see Tentative Draft No. 2, p. 153.

Section 301.6. Suspension or Probation Is Final Judgment for Other Purposes.

A judgment suspending sentence or sentencing a defendant to be placed on probation shall be deemed tentative, to the extent provided in this Article, but for all other purposes shall constitute a final judgment.

STATUS OF SECTION

Presented to the Institute in Tentative Draft No. 2 and considered at the May 1954 meeting.

Reprinted in Tentative Draft No. 4.

Resubmitted to the Institute in Proposed Final Draft No. 1 and approved at the May 1961 meeting.

For Commentary, see Tentative Draft No. 2, p. 155.

ARTICLE 302. FINES

Section 302.1. Time and Method of Payment; Disposition of Funds.

(1) When a defendant is sentenced to pay a fine, the Court may grant permission for the payment to be made within a specified period of time or in specified installments. If no such permission is embodied in the sentence, the fine shall be payable forthwith.

(2) When a defendant sentenced to pay a fine is also sentenced to probation, the Court may make the payment of the fine a condition of probation.

(3) The defendant shall pay a fine or any installment thereof to the [insert appropriate agency of the State or local subdivision]. In the event of default in payment, such agency shall take appropriate action for its collection.

(4) Unless otherwise provided by law, all fines collected shall be paid over to the [State Department of Taxation and Finance] and shall become part of the general funds of the State and shall be subject to general appropriation.

STATUS OF SECTION

Submitted to the Institute in Proposed Final Draft No. 1 and approved at the May 1961 meeting.

Section 302.2. Consequences of Non-Payment; Imprisonment for Contumacious Non-Payment; Summary Collection.

(1) When a defendant sentenced to pay a fine defaults in the payment thereof or of any installment, the Court, upon the motion of [insert appropriate agency of the State or local subdivision] or upon its own motion, may require

him to show cause why his default should not be treated as contumacious and may issue a summons or a warrant of arrest for his appearance. Unless the defendant shows that his default was not attributable to a willful refusal to obey the order of the Court, or to a failure on his part to make a good faith effort to obtain the funds required for the payment, the Court shall find that his default was contumacious and may order him committed until the fine or a specified part thereof is paid. The term of imprisonment for such contumacious non-payment of the fine shall be specified in the order of commitment and shall not exceed one day for each [five] dollars of the fine, thirty days if the fine was imposed upon conviction of a violation or a petty misdemeanor or one year in any other case, whichever is the shorter period. When a fine is imposed on a corporation or an unincorporated association, it is the duty of the person or persons authorized to make disbursements from the assets of the corporation or association to pay it from such assets and their failure so to do may be held contumacious under this Subsection. A person committed for non-payment of a fine shall be given credit towards its payment for each day of imprisonment, at the rate specified in the order of commitment.

(2) If it appears that the defendant's default in the payment of a fine is not contumacious, the Court may make an order allowing the defendant additional time for payment, reducing the amount thereof or of each installment, or revoking the fine or the unpaid portion thereof in whole or in part.

(3) Upon any default in the payment of a fine or any installment thereof, execution may be levied and such other measures may be taken for the collection of the fine or the unpaid balance thereof as are authorized for the collection of an unpaid civil judgment entered against the defendant in an action on a debt. The levy of execution for the col-

lection of a fine shall not discharge a defendant committed to imprisonment for non-payment of the fine until the amount of the fine has actually been collected.

STATUS OF SECTION

Submitted to the Institute in Proposed Final Draft No. 1 and approved at the May 1961 meeting.

The next to the last sentence in Subsection (1) has been added to deal with fines imposed on corporations or associations.

Section 302.3. Revocation of Fine.

A defendant who has been sentenced to pay a fine and who is not in contumacious default in the payment thereof may at any time petition the Court which sentenced him for a revocation of the fine or of any unpaid portion thereof. If it appears to the satisfaction of the Court that the circumstances which warranted the imposition of the fine have changed, or that it would otherwise be unjust to require payment, the Court may revoke the fine or the unpaid portion thereof in whole or in part.

STATUS OF SECTION

Submitted to the Institute in Proposed Final Draft No. 1 and approved at the May 1961 meeting.

ARTICLE 303. SHORT-TERM IMPRISONMENT

Section 303.1. State and Local Institutions for Short-Term Imprisonment; Review of Adequacy; Joint Use of Institutions; Approval of Plan of New Institutions.

(1) Within the appropriation allotted therefor, the several counties, cities and [other appropriate political subdivisions of the State] and the Department of Correction may construct, equip and maintain suitable buildings, structures and facilities for the operation and for the necessary expansion and diversification of local short-term institutions, including lockups, jails, houses of correction, work farms and such other institutions as may be required for the following purposes:

(a) the custody, control, correctional treatment and rehabilitation of persons sentenced or committed to imprisonment for a fixed term of one year or less;

(b) the custody, control and temporary detention of persons committed to the Department of Correction, until they are removed to the reception center or to another institution in the Department;

(c) the detention of persons charged with crime and committed for hearing or for trial;

(d) the detention of persons committed to secure their attendance as witnesses, and for other detentions authorized by law.

(2) The Director of Correction shall annually review, on the basis of visitation, inspection and reports pursuant to Section 401.11, the adequacy of the institutions for short-term imprisonment in the several counties, cities and [other

appropriate political subdivisions of the State] in the light of the number of persons committed thereto, the physical facilities thereof and programs conducted therein. No later than his next annual report, the Director shall report on any inadequacies of such facilities, including his recommendations for the alteration or expansion of existing institutions, for the construction of new institutions, for the combination of two or more local institutions of the same or of different political subdivisions of the State, or for such other measures to meet the situation as may be appropriate. In making his recommendations, the Director may indicate whether, in his opinion, the alteration, expansion or new construction can best be undertaken by the political subdivisions concerned, or by the Department of Correction.

(3) In reviewing the adequacy of the institutions for short-term imprisonment, the Director of Correction shall consider whether the facilities available in the several political subdivisions of the State afford adequate opportunity for the segregation and classification of prisoners, for the isolation and treatment of ill prisoners, for the treatment of alcoholic and drug-addicted prisoners, for diversified security and custody, and for opportunities for vocational and rehabilitative training.

(4) Upon the recommendation or with the approval of the Director of Correction, counties, cities, and [other appropriate political subdivisions of the State] having institutions for short-term imprisonment may establish joint institutions, or combine two or more existing facilities for short-term imprisonment, and may make such agreements for the sharing of the costs of construction and maintenance as may be authorized by law.

(5) No county, city, or [other appropriate political subdivision of the State] shall construct or establish an institution for short-term imprisonment, unless the plans for

§ 303.2

the establishment and construction of such institution are approved by the Director of Correction.

STATUS OF SECTION

Submitted to the Institute in Proposed Final Draft No. 1 and approved at the May 1961 meeting.

Section 303.2. Records of Prisoners; Classification; Transfer.

(1) **The Warden**, or other administrative head of an institution for short-term imprisonment, shall establish and maintain, in accordance with the regulations of the Department of Correction, a central file in the institution containing an individual file for each prisoner. Each prisoner's file shall as far as practicable include: (a) his admission summary; (b) his pre-sentence investigation report, if any; (c) the official records of his conviction and commitment, as well as earlier criminal records, if any; (d) progress reports from treatment and custodial staff; (e) reports of his disciplinary infractions and of their disposition; and (f) other pertinent data concerning his background, conduct, associations and family relationships. The content of the prisoners' files shall be confidential and shall not be subject to public inspection except by court order for good cause shown and shall not be accessible to prisoners in the institution.

(2) The [governing body of each] county, city [or other appropriate political subdivision of the State] having one or more institutions for short-term imprisonment shall appoint a Classification Committee consisting of [ ] members of the institutional staffs and of qualified citizens of the county, city or [other appropriate political subdivision]. If a physician has been appointed to serve the institutions, he shall be an ex officio member of the Committee.

All committee members shall serve without compensation but shall be paid their necessary expenses.

(3) As soon as practicable after a prisoner who has been sentenced to a definite term of thirty days or more is received in the institution, and no later than the expiration of the first third of his term, the Classification Committee shall study his file and interview him, and shall [determine] [aid the Warden or other administrative head of the institution in determining] the prisoner's program of treatment, training, employment, care and custody. The Classification Committee may also recommend the transfer of the prisoner to another institution which in its opinion is more suitable for him.

(4) The Warden or other administrative head of the institution may, on his own motion or upon the recommendation of the Classification Committee, apply to the Court for an order to transfer the prisoner to another institution for short-term imprisonment, within or outside of the county, city [or other appropriate political subdivision of the State].

STATUS OF SECTION

Submitted to the Institute in Proposed Final Draft No. 1 and approved at the May 1961 meeting.

Section 303.3. Segregation of Prisoners; Segregation and Transfer of Prisoners With Physical or Mental Diseases or Defects.

(1) In institutions for short-term imprisonment the following groups shall be segregated from each other:

    (a) female prisoners from male prisoners; and

    (b) prisoners under the age of twenty-two from older prisoners; and

(c) persons detained for hearing or trial from prisoners under sentence of imprisonment or committed for contumacious default in the payment of fines; and

(d) persons detained for hearing or trial or under sentence from material witnesses and other persons detained under civil commitment.

(2) When an institutional physician finds that a prisoner suffers from a physical disease or defect, or when an institutional physician or psychologist finds that a prisoner suffers from a mental disease or defect, the Warden or other administrative head may order such prisoner to be segregated from other prisoners, and if the physician or psychologist, as the case may be, is of the opinion that he cannot be given proper treatment at that institution, the Warden or other administrative head may transfer him to another institution in the county, city or [other appropriate political subdivision of the State] where proper treatment is available, or to a hospital, if any, operated by the county, city or [other appropriate political subdivision of the State] if such hospital has adequate facilities, including detention facilities when necessary, to receive and treat the prisoner. If proper treatment or facilities are not available in an institution or a hospital operated by the county, city, or [other appropriate political subdivision of the State] the Warden or other administrative head may transfer him to an institution or hospital operated by another county, city or [other appropriate political subdivision of the State], where such treatment and facilities are available, if such hospital or institution is ready to receive him, under such arrangements for reimbursement of costs as may be authorized by law. The Warden or other administrative head may request the Director of Correction to permit such prisoner to be transferred for examination, study and treatment to the medical-correctional facility, if any, or to another institution in the Department where proper treatment is available. The Director of Correction

shall permit such transfer whenever such institutions in the Department have available room to receive the prisoner.

(3) When an institutional physician finds upon examination that a prisoner suffers from a physical disease or defect that cannot, in his opinion, be properly treated in any institution or hospital of the county, city or [other appropriate political subdivision of the State] or of another county, city or [other appropriate subdivision of the State], or in the Department of Correction, such prisoner, upon the direction of the Warden or other administrative head [and with the approval of the Director of Correction], may receive treatment in, or may be transferred to, for the purpose of receiving treatment in, any other available hospital. The Warden or other administrative head, in accordance with regulations of the Department of Correction, shall make appropriate arrangements with other public or private agencies for the transportation to, and for the care, custody and security of the prisoner in such hospital. While receiving treatment in such hospital, the prisoner shall remain subject to the jurisdiction and custody of the institution to which he was committed, and shall be returned thereto when, prior to the expiration of his sentence, such hospital treatment is no longer necessary.

(4) When two psychiatrists approved by the Department of Mental Hygiene [or other appropriate department] find upon examination that a prisoner suffers from a mental disease or defect that cannot, in their opinion, be properly treated in any institution in the Department of Correction, such prisoner, upon the direction of the Warden or other administrative head [and with the approval of the Director of Correction], may be transferred for treatment, with the approval of the Department of Mental Hygiene [or other appropriate department], to a psychiatric facility in such department. The Warden or other administrative head, in accordance with the regulations of the Department of

Correction, shall make appropriate arrangements with the Department of Mental Hygiene [or other appropriate department] for the transportation to, and for the custody and security of the prisoner in such psychiatric facility. A prisoner receiving treatment in such a psychiatric facility shall remain subject to the jurisdiction and custody of the institution to which he was committed, and shall be returned thereto when, prior to the expiration of his sentence, treatment in such facility is no longer necessary. A prisoner receiving treatment in a psychiatric facility in the Department of Mental Hygiene [or other appropriate department] who continues in need of treatment at the time of his release or discharge shall be dealt with in accordance with Subsection (5) of this Section.

(5) When two psychiatrists approved by the Department of Mental Hygiene [or other appropriate department] find upon examination that a prisoner about to be discharged from an institution suffers from a mental disease or defect of such a nature that his release or discharge will endanger the public safety or the safety of the prisoner, the Warden or other administrative head, with the approval of the Director of Correction, shall transfer him to, or if he has already been transferred, permit him to remain in, the Department of Mental Hygiene [or other appropriate department] to be dealt with in accordance with law applicable to the civil commitment and detention of persons suffering from such disease or defect.

STATUS OF SECTION

Submitted to the Institute in Proposed Final Draft No. 1 and approved at the May 1961 meeting.

The words "commitment and" have been inserted before "detention."

Section 303.4. Medical Care; Food and Clothing.

(1) Upon admission to a facility for short-term imprisonment, each prisoner shall [whenever practicable] be

given a physical examination, and if he is suspected of having a communicable disease, he shall be quarantined until he is known to be free from such disease. Each prisoner shall receive such medical and dental care as may be necessary during his period of commitment [, but at his request, he may be permitted to provide such care for himself at his own expense].

(2) Each prisoner shall be adequately fed and clothed in accordance with regulations of the Department of Correction. No prisoner shall be required to wear stripes or other degrading apparel.

STATUS OF SECTION

Submitted to the Institute in Proposed Final Draft No. 1 and approved at the May 1961 meeting.

Section 303.5. Program of Rehabilitation.

The Warden or other administrative head of an institution for short-term imprisonment shall establish, subject to regulation of the Department of Correction, an appropriate program for his institution, designed as far as practicable to prepare and assist each prisoner to assume his responsibilities and to conform to the requirements of law. In developing such a program, the Warden or other administrative head shall seek to make available to each prisoner capable of benefiting therefrom academic or vocational training, participation in productive work, religious and recreational activities and such therapeutic measures as are practicable. No prisoner shall be ordered or compelled, however, to participate in religious activities.

STATUS OF SECTION

Submitted to the Institute in Proposed Final Draft No. 1 and approved at the May 1961 meeting.

In the last sentence the words "or recreational" have been eliminated.

Section 303.6. Discipline and Control.

(1) The Warden or other administrative head of each correctional institution shall be responsible for the discipline, control and safe custody of the prisoners therein. No prisoner shall be punished except upon the order of the Warden or other administrative head of the institution or of a deputy designated by him for the purpose; nor shall any punishment be imposed otherwise than in accordance with the provisions of this Section. The right to punish or to inflict punishment shall not be delegated to any prisoner or group of prisoners and no Warden or other administrative head shall permit any such prisoner or group of prisoners to assume authority over any other prisoner or group of prisoners.

(2) Except in flagrant or serious cases, punishment for a breach of discipline shall consist of deprivation of privileges. In case of assault, escape, or attempt to escape, or other serious or flagrant breach of discipline, the Warden or other administrative head may order that a prisoner's reduction of term for good behavior in accordance with Section 303.8 be forfeited. For serious or flagrant breach of discipline, the Warden or other administrative head may confine the prisoner, in accordance with the regulations of the Department of Correction, to a disciplinary cell for a period not to exceed [ten] days, and may order that the prisoner, during all or part of the period of such solitary confinement, be put on a monotonous but adequate and healthful diet. A prisoner in solitary confinement shall be visited by a physician at least once every twenty-four hours.

(3) No cruel, inhuman, or corporal punishment shall be used on any prisoner, nor is the use of force on any prisoner justifiable except as provided by Article 3 of the Code and the rules and regulations of the Department of Correction consistent therewith.

(4) The Warden or other administrative head of an institution shall maintain a record of breaches of rules, of the disposition of each case, and of the punishment, if any, for each such breach. Each breach of the rules by a prisoner shall be entered in his file, together with the disposition or punishment therefor.

STATUS OF SECTION

Submitted to the Institute in Proposed Final Draft No. 1 and approved at the May 1961 meeting.

Section 303.7. Employment and Labor of Prisoners.

(1) To establish good habits of work and responsibility, for the vocational training of prisoners, and to reduce the cost of institutional operation, prisoners shall be employed so far as possible in constructive and diversified activities in the production of goods, services and foodstuffs to maintain the institution and its inmates, for the use of the county, city or [other appropriate political subdivision of the State], State [and for other purposes expressly authorized by law]. To accomplish these purposes, the Warden or other administrative head, with the approval of the Director of Correction, shall establish and maintain work programs, including, to the extent practicable, prison industries and prison farms in his institution, and may enter into arrangements with the departments of the State, or of the county, city or [other appropriate political subdivision of the State], for the employment of prisoners in the improvement of public works and ways, and in the improvement and conservation of the natural resources owned by the State.

(2) No prisoner shall be required to engage in excessive labor, and no prisoner shall be required to perform any work for which he is declared unfit by the institutional physician.

§ 303.7

(3) The Director of Correction shall make rules and regulations governing the hours and conditions of labor of prisoners in correctional institutions of the counties, cities or [other appropriate political subdivision of the State] and the rates of prisoners' compensation for employment. In determining the rates of compensation, such regulations may take into consideration the quantity and quality of the work performed by a prisoner, whether or not such work was performed during regular working hours, the skill required for its performance, as well as the economic value of similar work outside of correctional institutions. Prisoners' wage payments shall be set aside by the Warden or other administrative head in a separate fund. The regulations may provide for the making of deductions from prisoners' wages to defray part or all of the cost of prisoner maintenance, but a sufficient amount shall remain after such deduction to enable the prisoner to contribute to the support of his dependents, if any, to make necessary purchases from the commissary, and to set aside sums to be paid to him at the time of his release from the institution.

(4) The labor or time of a prisoner shall not be sold, contracted or hired out, but prisoners may work for other departments of the State or of the county, city or [other appropriate political subdivision of the State] in accordance with arrangements made pursuant to Subsection (1) of this Section.

(5) All departments and agencies of the county, city or [other appropriate political subdivision of the State] and institutions and agencies which are supported in whole or in part by such political subdivision, shall purchase [or draw] from the correctional institution all articles and products required by them which are produced or manufactured by prison labor in such correctional institutions, unless excepted from this requirement by the [appropriate authority] of the county, city or [other appropriate politi-

cal subdivision of the State] in accordance with rules and regulations of such [appropriate authority] to carry out the purposes of this Subsection. Any surplus articles and products not so purchased shall be disposed of to the departments and agencies of the State and of other counties, cities or [other appropriate political subdivisions of the State]. The Governor [or other appropriate authority] may, by rule or regulation, provide for the manner in which standards and qualifications for such articles and products shall be set, for the manner in which the needs of departments, agencies and institutions of the State and its political subdivisions shall be estimated in advance, for the manner in which the price for such articles and products shall be determined, and for the manner in which purchases shall be made and payment credited.

(6) Within the appropriation allotted therefor, the Warden or other administrative head shall make appropriate arrangements for the compensation of prisoners for damages from injuries arising out of their employment.

STATUS OF SECTION

Submitted to the Institute in Proposed Final Draft No. 1 and approved at the May 1961 meeting.

Section 303.8. Reduction of Term for Good Behavior.

For good behavior and faithful performance of duties, the term of imprisonment of a prisoner sentenced or committed for a definite term of more than thirty days shall be reduced by [five] days for each month of such term. Such reductions of terms may be forfeited, withheld or restored by the Warden or other administrative head of the institution, in accordance with the regulations of the Department of Correction.

STATUS OF SECTION

Submitted to the Institute in Proposed Final Draft No. 1 and approved at the May 1961 meeting.

Section 303.9. Privilege of Leaving Institution for Work and Other Purposes; Conditions; Application of Earnings.

(1) When a defendant is sentenced or committed for a fixed term of one year or less, the Court may in its order grant him the privilege of leaving the institution during necessary and reasonable hours for any of the following purposes:

    (a) to work at his employment;

    (b) to seek employment;

    (c) to conduct his own business or to engage in other self-employment, including, in the case of a woman, housekeeping and attending to the needs of her family;

    (d) to attend an educational institution;

    (e) to obtain medical treatment;

    (f) to devote time to any other purpose approved by the Court.

(2) Whenever a prisoner who has been granted the privilege of leaving the institution under this Section is not engaged in the activity for which such leave is granted, he shall be confined in the institution.

(3) A prisoner sentenced to ordinary confinement may petition the Court at any time after sentence for the privilege of leaving the institution under this Section and may renew his petition in the discretion of the Court. The Court may withdraw the privilege at any time by order entered with or without notice.

(4) If the prisoner has been granted permission to leave the institution to seek or take employment, the Court's probation department shall assist him in obtaining suitable employment. Employment shall not be deemed

suitable if the wages or working conditions or other circumstances present a danger of exploitation or of interference in a labor dispute in the establishment in which the prisoner would be employed.

(5) If a prisoner is employed for wages or salary, the [probation service] [Warden or other administrative head] shall collect the same, or shall require the prisoner to turn over his wages or salary in full when received, and shall deposit the same in a trust account and shall keep a ledger showing the status of the account of each prisoner. Earnings levied upon pursuant to writ of attachment or execution or in other lawful manner shall not be collected hereunder, but when the [probation service] [Warden or other administrative head] has requested transmittal of earnings prior to levy, such request shall have priority. When an employer transmits such earnings to the [probation service] [Warden or other administrative head] pursuant to this Subdivision he shall have no liability to the prisoner for such earnings. From such earnings the probation service shall pay the prisoner's board and personal expenses both inside and outside the institution, shall deduct so much of the costs of administration of this Section as is allocable to such prisoner, and shall deduct installments on fines, if any, and, to the extent directed by the Court, shall pay the support of the prisoner's dependents. If sufficient funds are available after making the foregoing payments, the [probation service] [Warden or other administrative head] may, with the consent of the prisoner, pay, in whole or in part, any unpaid debts of the prisoner. Any balance shall be retained, and shall be paid to the prisoner at the time of his discharge.

(6) A prisoner who is serving his sentence pursuant to this Section shall be eligible for a reduction of his term for good behavior and faithful performance of duties in

accordance with Section 303.8 in the same manner as if he had served his term in ordinary confinement.

(7) The Warden or other administrative head may deny the prisoner the exercise of his privilege to leave the institution for a period not to exceed five days for any breach of discipline or other violation of regulations.

(8) The Court shall not make an order granting the privilege of leaving the institution under this Section unless it is satisfied [the Warden or other administrative head has certified] that there are adequate facilities for the administration of such privilege in the institution in which the defendant will be confined.

STATUS OF SECTION

Submitted to the Institute in Proposed Final Draft No. 1 and approved at the May 1961 meeting.

In Subsections (2) and (3) the words "under this Section" have been added.

In Subsection (8) the words "granting the privilege of leaving the institution" have been added.

Both changes were suggested at the meeting of the Institute.

The word "defendant" has been changed to "prisoner" in Subsections (2) to (7).

Section 303.10. Release from Institutions.

When a prisoner sentenced or committed for a definite term of one year or less is discharged from an institution, he shall be returned any personal possessions taken from him upon his commitment, and the Warden or other administrative head shall furnish him with a transportation ticket, or with the cost of transportation, to the place where he was sentenced, or to any other place not more distant.

STATUS OF SECTION

Submitted to the Institute in Proposed Final Draft No. 1 and approved at the May 1961 meeting.

ARTICLE 304. LONG-TERM IMPRISONMENT

Section 304.1. Reception Center; Reception Classification Boards; Reception Classification and Reclassification; Transfer of Prisoners.

(1) The Director of Correction shall, when practicable, establish, equip, and maintain one or more centers for the reception and classification of young adult offenders as defined in Section 6.05, and one or more such centers for other persons committed to the Department of Correction. When practicable, a reception center shall be a separate institution, but until it is established as such, it may be located in, or be contiguous to, another institution and may share its facilities. When a reception center shares the facilities of another institution, however, the administration and personnel of the center shall be independent of such other institution, and prisoners in such center shall be segregated from prisoners in the institution whose facilities it shares.

(2) The Director of Correction shall appoint a Reception Classification Board for each reception center, which shall include a representative of the Director of Correction, a physician, a psychiatrist or clinical psychologist, a representative of the treatment services, a representative of the custodial services, and such other persons as the Director may designate. Members of a Reception Classification Board shall serve at the pleasure of the Director of Correction.

(3) Reception Classification Boards shall examine and study all persons committed to the Department of Correction and may retain any prisoner in the reception center

§ 304.1

only for such period as may be required to complete such examination and study and to effect his transfer to another institution. The Board shall investigate each prisoner's medical, psychological, social, educational and vocational condition and history, and the motivation of his offense.

Upon the conclusion of its study of a prisoner, a Reception Classification Board shall submit its report, including its recommendations and the reasons therefor, to the Director of Correction. The Board's recommendation shall include [the classification of the prisoner according to such system of prisoner classification as the Director of Correction may establish by regulation,] the institution or unit to which the prisoner's transfer is recommended, the degree and kind of custodial control recommended for the protection of society, and the program of treatment for the rehabilitation of the prisoner, including in such program such recommendations for medical and psychological treatment and educational and vocational training as may be appropriate. The Board's report may, in addition, contain the dissenting views, if any, of any of its members.

(4) Upon receipt of the Reception Classification Board's report, the Director of Correction shall designate the institution or unit to which the prisoner shall be transferred.

(5) A reception center shall forward copies of the report of its Reception Classification Board to the institution to which the prisoner is transferred, [and] to the Division of Parole [and to the clerk of the court which sentenced the prisoner,] to be made a part of such prisoner's files.

(6) The Director of Correction may at any time order a prisoner transferred to a reception center for further

examination and study and for new recommendations concerning his classification, custodial control and rehabilitative treatment, or he may order such prisoner's immediate transfer to another institution without such further examination and study.

STATUS OF SECTION

Formerly numbered 305.1.

Presented to the Institute in Tentative Draft No. 12 and considered at the May 1960 meeting.

Resubmitted to the Institute, with verbal changes, in Proposed Final Draft No. 1 and approved at the May 1961 meeting.

For Commentary, see Tentative Draft No. 12, p. 23.

Section 304.2. Institutions; Review of Adequacy; Use of Institutions of Another Jurisdiction.

(1) Within the appropriation allotted therefor, the Director of Correction shall construct, equip and maintain suitable buildings, structures, and facilities for the operation, and for the necessary expansion and diversification, of the state correctional system, including prisons, reformatories, reception centers, parole and probation hostels, [state misdemeanant institutions] and such other institutions as may be required for the custody, control, correctional treatment and rehabilitation of persons committed to the Department of Correction.

(2) The Director of Correction shall annually review the adequacy of the state correctional system in the light of the number of persons committed thereto as well as in the light of the need for diversified facilities. No later than his next annual report, the Director shall report on any inadequacies of the state correctional system, including his recommendations for the alteration or expansion of the existing institutions, for the construction of new institutions, or for such other measures to meet the situation as may be

appropriate, whenever the system fails to provide, when practicable, the following institutions:

(a) one or more maximum security institutions accommodating in each such institution or in separate units thereof no more than [   ] prisoners;

(b) one or more medium security institutions accommodating in each such institution or in separate units thereof no more than [   ] prisoners;

(c) one or more minimum security institutions accommodating in each such institution or in separate units thereof no more than [   ] prisoners, which institutions may include unfenced farms, camps, colonies, housing for outside work areas, and similar facilities, and may, in addition to their regular uses, be employed also for parole preparation of prisoners and for the detention of prisoners during temporary suspension of parole, and for other similar purposes;

(d) special institutional facilities for the vocational and rehabilitative training of young adult offenders, as defined in Section 6.05, providing, if need be by separate units, for diversified security and custody;

(e) a medical-correctional facility to keep prisoners with difficult or chronic medical and psychiatric problems, which, if the number of persons committed to the Department reaches [   ], is a separate institution;

(f) one or more institutions for female prisoners committed to the Department, providing, if need be by separate units, for diversified security and custody[;

(g) one or more state misdemeanant institutions for misdemeanants committed to the Department [for an extended term], providing, if need be by separate units, for diversified security and custody].

(3) When the Director of Correction finds that certain classes or categories of persons committed to the Department require specialized treatment, or treatment of a kind that it is not feasible to provide within the state correctional system, the Director of Correction shall seek to place such prisoners in institutions providing such treatment in another jurisdiction, and may agree to pay reimbursement therefor. A prisoner so transferred to an out-of-state institution shall be subject to the rules and regulations of such institution concerning the custody, conduct and discipline of its inmates, but shall remain subject to the provisions of this Code concerning his term, reduction of term for good behavior, and release on parole.

STATUS OF SECTION

Formerly numbered 305.2.

Presented to the Institute in Tentative Draft No. 12 and considered at the May 1960 meeting.

Resubmitted to the Institute in Proposed Final Draft No. 1 and approved at the May 1961 meeting.

For Commentary, see Tentative Draft No. 12, p. 32.

Section 304.3. Central Prisoner File; Treatment, Classification and Reclassification in Institutions.

(1) The Warden or other administrative head of a correctional institution shall establish and maintain, in accordance with the regulations of the Department, a central file in the institution containing an individual file for each prisoner. Each prisoner's file shall include: (a) his admission summary; (b) his pre-sentence investigation report; (c) the report and recommendation of the Reception Classification Board; (d) the official records of his conviction and commitment as well as earlier criminal records, if any; (e) progress reports and admission-orientation reports from

treatment and custodial staff; (f) reports of his disciplinary infractions, and of their disposition; (g) his parole plan, prepared in accordance with Section 305.7; and (h) other pertinent data concerning his background, conduct, associations, and family relationships. Each prisoner's file shall be carefully reviewed before any decision is made concerning his classification, reclassification, or parole release. The content of the prisoners' files shall be confidential and shall not be subject to public inspection except by court order for good cause shown and shall not be accessible to prisoners in the institution.

(2) The Warden or other administrative head in each correctional institution shall appoint a Treatment Classification Committee with himself or his representative as chairman, and consisting of representatives of the treatment, custodial, and parole services, of medical, psychiatric or psychological personnel, of personnel concerned with the education and vocational training of inmates, and of such other persons as he may designate. Members of the Treatment Classification Committee shall serve at the pleasure of the Warden or other administrative head.

(3) When a prisoner is transferred to a correctional institution from a reception center or from any other institution, the Classification Committee of such receiving institution shall, within [two] months of receiving the prisoner, study his pre-sentence investigation report, his criminal history and escape record, if any, the report of the Reception Classification Board, the admission-orientation reports of the custodial and treatment officers of the institution, the attitudes and preferences of the prisoner, and such other relevant information as may be available in the prisoner's file or from other sources and shall aid the Warden or other administrative head of the institution in determining the prisoner's program of treatment, training, employment, care and custody.

(4) The Classification Committee, or a subcommittee thereof designated by the Warden or other administrative head, shall review the program of each prisoner at regular intervals and whenever a member of the Committee so requests, and shall recommend to the Warden such changes in the prisoner's program of treatment, training, employment, care and custody as it considers necessary or desirable.

(5) Approximately [three] months before a prisoner will be considered by the Board of Parole for release on parole, the Classification Committee shall re-examine the prisoner's individual file, shall prepare a report summarizing and evaluating the prisoner's progress, and may recommend to the Warden or other administrative head (a) that the prisoner be reclassified for pre-parole preparation at that institution or at another institution after transfer thereto or (b) that the prisoner's reclassification for pre-parole preparation be postponed, for a definite or indefinite period of time, stating the reason for such recommendation in the record. A copy of the Classification Committee's report shall be forwarded to the Board of Parole, and shall be available to such Board in advance of the prisoner's hearing before the Board of Parole.

(6) The Warden or other administrative head of the institution shall have final authority to determine matters of treatment classification within his institution and to recommend to the Director of Correction the transfer of any prisoner.

STATUS OF SECTION

Formerly numbered 305.3.

Presented to the Institute in Tentative Draft No. 12 and considered at the May 1960 meeting.

Resubmitted to the Institute in Proposed Final Draft No. 1 and approved at the May 1961 meeting.

In Subsection (1)(g) the cross-reference has been corrected.

For Commentary, see Tentative Draft No. 12, p. 45.

Section 304.4. Segregation and Transfer of Prisoners with Physical or Mental Diseases or Defects.

(1) When an institutional physician finds that a prisoner suffers from a physical disease or defect, or when an institutional physician or psychologist finds that a prisoner suffers from a mental disease or defect, the Warden or other administrative head may order such prisoner to be segregated from other prisoners, and if the physician or psychologist, as the case may be, is of the opinion that he cannot be given proper treatment at that institution, the Warden or other administrative head shall recommend to the Director of Correction that such prisoner be transferred for examination, study and treatment to the medical-correctional facility, if any, or to another institution in the Department where proper treatment is available.

(2) When an institutional physician finds upon examination that a prisoner suffers from a physical disease or defect that cannot, in his opinion, be properly treated in any institution in the Department of Correction, such prisoner, upon the recommendation of the Warden or other administrative head and the order of the Director of Correction, may receive treatment in, or may be transferred to, for the purpose of receiving treatment in, a hospital outside the Department of Correction. The Director of Correction shall make appropriate arrangements with other public or private agencies for the transportation to, and for the care, custody and security of the prisoner in, such outside hospital. While receiving treatment in such outside hospital, the prisoner shall remain subject to the jurisdic-

tion and custody of the Department of Correction, and shall be returned to the Department of Correction when, prior to the expiration of his sentence, such hospital treatment is no longer necessary.

(3) When two psychiatrists approved by the Department of Mental Hygiene [or other appropriate department] find upon examination that a prisoner suffers from a mental disease or defect that cannot, in their opinion, be properly treated in any institution in the Department of Correction, such prisoner, upon the recommendation of the Warden or other administrative head and the order of the Director of Correction, may be transferred for treatment, with the approval of the Department of Mental Hygiene [or other appropriate department], to a psychiatric facility in such department. The Director of Correction shall make appropriate arrangements with the Department of Mental Hygiene [or other appropriate department] for the transportation to, and for the custody and security of the prisoner in such psychiatric facility. A prisoner receiving treatment in such a psychiatric facility shall remain subject to the jurisdiction and custody of the Department of Correction, and shall be returned to the Department of Correction when, prior to the expiration of his sentence, treatment in such facility is no longer necessary. A prisoner receiving treatment in a psychiatric facility in the Department of Mental Hygiene [or other appropriate department] who continues in need of treatment at the time of his release or discharge shall be dealt with in accordance with Subsection (4) of this Section.

(4) When two psychiatrists approved by the Department of Mental Hygiene [or other appropriate department] find upon examination that a prisoner about to be released or discharged from an institution suffers from a mental disease or defect of such a nature that his release or discharge will endanger the public safety or the safety of the

prisoner, the Director of Correction shall transfer him to, or if he has already been transferred, permit him to remain in, the Department of Mental Hygiene [or other appropriate department] to be dealt with in accordance with law applicable to the civil commitment and detention of persons suffering from such disease or defect.

STATUS OF SECTION

Formerly numbered 305.4.

Presented to the Institute in Tentative Draft No. 12 and considered at the May 1960 meeting.

Resubmitted to the Institute, with verbal changes, in Proposed Final Draft No. 1 and approved at the May 1961 meeting.

The words "commitment and" have been inserted before "detention."

For Commentary, see Tentative Draft No. 12, p. 49.

Section 304.5. Medical Care, Food and Clothing.

(1) Upon admission to a state correctional institution, each prisoner shall be given a physical examination, and shall be kept apart from other prisoners for a period of quarantine until he is known to be free from communicable disease and until he has been classified in accordance with Section 304.3. Each prisoner shall have regular medical and dental care.

(2) Each prisoner shall be adequately fed and clothed in accordance with regulations of the Department. No prisoner shall be required to wear stripes or other degrading apparel.

STATUS OF SECTION

Formerly numbered 305.5.

Presented to the Institute in Tentative Draft No. 12 and considered at the May 1960 meeting.

Resubmitted to the Institute in Proposed Final Draft No. 1 and approved at the May 1961 meeting.

For Commentary, see Tentative Draft No. 12, p. 51.

Section 304.6. Program of Rehabilitation.

The Director of Correction shall establish an appropriate program for each institution, designed as far as practicable to prepare and assist each prisoner to assume his responsibilities and to conform to the requirements of law. In developing such programs, the Director shall seek to make available to each prisoner capable of benefiting therefrom academic or vocational training, participation in productive work, religious and recreational activities and such therapeutic measures as are practicable. No prisoner shall be ordered or compelled, however, to participate in religious activities.

STATUS OF SECTION

Formerly numbered 305.6.

Presented to the Institute in Tentative Draft No. 12 and considered at the May 1960 meeting.

Resubmitted to the Institute in Proposed Final Draft No. 1 and approved at the May 1961 meeting.

In the last sentence the words "or recreational" have been eliminated.

For Commentary, see Tentative Draft No. 12, p. 54.

Section 304.7. Discipline and Control.

(1) The Warden or other administrative head of each correctional institution shall be responsible for the discipline, control and safe custody of the prisoners therein. No prisoner shall be punished except upon the order of the Warden or other administrative head of the institution or of a deputy designated by him for the purpose; nor shall any punishment be imposed otherwise than in accordance with the provisions of this Section.

§ 304.7

(2) The Warden or other administrative head of each correctional institution shall appoint a Committee on Adjustment [disciplinary committee] from among the staff of the institution, which shall include a member of the treatment service, a member of the custodial service, and an institutional physician. The Warden or other administrative head may designate himself or a deputy as chairman of the Committee. The Committee shall give notice to any prisoner who has been reported for a breach of discipline, shall determine after a hearing whether the prisoner has committed an intentional breach of the rules, and shall recommend to the Warden or other administrative head an appropriate disposition of the matter subject to the provisions of this Section. No prisoner shall be punished until he has had such a hearing, but the recommendation of the Committee shall not be binding on the Warden or other administrative head or his deputy.

(3) Except in flagrant or serious cases, punishment for a breach of the rules shall consist of deprivation of privileges. In cases of assault, escape, or attempt to escape, or other serious or flagrant breach of the rules, the Committee on Adjustment [disciplinary committee] may recommend to the Warden or other administrative head, and he may order, that a prisoner's reduction of term for good behavior and faithful performance of duties be forfeited or withheld in accordance with Section 305.4. For serious or flagrant breach of the rules, the Committee on Adjustment [disciplinary committee], in accordance with the regulations of the Department, may also recommend, and the Warden or other administrative head may order, that the offender be confined in a disciplinary cell for a period not to exceed thirty days. The Committee on Adjustment [disciplinary committee] may recommend, and the Warden or other administrative head may order, that a prisoner, during all or part of the period of such solitary confinement, be put on a monotonous but adequate and healthful diet. A prisoner in

solitary confinement shall be visited by a physician at least once every twenty-four hours.

(4) No cruel, inhuman, or corporal punishment shall be used on any prisoner, nor is the use of force on any prisoner justifiable except as provided by Article 3 of the Code and the rules and regulations of the Department consistent therewith.

(5) The Warden or other administrative head of an institution shall maintain a record of breaches of rules, of the disposition of each case, and of the punishment, if any, for each such breach. Each breach of the rules by a prisoner shall be entered in his file, together with the disposition or punishment therefor.

(6) The Committee on Adjustment shall recommend to the Warden or other administrative head that a prisoner who is considered to be incorrigible by reason of frequent intentional breaches of discipline, or who is detrimental to the discipline or the morale of the institution, be reported to the Director of Correction for transfer to another institution for stricter safekeeping and closer confinement.

STATUS OF SECTION

Formerly numbered 305.7.

Presented to the Institute in Tentative Draft No. 12 and considered at the May 1960 meeting.

The first sentence of Subsection (1) was added.

Resubmitted to the Institute in Proposed Final Draft No. 1 and approved at the May 1961 meeting.

For Commentary, see Tentative Draft No. 12, p. 58.

Section 304.8. Employment and Labor of Prisoners.

(1) To establish good habits of work and responsibility, for the vocational training of prisoners, and to reduce the cost of prison operation, prisoners shall be employed so far

§ 304.8 280 Model Penal Code

as possible in constructive and diversified activities in the production of goods, services and foodstuffs to maintain the institution and its inmates, for state use [and for other purposes expressly authorized by law]. To accomplish these purposes, the Director of Correction shall establish and maintain prison industries and prison farms in appropriate correctional institutions, and may enter into arrangements with other departments for the employment of prisoners in the improvement of public works and ways, and in the improvement and conservation of the natural resources owned by the state.

(2) No prisoner shall be required to engage in excessive labor, and no prisoner shall be required to perform any work for which he is declared unfit by the medical department.

(3) The Director shall make rules and regulations governing the hours and conditions of labor of prisoners in correctional institutions, and the rates of prisoners' compensation for employment. In determining the rates of compensation, such regulations may take into consideration the quantity and quality of the work performed by a prisoner, whether or not such work was performed during regular working hours, the skill required for its performance, as well as the economic value of similar work outside of correctional institutions. Prisoners' wage payments shall be set aside by the Warden or other administrative head in a separate fund. The regulations may provide for the making of deductions from prisoners' wages to defray part or all of the cost of prisoner maintenance, but a sufficient amount shall remain after such deduction to enable the prisoner to contribute to the support of his dependents, if any, to make necessary purchases from the commissary, and to set aside sums to be paid to him at the time of his release from the institution.

(4) The labor or time of any prisoner committed to the Department of Correction shall not be sold, contracted or hired out, but prisoners may work for other departments of the State in accordance with arrangements made pursuant to Subsection (1) of this Section.

(5) All departments and agencies [and local subdivisions] of the State, and all institutions and agencies which are supported in whole or in part by the State shall purchase from the Department of Correction all articles and products required by them which are produced or manufactured by prison labor in state correctional institutions, unless excepted from this requirement by the Governor [or other appropriate authority] in accordance with rules and regulations promulgated by the Governor [or other appropriate authority] to carry out the purposes of this Subsection. The Governor [or other appropriate authority] may, by rule or regulation, provide for the manner in which standards and qualifications for such articles and products shall be set, for the manner in which the needs of departments, agencies and institutions shall be estimated in advance, for the manner in which the price for such articles and products shall be determined, and for the manner in which purchases shall be made and payment credited.

(6) Within the appropriation allotted therefor, the Director shall make appropriate arrangements for the compensation of prisoners for damages from injuries arising out of their employment.

STATUS OF SECTION

Formerly numbered 305.8.

Presented to the Institute in Tentative Draft No. 12 and considered at the May 1960 meeting.

Resubmitted to the Institute in Proposed Final Draft No. 1 and approved at the May 1961 meeting.

For Commentary, see Tentative Draft No. 12, p. 62.

Section 304.9. Compassionate Leave; Pre-Parole Furlough.

(1) The Director of Correction shall formulate rules or regulations governing compassionate leave from institutions and, in accordance with such rules or regulations, may permit any prisoner to leave his institution for short periods of time, either by himself or in the custody of an officer, to visit a close relative who is seriously ill, to attend the funeral of a close relative, to return to his home during what appears to be his own last illness, or to return to his home for other compelling reasons which strongly appeal to compassion.

(2) The rules or regulations shall provide for the manner in which compassionate leave shall be granted, for its duration, and for the custody, transportation and care of the prisoner during his leave. They shall also provide for the manner in which the expense connected with such leave shall be borne, and may allow the prisoner, or anyone in his behalf, to reimburse the state for such expense.

(3) The Director of Correction, on the recommendation of the Board of Parole, may grant a pre-parole furlough, not to exceed [two] weeks, to any prisoner whose parole release date has been fixed in accordance with Section 305.8 by the Board of Parole. The purpose of such a furlough shall be to enable the prisoner to secure employment, to find adequate living quarters for himself and his family, or, generally, to make more effective plans and arrangements towards his release on parole.

STATUS OF SECTION

Formerly numbered 305.9.

Presented to the Institute in Tentative Draft No. 12 and considered at the May 1960 meeting.

Subsection (3) was added and the Section heading changed to reflect the addition of provision for pre-parole furloughs.

Resubmitted to the Institute in Proposed Final Draft No. 1 and approved at the May 1961 meeting.

For Commentary, see Tentative Draft No. 12, p. 67.

Section 304.10. Release from Institutions.

When a prisoner is released from an institution, either on parole or upon final discharge, he shall be returned any personal possessions taken from him upon his commitment, and the Warden or other administrative head shall furnish him with decent clothing appropriate for the season of the year, a transportation ticket to the place where he will reside, the earnings set aside for him in the wage fund, and such additional sum of money as may be prescribed by regulation of the Department to enable him to meet his immediate needs. If at the time of his release a prisoner is too ill or feeble or otherwise unable to use public means of transportation, the Warden or other administrative head may, subject to the rules and regulations of the Department, make special arrangements for his transportation to the place where he will reside.

STATUS OF SECTION

Formerly numbered 305.10.

Presented to the Institute in Tentative Draft No. 12 and considered at the May 1960 meeting.

Resubmitted to the Institute in Proposed Final Draft No. 1 and approved at the May 1961 meeting.

For Commentary, see Tentative Draft No. 12, p. 68.

ARTICLE 305. RELEASE ON PAROLE

Section 305.1. Reduction of Prison Term for Good Behavior.

For good behavior and faithful performance of duties, the term of a prisoner sentenced to imprisonment for an indefinite term with a maximum in excess of one year, shall be reduced by [six] days for each month of such term. In addition, for especially meritorious behavior or exceptional performance of his duties, a prisoner may receive a further reduction, not to exceed [six] days, for any month of imprisonment. The total of all such reductions shall be deducted:

(1) from his minimum term of imprisonment, to determine the date of his eligibility for release on parole; and

(2) from his maximum term of imprisonment, to determine the date when his release on parole becomes mandatory.

STATUS OF SECTION

Formerly numbered 305.5.

Presented to the Institute in Tentative Draft No. 5 and considered at the May 1956 meeting.

Verbal changes were made to make clear that the ordinary reduction is to be made on an overall calculation rather than on a calculation made from month to month.

Resubmitted to the Institute in Proposed Final Draft No. 1 and approved at the May 1961 meeting.

For Commentary, see Tentative Draft No. 5, p. 83.

Section 305.2. Reduction of Parole Term for Good Behavior.

For good conduct in conformity with the conditions of parole, a parolee's parole term shall be reduced by [six] days for each month of such parole term. The total of such reductions shall be deducted:

(1) from his minimum parole term to determine the date of his eligibility for discharge from parole; and

(2) from the maximum of his parole term to determine the date when his discharge from parole becomes mandatory.

STATUS OF SECTION

Formerly numbered 305.6.

Presented to the Institute in Tentative Draft No. 5 and considered at the May 1956 meeting.

Resubmitted to the Institute, with verbal changes, in Proposed Final Draft No. 1 and approved at the May 1961 meeting.

For Commentary, see Tentative Draft No. 5, p. 83.

Section 305.3. Award of Reduction of Term for Good Behavior.

(1) Reductions of term of imprisonment in accordance with Section 305.1 shall be awarded by the **Warden of the institution** [Deputy Director for Treatment Services]. In the case of reductions for especially meritorious behavior, or exceptional performance of duties, the award shall be made only upon the recommendation of the **Committee on Adjustment** [or similar committee] of the institution.

(2) Reductions of parole terms in accordance with Section 305.2 shall be awarded by the **Board of Parole.**

STATUS OF SECTION

Formerly numbered 305.7.

Presented to the Institute in Tentative Draft No. 5 and considered at the May 1956 meeting.

Resubmitted to the Institute in Proposed Final Draft No. 1 and approved at the May 1961 meeting.

Minor verbal changes have been made.

For Commentary, see Tentative Draft No. 5, p. 83.

Section 305.4. Forfeiture, Withholding, and Restoration of Reduction of Term for Good Behavior.

(1) Reductions of terms of imprisonment for good behavior and faithful performance of duties may be forfeited, withheld and restored by the Warden of the institution [Deputy Director for Treatment Services] after hearing by the Committee on Adjustment [or disciplinary committee] of the institution, but no reduction of a prison term shall be forfeited or withheld after a prisoner is released on parole.

(2) Reductions of parole terms for good behavior may be forfeited, withheld and restored by the Board of Parole.

STATUS OF SECTION

Formerly numbered 305.8.

Presented to the Institute in Tentative Draft No. 5 and considered at the May 1956 meeting.

Section was revised to eliminate requirement of recommendation by Adjustment Committee, since responsibility is vested in the Warden.

Resubmitted to the Institute in Proposed Final Draft No. 1 and approved at the May 1961 meeting.

Minor verbal changes have been made.

For Commentary, see Tentative Draft No. 5, p. 83.

Section 305.5. Report of Reductions Granted, Forfeited and Restored.

The Warden of the institution [Deputy Director for Treatment Services] shall regularly report all reductions of prison terms for good behavior and faithful performance of duties, and all forfeitures and restorations of such reductions to the Director of Correction. On the basis of such report, the Director shall inform the **Board of Parole and the Parole Administrator** of all prisoners who are expected to become eligible for release on parole or whose release on parole will become mandatory within the next three months.

STATUS OF SECTION

Formerly numbered 305.9.

Presented to the Institute in Tentative Draft No. 5 and considered at the May 1956 meeting.

Resubmitted to the Institute, with verbal changes, in Proposed Final Draft No. 1 and approved at the May 1961 meeting.

For Commentary, see Tentative Draft No. 5, p. 83.

Section 305.6. Parole Eligibility and Hearing.

Every prisoner sentenced to an indefinite term of imprisonment shall be eligible for release on parole upon completion of his minimum term less reductions granted in accordance with Section 305.1, or, if there is no minimum, at any time. Within sixty days before the expiration of such minimum less reductions, or, if there is no minimum, within ninety days of his commitment, the prisoner shall have a hearing before the Board of Parole or a member or members designated by the Board, or, when appropriate, before the Young Adult Division of the Board. The hearing shall be conducted in an informal manner, but a verbatim record of the proceedings shall be made and preserved.

STATUS OF SECTION

Formerly numbered 305.10.

Presented to the Institute in Tentative Draft No. 5 and considered at the May 1956 meeting.

Section revised to take account of sentences of young adult offenders without a minimum under Section 6.05(2).

Resubmitted to the Institute in Proposed Final Draft No. 1 and approved at the May 1961 meeting.

For Commentary, see Tentative Draft No. 5, p. 85.

Section 305.7. Preparation for Hearing; Assistance to Prisoner.

(1) Each prisoner in advance of his parole hearing shall prepare a parole plan, setting forth the manner of life he intends to lead if released on parole, including such specific information as to where and with whom he will reside and what occupation or employment he will follow. The institutional parole staff shall render reasonable aid to the prisoner in the preparation of his plan and in securing information for submission to the Board of Parole.

(2) A prisoner shall be permitted to advise with any persons whose assistance he reasonably desires, including his own legal counsel, in preparing for a hearing before the Board of Parole.

STATUS OF SECTION

Formerly numbered 305.11.

Presented to the Institute in Tentative Draft No. 5 and considered at the May 1956 meeting.

As first presented to the Institute Subsection (2) read: "A prisoner shall be permitted to advise with his own legal counsel in preparing for a hearing before the Board of Parole." By a close vote the Institute approved an amendment to read as follows: "The prisoner shall be entitled to advise with his own legal counsel in preparing for a hearing before the Board of Parole and to have the assistance of counsel at the hearing, subject to the power of the Board to prevent abuse of that privilege." The Council reconsidered the question at its March 1957 meeting and resolved to recommend that the Institute reconsider its action and approve the formulation set forth above, which the Institute did at the May 1961 meeting in approving Proposed Final Draft No. 1.

For Commentary, see Tentative Draft No. 5, p. 89.

Section 305.8. Decision of Board of Parole; Reconsideration.

(1) The Board of Parole shall render its decision regarding a prisoner's release on parole within a reasonable time after hearing. The decision shall be by majority vote

[of a quorum] of the Board of Parole. The decision shall be based on the entire record before the Board, which shall include the opinion of the member who presided at the hearing. In its decision the Board shall either fix the prisoner's release date, or it shall defer the case for later reconsideration.

(2) If the Board fixes the release date, such date shall be not less than sixty days nor more than six months from the date of the prisoner's parole hearing, or from the date of last reconsideration of his case by the Board, unless there are special reasons for fixing an earlier or later release date.

(3) If the Board defers the case for later reconsideration, it shall review the record at least once a year until a release date is fixed. The Board may in its discretion order a reconsideration or a rehearing of the case at any time.

(4) If the Board fixes no earlier release date, a prisoner's release on parole shall become mandatory at the expiration of his maximum term of imprisonment, less reductions allowed in accordance with Section 305.1.

STATUS OF SECTION

Formerly numbered 305.12.

Presented to the Institute in Tentative Draft No. 5 and considered at the May 1956 meeting.

Resubmitted to the Institute in Proposed Final Draft No. 1 and approved at the May 1961 meeting.

For Commentary, see Tentative Draft No. 5, p. 93.

Section 305.9. Criteria for Determining Date of First Release on Parole.

(1) Whenever the Board of Parole considers the first release of a prisoner who is eligible for release on parole, it shall be the policy of the Board to order his release, unless the Board is of the opinion that his release should be deferred because:

(a) there is substantial risk that he will not conform to the conditions of parole; or

(b) his release at that time would depreciate the seriousness of his crime or promote disrespect for law; or

(c) his release would have a substantially adverse effect on institutional discipline; or

(d) his continued correctional treatment, medical care or vocational or other training in the institution will substantially enhance his capacity to lead a law-abiding life when released at a later date.

(2) In making its determination regarding a prisoner's release on parole, it shall be the policy of the Board of Parole to take into account each of the following factors:

(a) the prisoner's personality, including his maturity, stability, sense of responsibility and any apparent development in his personality which may promote or hinder his conformity to law;

(b) the adequacy of the prisoner's parole plan;

(c) the prisoner's ability and readiness to assume obligations and undertake responsibilities;

(d) the prisoner's intelligence and training;

(e) the prisoner's family status and whether he has relatives who display an interest in him, or whether he has other close and constructive associations in the community;

(f) the prisoner's employment history, his occupational skills, and the stability of his past employment;

(g) the type of residence, neighborhood or community in which the prisoner plans to live;

(h) the prisoner's past use of narcotics, or past habitual and excessive use of alcohol;

(i) the prisoner's mental or physical make-up, including any disability or handicap which may affect his conformity to law;

(j) the prisoner's prior criminal record, including the nature and circumstances, recency and frequency of previous offenses;

(k) the prisoner's attitude toward law and authority;

(l) the prisoner's conduct in the institution, including particularly whether he has taken advantage of the opportunities for self-improvement afforded by the institutional program, whether he has been punished for misconduct within six months prior to his hearing or reconsideration for parole release, whether he has forfeited any reductions of term during his period of imprisonment, and whether such reductions have been restored at the time of hearing or reconsideration;

(m) the prisoner's conduct and attitude during any previous experience of probation or parole and the recency of such experience.

STATUS OF SECTION

Formerly numbered 305.13.

Presented to the Institute in Tentative Draft No. 5 and considered at the May 1956 meeting.

As first presented to the Institute Subsection (1) provided that the Board "shall order his release, unless". With the approval of the Council at its March 1958 meeting, the Section was revised to declare that "it shall be the policy of the Board to order his release, unless". The purpose of the change is to make clear that the determination called for is to be made by the Board and is not subject to judicial review.

Resubmitted to the Institute, with verbal changes, in Proposed Final Draft No. 1 and approved at the May 1961 meeting.

For Commentary, see Tentative Draft No. 5, p. 97.

Section 305.10. Data to Be Considered in Determining Parole Release.

Before making a determination regarding a prisoner's release on parole, the Board of Parole shall cause to be brought before it all of the following records and information regarding the prisoner:

(1) a report prepared by the institutional parole staff, relating to his personality, social history and adjustment to authority, and including any recommendations which the institutional staff may make;

(2) all official reports of his prior criminal record, including reports and records of earlier probation and parole experiences;

(3) the pre-sentence investigation report of the sentencing Court;

(4) recommendations regarding his parole made at the time of sentencing by the sentencing judge or the prosecutor;

(5) the reports of any physical, mental and psychiatric examinations of the prisoner;

(6) any relevant information which may be submitted by the prisoner, his attorney, the victim of his crime, or by other persons;

(7) the prisoner's parole plan;

(8) such other relevant information concerning the prisoner as may be reasonably available.

STATUS OF SECTION

Formerly numbered 305.14.

Presented to the Institute in Tentative Draft No. 5 and considered at the May 1956 meeting.

Resubmitted to the Institute in Proposed Final Draft No. 1 and approved at the May 1961 meeting.

For Commentary, see Tentative Draft No. 5, p. 97.

Section 305.11. Eligibility for Discharge from Parole.

A parolee is eligible for discharge from parole upon the satisfactory completion of the minimum parole term less reductions for good behavior.

STATUS OF SECTION

Formerly numbered 305.15.

Presented to the Institute in Tentative Draft No. 5 and considered at the May 1956 meeting.

Resubmitted to the Institute, with verbal changes, in Proposed Final Draft No. 1 and approved at the May 1961 meeting.

For Commentary, see Tentative Draft No. 5, p. 72.

Section 305.12. Termination of Supervision; Discharge from Parole.

If, in the opinion of the Board of Parole, a parolee does not require guidance and supervision, the Board may dispense with or terminate such supervision. When a parolee is eligible for discharge from parole in accordance with Section 305.11, the Board may discharge him from parole, if, in its opinion, such discharge is not incompatible with the protection of the public. A parolee's discharge from parole or from recommitment for violation of parole becomes mandatory upon completion of the maximum parole term less reductions for good behavior.

STATUS OF SECTION

Formerly numbered 305.16.

Presented to the Institute in Tentative Draft No. 5 and considered at the May 1956 meeting.

Section revised with the approval of the Council at its March 1957 meeting to make clear that the Board may initially dispense with supervision that it deems to be unnecessary.

Resubmitted to the Institute in Proposed Final Draft No. 1 and approved at the May 1961 meeting.

For Commentary, see Tentative Draft No. 5, p. 100.

Section 305.13. Conditions of Parole.

(1) When a prisoner is released on parole, the Board of Parole shall require as a condition of his parole that he refrain from engaging in criminal conduct. The Board of Parole may also require, either at the time of his release on parole or at any time and from time to time while he remains under parole, that he conform to any of the following conditions of parole:

(a) meet his specified family responsibilities;

(b) devote himself to an approved employment or occupation;

(c) remain within the geographic limits fixed in his Certificate of Parole, unless granted written permission to leave such limits;

(d) report, as directed, in person and within thirty-six hours of his release, to his parole officer;

(e) report in person to his parole officer at such regular intervals as may be required;

(f) reside at the place fixed in his Certificate of Parole and notify his parole officer of any change in his address or employment;

(g) have in his possession no firearm or other dangerous weapon unless granted written permission;

(h) submit himself to available medical or psychiatric treatment, if the Board shall so require;

(i) refrain from associating with persons known to him to be engaged in criminal activities or, without permission of his parole officer, with persons known to him to have been convicted of a crime;

(j) satisfy any other conditions specially related to the cause of his offense and not unduly restrictive of his liberty or incompatible with his freedom of conscience.

(2) Before release on parole, a parolee shall be provided with a Certificate of Parole setting forth the conditions of his parole.

STATUS OF SECTION

Formerly numbered 305.17.

Presented to the Institute in Tentative Draft No. 5 and considered at the May 1956 meeting.

Section revised with the approval of the Council at its March 1957 meeting to add paragraph (1)(j).

Resubmitted to the Institute in Proposed Final Draft No. 1 and approved at the May 1961 meeting.

For Commentary, see Tentative Draft No. 5, p. 103.

Section 305.14. Parole Residence Facilities.

The Board of Parole may in appropriate cases require a parolee, as a condition of his parole, either at the time of his release on parole or at any time and from time to time while he remains under parole supervision, to reside in a parole hostel, boarding home, hospital, or other special residence facility, for such a period and under such supervision or treatment as the Board may deem appropriate.

STATUS OF SECTION

Formerly numbered 305.18.

Presented to the Institute in Tentative Draft No. 5 and considered at the May 1956 meeting.

Resubmitted to the Institute in Proposed Final Draft No. 1 and approved at the May 1961 meeting.

For Commentary, see Tentative Draft No. 5, p. 106.

Section 305.15. Revocation of Parole for Violation of Condition; Hearing.

(1) When a parolee has been returned to the institution, the Board of Parole shall hold a hearing within sixty days of his return to determine whether his parole should be revoked. The parolee shall have reasonable notice of the charges filed. The institutional parole staff shall render reasonable aid to the parolee in preparation for the hearing and he shall be permitted to advise with his own legal counsel. At the hearing the parolee may admit, deny, or explain the violation charged, and he may present proof, including affidavits and other evidence, in support of his contention. A verbatim record of the hearing shall be made and preserved.

(2) The Board may order revocation of parole if it is satisfied, upon substantial evidence, that:

    (a) the parolee has failed, without a satisfactory excuse, to comply with a substantial requirement imposed as a condition of his parole; and

    (b) the violation of condition involves:

        (i) the commission of another crime; or

        (ii) conduct indicating a substantial risk that the parolee will commit another crime; or

        (iii) conduct indicating that the parolee is unwilling to comply with proper conditions of parole.

(3) Parole revocation shall be by majority vote of the Board.

STATUS OF SECTION

Formerly numbered 305.21.

Presented to the Institute in Tentative Draft No. 5 and considered at the May 1956 meeting.

Resubmitted to the Institute in Proposed Final Draft No. 1 as Section 305.16 and approved at the May 1961 meeting.

For Commentary, see Tentative Draft No. 5, p. 114.

Section 305.16. Sanctions Short of Revocation for Violation of Condition of Parole.

(1) If the Parole Administrator has reasonable cause to believe that a parolee has violated a condition of parole, he shall notify the Board of Parole, and shall cause the appropriate district parole supervisor to submit the parolee's record to the Board. After consideration of the records submitted, and after such further investigation as it may deem appropriate, the Board may order:

    (a) that the parolee receive a reprimand and warning from the Board;

    (b) that parole supervision and reporting be intensified;

    (c) that reductions for good behavior be forfeited or withheld;

    (d) that the parolee be remanded, without revocation of parole, to a residence facility specified in Section 305.14 for such a period and under such supervision or treatment as the Board may deem appropriate;

    (e) that the parolee be required to conform to one or more additional conditions of parole which may be imposed in accordance with Section 305.13;

    (f) that the parolee be arrested and returned to prison, there to await a hearing to determine whether his parole should be revoked.

(2) If a parole officer or district parole supervisor has reasonable cause to believe that a parolee has violated or is

§ 305.16

about to violate a condition of his parole and that an emergency situation exists, so that awaiting action by the Board of Parole under Subsection (1) of this Section would create an undue risk to the public or to the parolee, such parole officer or district parole supervisor may arrest such parolee without a warrant, and may call on any peace officer to assist him in so doing. The parolee, whether arrested hereunder with or without a warrant, shall be detained in the local jail, lockup, or other detention facility, pending action by the Board of Parole. Immediately after such arrest and detention, the parole officer or district parole supervisor concerned shall notify the Board and submit a written report of the reason for such arrest. After consideration of such written report, the Board [or a member of the Board] shall, with all practicable speed, make a preliminary determination, and shall either order the parolee's release from detention or order his return to the institution from which he was paroled, there to await a hearing to determine whether or not his parole shall be revoked. The Board's preliminary determination to order the parolee's release from detention shall not, however, be deemed to bar further proceedings under Subsection (1) of this Section.

STATUS OF SECTION

Formerly numbered 305.19.

Presented to the Institute in Tentative Draft No. 5 and considered at the May 1956 meeting.

Subsection (2) was revised to eliminate alternative calling for production of arrested parolee before a magistrate, and to eliminate the provision authorizing parole officers to issue warrants for the arrest of parole violators, substituting therefor a provision allowing parole officers to call upon any peace officer to assist them in making such an arrest.

Resubmitted to the Institute in Proposed Final Draft No. 1 as Section 305.15 and approved at the May 1961 meeting.

Verbal changes have been made.

For Commentary, see Tentative Draft No. 5, p. 109.

Section 305.17. Duration of Re-imprisonment and Re-parole after Revocation.

(1) A parolee whose parole is revoked for violation of the conditions of parole shall be recommitted for the remainder of his maximum parole term, after credit thereon for the period served on parole prior to the violation and for reductions for good behavior earned while on parole.

(2) A parolee whose parole has been revoked may be considered by the Board of Parole for re-parole at any time. He shall be entitled to a hearing and consideration for re-parole after serving a further period of imprisonment equal to one third of the remainder of his maximum parole term, or after serving a period of six months, whichever is longer.

(3) Except in the case of a parolee who has absconded from the jurisdiction or from his place of residence, action revoking a parolee's parole and recommitting him for violation of the conditions of parole must be taken before the expiration of his maximum parole term less reductions for good behavior. A parolee who has absconded from the jurisdiction, or from his place of residence, shall be treated as a parole violator and whenever he is apprehended shall be subject to recommitment or to supervision for the balance of his parole term remaining on the date when he absconded.

STATUS OF SECTION

Formerly numbered 305.22.

Presented to the Institute in Tentative Draft No. 5 and considered at the May 1956 meeting.

Revised to take account of changes in parole term under Section 6.10, made with the approval of the Council at its March 1957 meeting.

Resubmitted to the Institute, with verbal changes, in Proposed Final Draft No. 1 and approved at the May 1961 meeting.

For Commentary, see Tentative Draft No. 5, p. 125.

Section 305.18. Parole to Detainers.

(1) If a warrant or detainer is placed against a prisoner by a court, parole agency or other authority of this or any other jurisdiction, the Parole Administrator shall inquire, and seek to determine, before such prisoner becomes eligible for parole, whether the authority concerned intends to execute or withdraw the writ when the prisoner is released.

(2) If the authority notifies the Parole Administrator that it intends to execute such writ when the prisoner is released, the Parole Administrator shall advise the authority concerned of the sentence under which the prisoner is held, the time of parole eligibility, any decision of the Board of Parole relating to the prisoner, and of the nature of his adjustment during imprisonment, and shall give reasonable notice to such authority of the prisoner's release date.

(3) The Board of Parole may parole a prisoner who is eligible for release to a warrant or detainer. If a prisoner is paroled to such a warrant or detainer the Board of Parole may provide, as a condition of his release, that if the charges on which the warrant or detainer is based are dismissed, or are satisfied after conviction and sentence, prior to the expiration of his maximum parole term, the authority to whose warrant or detainer he is released shall return him to serve the remainder of his maximum parole term or such part thereof as the Board may determine.

(4) If a person paroled to a warrant or detainer is thereafter sentenced and placed on probation, or released on parole in another jurisdiction prior to the expiration of his maximum parole term less reduction for good behavior in

this State, the Board of Parole may permit him to serve the remainder of his parole term, or such part thereof as the Board may determine, concurrently with his new probation or parole term. Such concurrent terms may be served in either of the two jurisdictions, and supervision shall be administered in accordance with the provisions of the Interstate Compact for the Supervision of Parolees and Probationers.

STATUS OF SECTION

Formerly numbered 305.24.

Presented to the Institute in Tentative Draft No. 5 and considered at the May 1956 meeting.

Resubmitted to the Institute in Proposed Final Draft No. 1 and approved at the May 1961 meeting.

For Commentary, see Tentative Draft No. 5, p. 129.

Section 305.19. Finality of Determinations with Respect to Reduction of Terms for Good Behavior and Parole.

No court shall have jurisdiction to review or set aside, except for the denial of a hearing when a right to be heard is conferred by law:

(1) the action of an authorized official of the Department of Correction or of the Board of Parole withholding, forfeiting or refusing to restore a reduction of a prison or parole term for good behavior; or

(2) the orders or decisions of the Board of Parole regarding, but not limited to, the release or deferment of release on parole of a prisoner whose maximum prison term has not expired, the imposition or modification of conditions of parole, the revocation of parole,

the termination or restoration of parole supervision or the discharge from parole or from re-imprisonment before the end of the parole term.

STATUS OF SECTION

Formerly numbered 305.25.

Presented to the Institute in Tentative Draft No. 5 and considered at the May 1956 meeting.

Resubmitted to the Institute, with verbal changes, in Proposed Final Draft No. 1 and approved at the May 1961 meeting.

For Commentary, see Tentative Draft No. 5, p. 128.

Two of the sections in Article 305, as it was presented in Tentative Draft No. 5, were eliminated in Proposed Final Draft No. 1. They were former Section 305.20, entitled Automatic Revocation of Parole Upon Conviction of New Crime, and former Section 305.23, entitled Revocation of Parole; Reconsideration. See Tentative Draft No. 5, pp. 112, 127; Proposed Final Draft No. 1, p. 117.

ARTICLE 306. LOSS AND RESTORATION OF RIGHTS INCIDENT TO CONVICTION OR IMPRISONMENT

Section 306.1. Basis of Disqualification or Disability.

(1) No person shall suffer any legal disqualification or disability because of his conviction of a crime or his sentence on such conviction, unless the disqualification or disability involves the deprivation of a right or privilege which is:

    (a) necessarily incident to execution of the sentence of the Court; or

    (b) provided by the Constitution or the Code; or

    (c) provided by a statute other than the Code, when the conviction is of a crime defined by such statute; or

    (d) provided by the judgment, order or regulation of a court, agency or official exercising a jurisdiction conferred by law, or by the statute defining such jurisdiction, when the commission of the crime or the conviction or the sentence is reasonably related to the competency of the individual to exercise the right or privilege of which he is deprived.

(2) Proof of a conviction as relevant evidence upon the trial or determination of any issue, or for the purpose of impeaching the convicted person as a witness is not a disqualification or disability within the meaning of this Article.

STATUS OF SECTION

Submitted to the Institute in Proposed Final Draft No. 1 and approved at the May 1961 meeting.

Verbal changes have been made in response to a suggestion made at the 1961 Institute meeting.

Section 306.2. Forfeiture of Public Office.

A person holding any public office who is convicted of a crime shall forfeit such office if:

(1) he is convicted under the laws of this State of a felony or under the laws of another jurisdiction of a crime which, if committed within this State, would be a felony; or

(2) he is convicted of a crime involving malfeasance in such office, or dishonesty; or

(3) the Constitution or a statute other than the Code so provides.

STATUS OF SECTION

Submitted to the Institute in Proposed Final Draft No. 1 and considered at the May 1961 meeting.

The words "or employment" have been delected from the Section, and in Subsection (1) the words "under the laws of this State" and "or under the laws of another jurisdiction of a crime which, if committed within this State, would be a felony" have been added, in accordance with the action of the Institute at the May 1961 meeting.

Section 306.3. Voting and Jury Service.

Notwithstanding any other provision of law, a person who is convicted of a crime shall be disqualified

(1) from voting in a primary or election if and only so long as he is committed under a sentence of imprisonment; and

(2) from serving as a juror until he has satisfied his sentence.

STATUS OF SECTION

Submitted to the Institute in Proposed Final Draft No. 1 and approved at the May 1961 meeting.

Section 306.4. Testimonial Capacity; Testimony of Prisoners.

(1) Notwithstanding any other provision of law, the fact that a person has been convicted of a crime or that he is under sentence therefor, whether of imprisonment or otherwise, does not render him incompetent to testify in a legal proceeding.

(2) Upon the order of the ——————— Court, the Warden or other administrative head of an institution in which a prisoner is confined shall arrange for the production of the prisoner to testify at the place designated in the order. Such order shall be issued whenever the Court is satisfied that the testimony of the prisoner is required in a judicial or administrative proceeding and that the ends of justice can not be satisfied by taking his deposition at the institution where he is confined.

(3) Subject to regulations of the Department of Correction as to institutions subject to its jurisdiction, the Warden or other administrative head of an institution in which a prisoner is confined may, in his discretion, permit the prisoner to leave the institution, either alone or in the custody of an officer, for the purpose of testifying in a legal proceeding in which he is a party or has been called as a witness. In granting such permission, the Warden or administrative head may require that the prisoner or party calling him to testify defray the reasonable costs of providing for his custody while absent from the institution.

(4) Subject to regulations of the Department of Correction as to institutions subject to its jurisdiction, the Warden or other administrative head of an institution in which a prisoner is confined shall permit the prisoner to give testimony by deposition or in response to interrogatories, when such testimony is desired in a legal proceeding,

and shall make suitable arrangements to facilitate the taking of such deposition in the institution.

STATUS OF SECTION

Submitted to the Institute in Proposed Final Draft No. 1 and approved at the May 1961 meeting.

Section 306.5. Appointment of Agent, Attorney-in-Fact or Trustee for Prisoner.

(1) A person confined under a sentence of imprisonment shall have the same right to appoint an agent, attorney-in-fact or trustee to act in his behalf with respect to his property or economic interests as if he were not so confined.

(2) Upon the application of a person confined or about to be confined under a sentence of imprisonment, the ———— Court [insert appropriate court of record] of the county where the prisoner resided at the time of sentence or where the sentence was imposed may appoint a trustee to safeguard his property and economic interests during the period of his commitment. The trustee shall have such power and authority as the Court designates in the order of appointment but, unless the order otherwise provides, shall have all the power and authority conferred by a general power of attorney.

STATUS OF SECTION

Submitted to the Institute in Proposed Final Draft No. 1 and approved at the May 1961 meeting.

Section 306.6. Order Removing Disqualifications or Disabilities; Vacation of Conviction; Effect of Order of Removal or Vacation.

(1) In the cases specified in this Subsection the Court may order that so long as the defendant is not convicted of

another crime, the judgment shall not thereafter constitute a conviction for the purpose of any disqualification or disability imposed by law because of the conviction of a crime:

    (a) in sentencing a young adult offender to the special term provided by Section 6.05(2) or to any sentence other than one of imprisonment; or

    (b) when the Court has theretofore suspended sentence or has sentenced the defendant to be placed on probation and the defendant has fully complied with the requirements imposed as a condition of such order and has satisfied the sentence; or

    (c) when the Court has theretofore sentenced the defendant to imprisonment and the defendant has been released on parole, has fully complied with the conditions of parole and has been discharged; or

    (d) when the Court has theretofore sentenced the defendant, the defendant has fully satisfied the sentence and has since led a law-abiding life for at least [two] years.

(2) In the cases specified in this Subsection, the Court which sentenced a defendant may enter an order vacating the judgment of conviction:

    (a) when an offender [a young adult offender] has been discharged from probation or parole before the expiration of the maximum term thereof[; or

    (b) when a defendant has fully satisfied the sentence and has since led a law-abiding life for at least [five] years].

(3) An order entered under Subsection (1) or (2) of this Section:

    (a) has only prospective operation and does not require the restoration of the defendant to any office, employment or position forfeited or lost in accordance with this Article; and

(b) does not preclude proof of the conviction as evidence of the commission of the crime, whenever the fact of its commission is relevant to the determination of an issue involving the rights or liabilities of someone other than the defendant; and

(c) does not preclude consideration of the conviction for purposes of sentence if the defendant subsequently is convicted of another crime; and

(d) does not preclude proof of the conviction as evidence of the commission of the crime, whenever the fact of its commission is relevant to the exercise of the discretion of a court, agency or official authorized to pass upon the competency of the defendant to perform a function or to exercise a right or privilege which such court, agency or official is empowered to deny, except that in such case the court, agency or official shall also give due weight to the issuance of the order; and

(e) does not preclude proof of the conviction as evidence of the commission of the crime, whenever the fact of its commission is relevant for the purpose of impeaching the defendant as a witness, except that the issuance of the order may be adduced for the purpose of his rehabilitation; and

(f) does not justify a defendant in stating that he has not been convicted of a crime, unless he also calls attention to the order.

STATUS OF SECTION

Presented to the Institute in Proposed Final Draft No. 1 and approved at the May 1961 meeting.

In paragraph (f) of Subsection (3) the words "when the truthfulness of such a statement is in issue" have been eliminated, in accordance with the action of the Institute at the May 1961 meeting.

PART IV. ORGANIZATION OF CORRECTION

ARTICLE 401. DEPARTMENT OF CORRECTION

Section 401.1. Department of Correction; Creation; Responsibilities.

There shall be in the state government a **Department of Correction**, which shall be charged with the following responsibilities:

(1) to maintain, administer, and to establish state correctional institutions, including prisons, reformatories, reception centers, parole and probation hostels, state misdemeanant institutions and such other facilities as may be required for the custody, control, correctional treatment and rehabilitation of committed offenders, and for the safekeeping of such other persons as may be remanded thereto in accordance with law;

(2) to administer the release of prisoners under parole supervision and to administer parole services in the institutions and in the community;

(3) to establish personnel standards and supervision policies for all probation services in the State, and to administer probation field services in any county or other governmental subdivision of this State which has no probation service of its own;

[Alternative: (3) to administer probation services in the community;] *

(4) to develop policies and programs for the correctional treatment and rehabilitation of offenders committed to institutions in the Department;

---

* The alternative should be used in jurisdictions adopting Alternative Article 404 establishing a Division of Probation and Parole.

(5) to establish standards for the management, operation, personnel and program of, and to exercise powers of supervision, visitation and inspection over, all institutions in the State for the detention of persons charged with or convicted of an offense, or for the safekeeping of such other persons as may be remanded thereto in accordance with law, and to close any such institution which is inadequate.

STATUS OF SECTION

Presented to the Institute in Tentative Draft No. 5 and considered at the May 1956 meeting.

The word "supervision" was added to Subsection (5).

Resubmitted to the Institute in Proposed Final Draft No. 1 and approved at the May 1961 meeting.

Bracketed alternative Subsection (3) was added for technical conformity with other alternative provisions.

For Commentary, see Tentative Draft No. 5, p. 147.

Section 401.2. Director of Correction; Appointment; Powers and Duties.

(1) The Department of Correction shall be under the direction of the Director of Correction, who shall be appointed by the Governor for a term of ———— years. His salary shall be fixed by the Governor within the appropriation therefor.

(2) The Director of Correction shall:

(a) supervise and be responsible for the administration of the Department;

(b) establish and administer, with the advice of the Commission of Correction and Community Services, programs and policies for the operation of the institutions in the Department, and for the correction and rehabilitation of prisoners;

(c) appoint and remove deputy directors as provided by law and delegate appropriate powers and duties to them;

(d) appoint and remove subordinate officers of the Department, other than the Board and Division of Parole [Division of Probation and Parole], in accordance with law, and delegate appropriate powers and duties to them;

(e) make rules and regulations for the government, correctional treatment and rehabilitation of prisoners, the administration of institutions in the Department, and the regulation of officers and employees under his jurisdiction;

(f) order the assignment and transfer of prisoners committed to the custody of the Department of Correction to institutions of the Department;

(g) collect, develop and maintain statistical information concerning offenders, sentencing practices and correctional treatment as may be useful in practical penological research or in the development of treatment programs;

(h) exercise, in accordance with law, supervisory power over all institutions in the State for the detention of persons charged with or convicted of an offense, or for the safekeeping of such other persons as may be remanded thereto in accordance with law;

(i) transmit to the Governor annually, on or before the ——— day of ———————, a detailed report of the operations of the Department for the preceding calendar year, which report shall be transmitted by the Governor to the legislature;

(j) exercise all powers and perform all duties necessary and proper in carrying out his responsibilities.

§ 401.3

STATUS OF SECTION

Presented to the Institute in Tentative Draft No. 5 and considered at the May 1956 meeting.

Alternative providing that Director serves during the pleasure of the Governor was eliminated by vote of the Institute.

Paragraph (2)(d) was revised to exclude officers of the Board and Division of Parole from the Director's appointment and removal power;

Paragraph (2)(f) was added and subsequent paragraphs renumbered accordingly;

Paragraph (2)(h) was revised to conform with change in Section 401.1(5).

Resubmitted to the Institute in Proposed Final Draft No. 1 and approved at the May 1961 meeting.

For Commentary, see Tentative Draft No. 5, p. 147.

Section 401.3. Organization of Department of Correction.

(1) There shall be in the Department of Correction the following divisions and independent boards:

(a) Division of Treatment Services;

(b) Division of Custodial Services;

(c) Division of Young Adult Correction;

(d) Division of Fiscal Control;

(e) Division of Prison Industries;

(f) Division of Research and Training;

(g) Division of Parole;

(h) Division of Probation;

Alternate: Division of Probation and Parole;

(i) Commission of Correction and Community Services;

(j) Board of Parole.

The Director of Correction may, after consultation with and on the advice of the Commission of Correction and Community Services, establish additional divisions, consolidate such additional divisions with other divisions, or abolish them, and he may establish, consolidate or abolish bureaus or other administrative subdivisions in any division.

(2) There shall be in each institution in the Department of Correction a warden or other administrative head and [two] associate wardens or administrative heads [designated, respectively, as associate warden on treatment and associate warden on custody]. The Warden in each institution shall be responsible to the Director of Correction for the custody, control and correctional treatment of prisoners and for the general administration of the institution. Associate wardens in each institution shall advise and be responsible to the Warden, and shall have such powers and duties as the Warden may delegate to them in accordance with law or pursuant to the directions of the Director of Correction.

STATUS OF SECTION

Presented to the Institute in Tentative Draft No. 5 and considered at the May 1956 meeting.

Resubmitted to the Institute, with verbal changes, in Proposed Final Draft No. 1 and approved at the May 1961 meeting.

For Commentary, see Tentative Draft No. 5, p. 147.

Section 401.4. Division of Treatment Services; Deputy Director for Treatment Services.

(1) The Division of Treatment Services shall be charged with the supervision of programs of education and training, including academic, vocational and industrial

§ 401.5   Model Penal Code

training, and correctional treatment and rehabilitation, and parole preparation in the institutions of the Department, excepting only institutions for young adult offenders.

(2) The Division of Treatment Services shall be headed by the Deputy Director of Treatment Services, who shall act as the staff advisor of the Director of Correction in regard to correctional treatment, and who shall exercise such power and perform such duties as the Director of Correction may delegate to him. The Deputy Director of Treatment Services shall be appointed by, and serve during the pleasure of, the Director of Correction. He shall be a person with appropriate experience in the field of education, correctional treatment or rehabilitation, and appropriate training in relevant disciplines. His salary shall be fixed by the Governor [the Director of Correction] within the appropriation therefor.

STATUS OF SECTION

Presented to the Institute in Tentative Draft No. 5 and considered at the May 1956 meeting.

Resubmitted to the Institute, with verbal changes, in Proposed Final Draft No. 1 and approved at the May 1961 meeting.

For Commentary, see Tentative Draft No. 5, p. 147.

Section 401.5. Division of Custodial Services; Deputy Director for Custodial Services.

(1) The Division of Custodial Services shall be charged with the custody, control, safekeeping, protection and discipline of prisoners in the institutions of the Department, excepting only institutions for young adult offenders.

(2) The Division of Custodial Services shall be headed by the Deputy Director for Custodial Services, who shall act as the staff advisor of the Director of Correction in regard to matters of custody and discipline, and who shall exercise

such powers and perform such duties as the Director of Correction may delegate to him. The Deputy Director for Custodial Services shall be appointed by, and serve during the pleasure of, the Director of Correction. He shall be a person with appropriate experience in a position of responsibility in the management of institutions or in law enforcement work. His salary shall be fixed by the Governor [the Director of Correction] within the appropriation therefor.

STATUS OF SECTION

Presented to the Institute in Tentative Draft No. 5 and considered at the May 1956 meeting.

Resubmitted to the Institute in Proposed Final Draft No. 1 and approved at the May 1961 meeting.

For Commentary, see Tentative Draft No. 5, p. 147.

Section 401.6. Division of Young Adult Correction; Deputy Director for Young Adult Correction.

(1) The Division of Young Adult Correction shall be charged with the supervision of institutions and facilities for the custody, control, treatment and rehabilitation of young adult offenders, and in cooperation with the Commission of Correction and Community Services, with the planning and establishment of diversified facilities and programs for the treatment and rehabilitation of young adult offenders.

(2) The Division of Young Adult Correction shall be headed by the Deputy Director for Young Adult Correction, who shall act as the staff advisor of the Director of Correction in regard to matters of custody, control and treatment of young adult offenders, and who shall exercise such powers and perform such duties as the Director of Correction may delegate to him. The Deputy Director for Young Adult Correction shall be appointed by, and serve during the pleasure of, the Director of Correction. He shall be a

§ 401.7

person with appropriate experience in the fields of youth guidance, correctional treatment and rehabilitation, or appropriate training in relevant disciplines at a recognized university. His salary shall be fixed by the Governor [the Director of Correction] within the appropriation therefor.

STATUS OF SECTION

Presented to the Institute in Tentative Draft No. 5 and considered at the May 1956 meeting.

Resubmitted to the Institute in Proposed Final Draft No. 1 and approved at the May 1961 meeting.

The word "control" has been added to each subsection in response to a suggestion made at the 1961 Institute meeting.

For Commentary, see Tentative Draft No. 5, p. 147.

Section 401.7. Division of Prison Industries; Deputy Director for Prison Industries.

(1) The Division of Prison Industries shall be charged with the general supervision of industries in the institutions of the Department.

(2) The Division of Prison Industries shall be headed by the Deputy Director for Prison Industries, who shall be the staff advisor of the Director of Correction in regard to the industries in the institutions of the Department, and who shall exercise such powers and perform such duties as the Director of Correction may delegate to him. The Deputy Director for Prison Industries shall be appointed by, and serve during the pleasure of, the Director of Correction. He shall be a person with appropriate experience in the management of institutional industries, or in industrial management. His salary shall be fixed by the Governor [the Director of Correction] within the appropriation therefor.

STATUS OF SECTION

Presented to the Institute in Tentative Draft No. 5 and considered at the May 1956 meeting.

Resubmitted to the Institute in Proposed Final Draft No. 1 and approved at the May 1961 meeting.

For Commentary, see Tentative Draft No. 5, p. 147.

Section 401.8. Division of Fiscal Control; Deputy Director for Fiscal Control.

(1) The Division of Fiscal Control shall be charged with the establishment and maintenance of an accounting and auditing system [in accordance with the state finance law] for the Department of Correction, its institutions, and all of its divisions, and boards other than the Division of Parole and the Board of Parole. The Division of Fiscal Control shall also be responsible for the preparation of the Department's proposed annual budget, except for the annual budget of the Division of Parole and the Board of Parole, which shall be prepared in accordance with Section 404.1.

(2) The Division of Fiscal Control shall be headed by the Deputy Director for Fiscal Control, who shall be the staff advisor of the Director of Correction in regard to fiscal matters, and who shall exercise such powers and perform such duties as the Director of Correction may delegate to him. The Deputy Director for Fiscal Control shall be appointed by, and serve during the pleasure of, the Director of Correction. He shall be a person with appropriate experience in a position of responsibility in accounting or managerial work, or with appropriate training in relevant disciplines at a recognized university or school of business or administration. His salary shall be fixed by the Governor [the Director of Correction] within the appropriation therefor.

§ 401.9

STATUS OF SECTION

Presented to the Institute in Tentative Draft No. 5 and considered at the May 1956 meeting.

Subsection (1) revised to except the Division and Board of Parole from the scope of the Section, so as to conform to the amendment of Section 404.1 granting the Division of Parole control of its own budget. The amendment reflects the advice of parole administrators.

Resubmitted to the Institute in Proposed Final Draft No. 1 and approved at the May 1961 meeting.

For Commentary, see Tentative Draft No. 5, p. 147.

Section 401.9. Division of Research and Training; Deputy Director for Research and Training.

(1) The Division of Research and Training shall be charged:

(a) with the collection, development and maintenance of statistical and other information concerning the dispositions by criminal courts of the State, length of sentences imposed and length of sentences actually served, release on parole, success or failure on parole, discharge from parole supervision, success or failure on probation, recidivism, and concerning such other aspects of sentencing practice and correctional treatment as may be useful in practical penological research or in the development of treatment programs; and

(b) with the conduct of training programs designed to equip personnel for duty in the correctional institutions and services of the State and to raise and maintain the educational standards and the level of performance of correctional personnel.

(2) The Division of Research and Training shall be headed by the Deputy Director for Research and Training, who shall be the staff advisor of the Director of Correction

Art. 401 319 § 401.10

in regard to all matters of penological research in the Department and who shall exercise such powers and perform such duties as the Director of Correction may delegate to him. The Deputy Director for Research and Training shall be appointed by, and serve during the pleasure of, the Director of Correction. He shall be a person with appropriate experience in statistical research or research in the social sciences, with appropriate training in relevant disciplines. His salary shall be fixed by the Governor [the Director of Correction] within the appropriation therefor.

STATUS OF SECTION

Presented to the Institute in Tentative Draft No. 5 and considered at the May 1956 meeting.

Resubmitted to the Institute, with verbal changes, in Proposed Final Draft No. 1 and approved at the May 1961 meeting.

For Commentary, see Tentative Draft No. 5, p. 147.

Section 401.10. Commission of Correction and Community Services; Organization; Functions.

(1) The Commission of Correction and Community Services shall consist of the Director of Correction, the Chairman of the Board of Parole, the Parole Administrator, the Probation Administrator [alternate: the Probation and Parole Administrator], the Deputy Director for Treatment Services, the Deputy Director for Young Adult Correction, two judges sitting in courts of general criminal jurisdiction [or special parts of courts dealing with young adult offenders], designated by the Governor, and four public members, appointed by the Governor, one of whom shall be a psychiatrist and one a professional educator. The judicial and public members shall be appointed for a term of ———— years [alternate: serve for the remainder of the term of office of the Governor during whose incumbency they were appointed, unless sooner removed for cause]; all other

members shall serve during their terms of office. The Director of Correction shall act as chairman of the Commission. All members of the Commission shall serve without compensation, but each member shall be reimbursed for his necessary travel and other expenses actually incurred in the discharge of his duties on the Commission.

(2) The Commission of Correction and Community Services shall meet at least every three months, and whenever called into session by the chairman, at the request of the Governor, of the Deputy Director for Young Adult Correction under Subsection (4) of this Section, of any two or more members of the Commission, or on his own motion.

(3) The Commission of Correction and Community Services shall advise the Governor and the Director of Correction concerning correctional policy and programs, including particularly the following:

    (a) the need for, and the development of new or specialized institutions, facilities, or programs;

    (b) the need for, and the effectuation of collaboration and liaison within the Department, and between the Department and community agencies and resources, in order to promote the readjustment and rehabilitation of offenders in institutions or under parole or probation supervision in the community;

    (c) the need for, and the development of useful researches in penology, correctional treatment, criminal law, or in the disciplines relevant thereto.

(4) Whenever requested by the Deputy Director for Young Adult Correction, the Commission of Correction and Community Services shall meet to consider, and to advise

the Department of Correction concerning the need for, and the development of, services and facilities for young adult offenders, and concerning researches necessary or useful in evaluating the effectiveness of correctional treatment of such offenders.

(5) The Commission or one or more of its members may visit and inspect any institution, state or local, for the detention of persons charged with or convicted of an offense, and for the safekeeping of such other persons as may be remanded thereto in accordance with law, and may inform and advise the Director of Correction in regard to any such institution's physical or other condition, its discipline, management, program, and its general adequacy or inadequacy. The Commission or one or more of its members shall have full access to the grounds and buildings and to the books and records belonging or relating to any such institution, as well as the right to subpoena witnesses, take proof or hear testimony under oath relating to any such institution.

(6) The Commission may employ a staff director and such other personnel as may be necessary to help perform its functions, and may prescribe their duties.

STATUS OF SECTION

Presented to the Institute in Tentative Draft No. 5 and considered at the May 1956 meeting.

Resubmitted to the Institute in Proposed Final Draft No. 1 and approved at the May 1961 meeting.

For Commentary, see Tentative Draft No. 5, p. 147.

Section 401.11. Visitation and Inspection of Institutions.

(1) The Director of Correction, or any person to whom he has delegated such power in writing, shall visit and in-

spect any institution in the State for the detention of persons charged with or convicted of an offense, or for the safekeeping of such other persons as may be remanded thereto in accordance with law. He shall have full access to the grounds, buildings, books and records belonging or relating to any such institution, and may require the Warden or other head of such institution to provide information relating thereto in person or in written response to a questionnaire. He shall have the power, in connection with the inspection of any such institution, to issue subpoenas, compel the attendance of witnesses and the production of books, papers and other documents relating to such institution or its officers, and to administer oaths and to take the testimony of persons under oath.

(2) If the Director of Correction finds, after inspection of an institution, that the laws or regulations relating to the construction, management and affairs of such institution and the care, custody, treatment and discipline of its prisoners are being violated, or that the prisoners are cruelly, negligently or improperly treated, or that there is improper or inadequate provision for their sustenance, clothing, care or other condition necessary to their discipline and welfare, the Director may in writing order the Warden or other head of such institution to remedy the situation within such period of time as the Director may deem appropriate under the circumstances. If the Director's order is not complied with within the time provided, the Director may order the institution to be closed until such time as he finds that his order has been or is being complied with. When an order closing an institution is made, it shall be unlawful to detain or confine any person therein. Whenever an inspection of an institution discloses violation of law in its management or conduct, the Director of Correction shall report such violation to the appropriate law enforcement official.

STATUS OF SECTION

Presented to the Institute in Tentative Draft No. 5 and considered at the May 1956 meeting.

Revised to make inspection mandatory rather than permissive and to include reference to "regulations."

Resubmitted to the Institute in Proposed Final Draft No. 1 and approved at the May 1961 meeting.

For Commentary, see Tentative Draft No. 5, p. 147.

Section 401.12. Appointment and Promotion of Employees; Department Under Civil Service Law [Merit System].

Except as otherwise provided by the Code, the officers and employees of the Department, its divisions and boards, shall be appointed, promoted and discharged in accordance with the state civil service law [merit system], and the Civil Service Commission [or other appropriate body] shall set standards, in accordance with law, for the appointment and promotion of such personnel.

STATUS OF SECTION

Presented to the Institute in Tentative Draft No. 5 and considered at the May 1956 meeting.

Revised for technical conformity with other provisions.

Resubmitted to the Institute in Proposed Final Draft No. 1 and approved at the May 1961 meeting.

For Commentary, see Tentative Draft No. 5, p. 147.

ARTICLE 402. BOARD OF PAROLE

Section 402.1. Board of Parole; Composition and Tenure.

(1) There is hereby created within the Department of Correction an independent Board of Parole, to consist of ———— members [not less than three or more than nine], to be appointed by the Governor with the advice of [from a panel of candidates submitted by] the Commission of Correction and Community Services. Members selected shall be persons of good character and judicious temperament who possess specialized skills evidenced by training or past experience in fields related to correctional administration and criminology. At least one member of the Board shall be a member of the bar of this State. The term of office of each member of the Board shall be six years and until his successor is appointed, except that of the members first appointed to the Board, ———— shall be appointed to serve for a term of two years, ———— for a term of four years, and ———— for a term of six years. A member appointed to fill a vacancy occurring other than by expiration of a term shall be appointed for the remainder of the unexpired term of the member whom he succeeds. Members may be reappointed for additional six-year terms. They may be removed by the Governor solely for corruption or disability, and after an opportunity to be heard. The Governor shall, from time to time, designate one of the members to serve as chairman of the Board during such member's term of office.

(2) Each member shall devote full time to the duties of his office, and shall not engage in any other business or profession, or hold any other public office. No member shall, at the time of his appointment or during his tenure, serve as the representative of any political party, or of any executive committee or governing body thereof, or as an executive officer or employee of any political party, organization, association, or committee. Each member of the

Board shall receive an annual salary to be fixed by the Governor, within the appropriation therefor, at not less than ———— and shall be reimbursed for his necessary travel and other expenses actually incurred in the discharge of his duties.

STATUS OF SECTION

Presented to the Institute in Tentative Draft No. 5 and considered at the May 1956 meeting.

Resubmitted to the Institute in Proposed Final Draft No. 1 and approved at the May 1961 meeting.

For Commentary, see Tentative Draft No. 5, p. 165.

Section 402.2. Powers and Duties of the Board of Parole.

(1) The Board of Parole shall, in accordance with Article 305:

(a) determine the time of release on parole of prisoners eligible for such release;

(b) fix the conditions of parole, revoke parole, issue or authorize the issuance of warrants for the arrest of parole violators, and impose other sanctions short of revocation for violation of conditions of parole;

(c) determine the time of discharge from parole [;

(d) appoint the Parole Administrator in accordance with Article 404, and establish policies for the Division of Parole and supervise their execution].*

(2) The Board of Parole shall, when requested by the Governor, advise him concerning applications for pardon, reprieve, or commutation, and shall when so requested make such investigation and collect such records concerning the facts and circumstances of a prisoner's crime, his past criminal record, social history, and physical, mental or psychiatric condition as may bear on such application.

---

* As indicated in the status notes, the alternative provisions in Sections 402.2(1)(d), 404.1(2) and 404.2 serve in the aggregate to vest control of the Division of Parole in the Board of Parole rather than in the Director of Correction. They must therefore be considered in combination.

§ 402.3   Model Penal Code

(3) The Board of Parole shall cooperate with the Commission of Correction and Community Services in the development and promotion of effective parole policies.

(4) The Board of Parole shall annually, on or before the ———— day of ——————, transmit to the Director of Correction a detailed report of its work for the preceding calendar year. The annual report shall be transmitted by the Director of Correction to the Governor for submission to the legislature.

(5) The Board or any member thereof shall have the power, in the performance of official duties, to issue subpoenas, compel the attendance of witnesses, and the production of books, papers and other documents pertinent to the subject of its inquiry, and to administer oaths and to take the testimony of persons under oath.

STATUS OF SECTION

Presented to the Institute in Tentative Draft No. 5 and considered at the May 1956 meeting.

Paragraph (1)(d), which appears in brackets, was added as an alternative provision. The effect of the bracketed paragraph, taken together with the bracketed provisions in Sections 404.1(2) and 404.2, is to establish control of the Division of Parole by the Board of Parole, as an alternative to vesting such control in the Director of Correction.

Resubmitted to the Institute, with verbal changes, in Proposed Final Draft No. 1 and approved at the May 1961 meeting.

Paragraph (b) of Subsection (1) has been revised to allow greater flexibility with respect to the manner in which warrants for the arrest of parole violators may be issued, and more clearly to articulate other powers of the Board of Parole.

Paragraph (c) of Subsection (1) has been revised for technical conformity with other provisions.

For Commentary, see Tentative Draft No. 5, p. 165.

Section 402.3. Young Adult Division of Board of Parole.

(1) The Board of Parole may from time to time designate one or more of its members to serve as a Young Adult

Division of the Board. All decisions of the Young Adult Division shall be by majority vote, but if the Young Adult Division consists of less than three members, its decisions shall not be effective until voted by a majority of a quorum of the whole Board of Parole. When the Young Adult Division has been established, it shall have all of the powers and duties of the Board in respect to young adult offenders committed to the custody of the Division of Young Adult Correction of the Department of Correction.

(2) The Board of Parole, or if the Young Adult Division has been established, the Division shall:

    (a) hold a parole hearing of every young adult offender sentenced in accordance with Section 6.05(2) to a term of imprisonment without a minimum and with a maximum of four years, within ninety days of such offender's date of commitment, in order to fix his release date or to defer the case for later reconsideration;

    (b) interview every young adult offender who has been remanded to the Department of Correction prior to sentence for observation and study in a reception center, study his record and advise the Court of its findings and recommendations before sentence;

    (c) consult with the Deputy Director of Young Adult Correction concerning correctional policy and programs in institutions and treatment facilities serving young adult offenders, and concerning such special programs of intensive correctional and rehabilitative treatment as may be required for such offenders.

STATUS OF SECTION

Presented to the Institute in Tentative Draft No. 7 and considered at the May 1957 meeting.

Resubmitted to the Institute, with verbal changes, in Proposed Final Draft No. 1 and approved at the May 1961 meeting.

For Commentary, see Tentative Draft No. 7, p. 33.

ARTICLE 403. ADMINISTRATION OF INSTITUTIONS

Section 403.1. Appointment of Personnel.

(1) The Director of Correction by and with the advice of the Commission of Correction and Community Services and in accordance with the state civil service law [merit system] shall appoint and assign the Wardens or other administrative heads for each of the correctional institutions of the Department. The Director shall appoint professional, technical, skilled, and other subordinate officers and employees as may be required for the effective administration of the correctional institutions of the Department in accordance with the state civil service law [merit system] and in the case of institutional employees he shall consider the recommendations of the respective Wardens or other administrative heads of institutions.

(2) The [appropriate authority] of the county, city or [other appropriate political subdivision of the state] shall appoint and assign the Wardens or other administrative heads for each of the correctional institutions of such political subdivision, in accordance with the state civil service law [merit system] and subject to approval by the Director of Correction. In the case of correctional institutions serving more than one such political subdivision of the State, the appointment shall be made in the same manner by the [appropriate authorities] of such subdivisions acting jointly. The Warden or other administrative head of such correctional institution shall appoint professional, technical, skilled, and other subordinate officers and employees as may be required for the effective administration of the correctional institution in accordance with the state civil service law [merit system] and with the regulations of the Department of Correction.

(3) Personnel in the custodial and treatment program of institutions shall have such special training or experience in correctional matters as the [State Civil Service Commission] may require upon the advice of the Director of Correction.

(4) No male person shall be appointed or assigned to positions involving the immediate supervision and control of female prisoners.

(5) Civilian instructors certified by the [State Department of Education] shall, as far as practicable, be employed for the academic and vocational training of prisoners.

(6) Each new officer or employee in the custodial or treatment program of a correctional institution shall participate in an institutional training program for new employees. Every officer and employee in the Department of Correction shall participate in such in-service training programs as the Director of Correction may require from time to time.

STATUS OF SECTION

Presented to the Institute in Tentative Draft No. 12 and considered at the May 1960 meeting.

Revised to take account of local institutions and their relation to the Department of Correction under Article 303.

Resubmitted to the Institute in Proposed Final Draft No. 1 and approved at the May 1961 meeting.

A sentence in Subsection (3) requiring appointments and assignments without reference to race, color or religion has been eliminated as implicit in the general requirement of conformity to State civil service law or merit system.

For Commentary, see Tentative Draft No. 12, p. 71.

Section 403.2. Powers and Duties of Wardens and Other Administrative Heads of State and Local Institutions.

The Warden or other administrative head of each correctional institution in the Department of Correction and of each correctional institution of a county, city or [other appropriate political subdivision of the State] shall be its chief executive officer, and, subject to the supervisory authority conferred by law on the Director of Correction, shall be responsible for its efficient and humane maintenance and operation, and for its security. The duties and powers of his office shall include the following:

(1) to receive, retain in imprisonment, and to release, in accordance with law, prisoners duly committed to the Department and transferred to the institution, or duly committed to the institution;

(2) to enforce the provisions of law and the regulations of the Department for the administration of the institution, the government of its officers, and the treatment, training, employment, care, discipline and custody of the prisoners;

(3) to take proper measures to protect the safety of the prisoners and personnel of the institution;

(4) to take proper measures to prevent the escape of prisoners and to effect their recapture;

(5) to maintain and improve the buildings, grounds and appurtenances of the institution;

(6) to make recommendations to the Director concerning the appointment of professional, technical, skilled and other subordinate officers and employees, in accordance with Section 403.1(1) in the case of institutions in the Department of Correction, and to appoint such subordinate officers and employees, in accordance with Section 403.1(2) in the case of institutions of counties, cities, or [other appropriate political subdivision of the State].

(7) to establish and administer rules, including rules for the operation of the institution and for the

proper classification and separation of prisoners therein, consistent with the provisions of this Code, the general policies and regulations of the Department, and subject to the prior approval of such rules by the Director of Correction;

(8) to maintain and preserve the central prisoner file, in accordance with Section 303.2 or Section 304.3, and to maintain and preserve records on the management and operation of the institution, including records concerning its industries and the wage funds of prisoners, and to report thereon to the Director of Correction at such times as the Director may require.

STATUS OF SECTION

Presented to the Institute in Tentative Draft No. 12 and considered at the May 1960 meeting.

Subsections (3) and (4) were added. The initial paragraph and Subsections (1), (6) and (8) were revised to reflect inclusion of local institutions within the scope of the Section. Verbal changes were made and Subsections renumbered.

Resubmitted to the Institute in Proposed Final Draft No. 1 and approved at the May 1961 meeting.

For Commentary, see Tentative Draft No. 12, p. 77.

Section 403.3. Separation of Female Prisoners.

No female prisoner committed to the Department shall be kept in any correctional institution used for the imprisonment of men.

STATUS OF SECTION

Presented to the Institute in Tentative Draft No. 12 and considered at the May 1960 meeting.

Resubmitted to the Institute in Proposed Final Draft No. 1 and approved at the May 1961 meeting.

For Commentary, see Tentative Draft No. 12, p. 85.

ARTICLE 404. DIVISION OF PAROLE

Section 404.1. Division of Parole; Parole Administrator.

(1) The Division of Parole shall be charged with the administration of parole services in the community. The Division shall consist of the field parole service and of such other employees as may be necessary in carrying out its functions.

(2) The Division of Parole shall be under the direction of the Parole Administrator, who shall be appointed by, and serve during the pleasure of, the Governor [the Director of Correction] [alternative: the Board of Parole].* The Parole Administrator shall be a person with appropriate experience in a field of correctional administration, or appropriate training in relevant disciplines at a recognized university. His salary shall be fixed by the Governor [the Director of Correction] [the Board] within the appropriation therefor.

(3) The Division of Parole shall establish and maintain its own accounting and auditing system [in accordance with the state finance law] and shall prepare and submit its own proposed annual budget, including therein the proposed annual budget of the Board of Parole, separate from the proposed annual budget of the Department of Correction.

STATUS OF SECTION

Presented to the Institute in Tentative Draft No. 5 and considered at the May 1956 meeting.

---

* As indicated in the status notes, the alternative provisions in Sections 402.2(1)(d), 404.1(2), and 404.2 serve in the aggregate to vest control of the Division of Parole in the Board of Parole rather than in the Director of Correction. They must therefore be considered in combination.

The alternative provision in Subsection (2), consisting of the words "the Board of Parole," was added. The effect of the bracketed alternative, taken together with the bracketed provisions in Sections 402.2(1)(d) and 404.2, is to establish control of the Division of Parole by the Board of Parole, as an alternative to vesting such control in the Director of Correction.

Subsection (3) was added to grant to the Division of Parole control of its auditing and accounting system, and of its own budget. The addition reflects the advice of parole administrators.

Resubmitted to the Institute in Proposed Final Draft No. 1 and approved at the May 1961 meeting.

Verbal changes have been made for technical conformity with other provisions.

For Commentary, see Tentative Draft No. 5, p. 176.

Section 404.2. Powers and Duties of the Parole Administrator.

[Subject to the policy direction of the Board of Parole,] * the Parole Administrator shall:

(1) establish and administer standards, policies and procedures for the field parole service;

(2) appoint district parole supervisors, field parole officers and such other employees as may be required to carry out adequate parole supervision of all parolees from correctional institutions of the State, and prescribe their powers and duties;

(3) cooperate closely with the Board of Parole, the criminal courts, the Deputy Director for Treatment Services, the institutional parole staffs, and other institutional personnel;

---

* As indicated in the status notes, the alternative provisions in Sections 402.2(1)(d), 404.1(2), and 404.2 serve in the aggregate to vest control of the Division of Parole in the Board of Parole rather than in the Director of Correction. They must therefore be considered in combination.

§ 404.3

(4) make recommendations to the Board of Parole in cases of violation of the conditions of parole, issue warrants for the arrest of parole violators when so instructed by the Board, notify the Wardens or other administrative heads of institutions of determinations made by the Board, and upon instruction of the Board issue certificates of parole and of parole revocation to the institutions, and certificates of discharge from parole to parolees;

(5) carry out the provisions of Section 404.1(3) in cooperation with the Board of Parole.

STATUS OF SECTION

Presented to the Institute in Tentative Draft No. 5 and considered at the May 1956 meeting.

The alternative language at the beginning of the Section, which appears in brackets, was added. The effect of the bracketed portion, taken together with the bracketed provisions in Section 402.2(1)(d) and alternative 404.1(2), is to establish control of the Division of Parole by the Board of Parole, as an alternative to vesting such control in the Director of Correction.

Subsection (5) was added to conform the Section to the changes in Section 404.1.

Resubmitted to the Institute in Proposed Final Draft No. 1 and approved at the May 1961 meeting.

Verbal changes have been made for technical conformity with other provisions.

For Commentary, see Tentative Draft No. 5, p. 176.

Section 404.3. Field Parole Service; Organization and Duties.

(1) The field parole service, consisting of field parole officers working under the immediate direction of district parole supervisors, and under the ultimate direction of the Parole Administrator, shall be responsible for the investi-

gation, supervision and assistance of parolees. The field parole service shall be sufficient in size to assure that no parole officer carries a case load larger than is compatible with adequate parole investigation or supervision.

(2) Field parole officers shall:

(a) make investigations, prior to a prisoner's release on parole, in cooperation with institutional parole officers and the Board of Parole, to determine the adequacy of parole plans submitted by prisoners who are candidates for parole, and make reasonable advance preparations for their release on parole;

(b) help parolees in conforming to the conditions of parole, and in making a successful adjustment in the community;

(c) supervise parolees, and in supervising them visit each parolee's home from time to time, and require that each parolee report to his parole officer as frequently as may be required in the light of his personality and adjustment, but no less frequently than twice a month during the first year of parole, except in unusual cases;

(d) admonish parolees who appear in danger of violating the conditions of parole, and report to the appropriate district supervisor serious or persistent violations which may require action by the Board of Parole, and, in emergency situations, exercise the power of arrest as provided in Section 305.16.

(3) District parole supervisors shall:

(a) make regular reports to the Parole Administrator concerning the adjustment of parolees under their supervision;

(b) inform the Parole Administrator when, in the district parole supervisor's opinion, any eligible parolee's conduct and attitude warrant his discharge from supervision, or when any parolee's violation of the conditions of parole is of sufficient seriousness to require action by the Board of Parole, and, in emergency situations, exercise the power of arrest as provided in Section 305.16.

STATUS OF SECTION

Formerly numbered 404.4.

Presented to the Institute in Tentative Draft No. 5 and considered at the May 1956 meeting.

Resubmitted to the Institute, with verbal changes, in Proposed Final Draft No. 1 and approved at the May 1961 meeting.

Verbal changes have been made for technical conformity with other provisions.

Former Section 404.3 of Tentative Draft No. 5, entitled Division of Parole Under Civil Service Law [Merit System], was eliminated in Proposed Final Draft No. 1 because its subject matter is covered by the general provision in Section 401.12. See Tentative Draft No. 5, p. 171; Proposed Final Draft No. 1, p. 151.

For Commentary, see Tentative Draft No. 5, p. 176.

ALTERNATIVE ARTICLE 404. DIVISION OF PROBATION AND PAROLE

Section 404.1. Division of Probation and Parole; Probation and Parole Administrator.

(1) The Division of Probation and Parole shall be charged with the administration of probation and parole services in the community. The Division shall consist of the field probation and parole service and of such other employees as may be necessary in carrying out its functions.

(2) The Division of Probation and Parole shall be under the direction of the Probation and Parole Administrator, who shall be appointed by, and serve during the pleasure of, the Governor [the Director of Correction]. The Probation and Parole Administrator shall be a person with appropriate experience in a field of correctional administration, or appropriate training in relevant disciplines at a recognized university. His salary shall be fixed by the Governor [the Director of Correction] within the appropriation therefor.

STATUS OF SECTION

Presented to the Institute in Tentative Draft No. 5 and considered at the May 1956 meeting.

Resubmitted to the Institute in Proposed Final Draft No. 1 and approved at the May 1961 meeting.

For Commentary, see Tentative Draft No. 5, p. 176.

Section 404.2. Powers and Duties of the Probation and Parole Administrator.

The Probation and Parole Administrator shall:

(1) supervise the administration of probation and parole services in the State and, with the advice of the

Commission of Correction and Community Services, establish policies, standards and procedures, and make rules and regulations for the field probation and parole service, regarding probation and parole investigations, supervision, case work and case loads and record keeping;

(2) appoint district probation and parole supervisors, field probation and parole officers, and such other employees as may be required to carry out adequate probation supervision of persons sentenced to probation and adequate parole supervision of all parolees, and prescribe their powers and duties;

(3) cooperate closely with the Commission of Correction and Community Services, the Board of Parole, the criminal courts, the Deputy Director for Treatment Services, the institutional parole staffs, and other institutional personnel;

(4) make recommendations to the Board of Parole in cases of violation of the conditions of parole, issue warrants for the arrest of parole violators when so instructed by the Board, notify the Wardens or other administrative heads of institutions of determinations made by the Board, and upon instruction of the Board, issue certificates of parole and of parole revocation to the institutions, and certificates of discharge from parole to parolees.

STATUS OF SECTION

Presented to the Institute in Tentative Draft No. 5 and considered at the May 1956 meeting.

Resubmitted to the Institute, with verbal changes, in Proposed Final Draft No. 1 and approved at the May 1961 meeting.

Verbal changes have been made for technical conformity with other provisions.

For Commentary, see Tentative Draft No. 5, p. 176.

Section 404.3. Field Probation and Parole Service; Organization and Duties.

(1) The field probation and parole service, consisting of field probation and parole officers working under the immediate direction of district probation and parole supervisors, and under the ultimate direction of the Probation and Parole Administrator, shall be responsible for the investigation, supervision and assistance of parolees, presentence and other probation investigations, and for the supervision of persons sentenced to probation. The field probation and parole service shall be sufficient in size to assure that no probation and parole officer carries a case load larger than is compatible with adequate investigation or supervision.

(2) Field Probation and Parole Officers shall:

(a) make pre-sentence and other probation investigations as may be required by law or directed by the Court in which they are serving, and make investigations, prior to a prisoner's release on parole, in cooperation with institutional parole officers and the Board of Parole to determine the adequacy of parole plans submitted by prisoners who are candidates for parole, make reasonable advance preparation for their release on parole, help them in conforming to the conditions of parole, and in making a successful adjustment in the community;

(b) supervise probationers and parolees, and in supervising them visit each probationer's or parolee's home from time to time, and require that he report to the officer as frequently as may be required, in the case of a probationer, by the order of the Court in accordance with Section 301.1, or as may be required in the case of probationers and parolees, by the officer himself, in the light of such probationer's or parolee's personality and adjustment, but no less frequently than twice a month during the first year of probation or parole, except in unusual cases;

(c) admonish probationers who appear in danger of violating the conditions of the order of probation, in accordance with Section 301.1, and report, in accordance with procedures established by the appropriate district supervisor, serious or persistent violations to the sentencing court, and advise the sentencing court, in accordance with procedures established by the appropriate district supervisor, when the situation of a probationer requires a modification of the conditions of the order of probation, or when the probationer's adjustment is such as to warrant termination of probation, in accordance with Section 301.2;

(d) admonish parolees who appear in danger of violating the conditions of parole, and report to the appropriate district supervisor serious or persistent violations which may require action by the Board of Parole and, in emergency situations, exercise the power of arrest as provided in Section 305.16.

(3) District probation and parole supervisors shall:

(a) establish procedures for the direction and guidance of probation and parole officers under their jurisdiction and advise such officers in regard to the most effective performance of their duties;

(b) supervise probation and parole supervisors under their jurisdiction and evaluate the effectiveness of their case work;

(c) make regular reports to the Probation and Parole Administrator concerning the activities of probation and parole officers under their jurisdiction and concerning the adjustment of probationers and parolees under their supervision;

(d) inform the Probation and Parole Administrator when, in the district probation and parole supervisor's opinion, any eligible parolee's conduct and attitude warrant his discharge from supervision, or when any parolee's violation of the conditions of parole is of sufficient seriousness to require action by the Board of Parole, and, in emergency situations, exercise the power of arrest as provided in Section 305.16.

STATUS OF SECTION

Presented to the Institute in Tentative Draft No. 5 and considered at the May 1956 meeting.

Resubmitted to the Institute, with verbal changes, in Proposed Final Draft No. 1 and approved at the May 1961 meeting.

Verbal changes have been made for technical conformity with other provisions.

For Commentary, see Tentative Draft No. 5, p. 176.

ARTICLE 405. DIVISION OF PROBATION

Section 405.1. Division of Probation; Probation Administrator.

(1) The Division of Probation shall be charged with the general supervision of the administration of probation services in the State, with the establishment of probation policies and standards, and with the administration of field probation services in any county or other governmental subdivision of this State which has no probation service of its own. The Division shall consist of the field probation service and of such other employees as may be necessary in carrying out its functions.

(2) The Division of Probation shall be under the direction of the Probation Administrator, who shall be appointed by, and serve during the pleasure of, the Governor [the Director of Correction]. The Probation Administrator shall be a person with appropriate experience in a field of correctional administration, or appropriate training in relevant disciplines at a recognized university. His salary shall be fixed by the Governor [the Director of Correction] within the appropriation therefor.

STATUS OF SECTION

Presented to the Institute in Tentative Draft No. 5 and considered at the May 1956 meeting.

Resubmitted to the Institute in Proposed Final Draft No. 1 and approved at the May 1961 meeting.

Verbal changes have been made for technical conformity with other provisions.

For Commentary, see Tentative Draft No. 5, p. 185.

Section 405.2. Powers and Duties of the Probation Administrator.

The Probation Administrator shall:

(1) supervise the administration of probation services in the State and, with the advice of the Commission of Correction and Community Services, establish policies and standards and make rules and regulations regarding probation investigation, supervision, case work and case loads, record keeping, and the qualification of probation officers;

(2) keep informed of the operations of all probation departments throughout the State and inquire into their conduct and efficiency, and, in this connection, he shall have access to all probation records and probation offices in the State, and he may issue subpoenas to compel the attendance of witnesses or the production of books and papers;

(3) recommend, in an appropriate case, the removal of any probation officer from any probation department in the State;

(4) appoint district probation supervisors, field probation officers and such other employees as may be required to carry out adequate probation supervision of persons sentenced to probation in any county or other governmental subdivision of this State which has no probation service of its own, and prescribe their powers and duties;

(5) cooperate closely with the Commission of Correction and Community Services and with the criminal courts.

STATUS OF SECTION

Presented to the Institute in Tentative Draft No. 5 and considered at the May 1956 meeting.

Resubmitted to the Institute in Proposed Final Draft No. 1 and approved at the May 1961 meeting.

Verbal changes have been made for technical conformity with other provisions.

For Commentary, see Tentative Draft No. 5, p. 185.

Section 405.3. Extension of Probation Field Services by Division of Probation.

The Probation Administrator, with the advice of the Commission of Correction and Community Services, may direct the extension of probation field services to any county or other governmental subdivision if he finds that such county or other governmental subdivision is not supplying adequate probation services to its criminal courts. The Administrator shall determine, after consultation with the [criminal courts in the county or other governmental subdivision concerned], the extent and duration of such services to be furnished. The Administrator may make agreements with the appropriate authorities concerning partial or full reimbursement to the Department of Correction for the costs of such services.

STATUS OF SECTION

Presented to the Institute in Tentative Draft No. 5 and considered at the May 1956 meeting.

Resubmitted to the Institute in Proposed Final Draft No. 1 and approved at the May 1961 meeting.

For Commentary, see Tentative Draft No. 5, p. 185.

Section 405.4. Field Probation Service; Organization and Duties.

(1) The field probation service, consisting of probation officers working under the immediate direction of district probation supervisors, and under the ultimate direction of

the Probation Administrator, shall be responsible for presentence and other probation investigations and for the supervision of persons sentenced to probation by a court in any county or other governmental subdivision which receives field probation services in accordance with Section 405.3. The field probation service shall be sufficient in size to assure that no probation officer carries a case load larger than is compatible with adequate probation investigation or supervision.

(2) Probation officers shall:

(a) make pre-sentence and other probation investigations, as may be required by law or directed by the Court in which they are serving;

(b) supervise probationers, and in supervising them visit each probationer's home from time to time, and require that he report to the probation officer as frequently as may be required by the order of the Court in accordance with Section 301.1, or as may be required by the probation officer himself in the light of the probationer's personality and adjustment, but no less frequently than twice a month during the first year of probation, except in unusual cases;

(c) admonish probationers who appear in danger of violating the conditions of the order of probation, in accordance with Section 301.1, and report, in accordance with procedures established by the appropriate district probation supervisor, serious or persistent violations to the sentencing court;

(d) advise the sentencing court, in accordance with procedures established by the appropriate district probation supervisor, when the situation of a probationer requires a modification of the conditions of the order of probation, or when a probationer's adjustment is such as to warrant termination of probation, in accordance with Section 301.2.

§ 405.4   Model Penal Code

(3) District probation supervisors shall:

(a) establish procedures for the direction and guidance of probation officers under their jurisdiction, and advise such officers in regard to the most effective performance of their duties;

(b) supervise probation officers under their jurisdiction and evaluate the effectiveness of their case work;

(c) make regular reports to the Probation Administrator concerning the activities of probation officers under their jurisdiction and concerning the adjustment of probationers under their supervision.

STATUS OF SECTION

Presented to the Institute in Tentative Draft No. 5 and considered at the May 1956 meeting.

Resubmitted to the Institute in Proposed Final Draft No. 1 and approved at the May 1961 meeting.

Minor verbal changes have been made.

For Commentary, see Tentative Draft No. 5, p. 185.